BEFORE STANISLAVSKY

American Professional Acting Schools and Acting Theory 1875–1925

by

JAMES H. McTEAGUE

The Scarecrow Press, Inc.
Metuchen, N.J., & London
1993

British Library Cataloguing-in-Publication data available

Library of Congress Cataloging-in-Publication Data

McTeague, James, 1931–
    Before Stanislavsky : American professional acting
schools and acting theory, 1875–1925 / by James H.
McTeague.
        p.   cm.
    Includes bibliographical references and index.
    ISBN 0-8108-2657-7 (acid-free)
    1. Acting—Study and teaching—United States—
History. I. Title.
    PN2078.U6M37   1993
    792'.028'07073—dc20   93-26669

ELEANOR
for her many sacrifices,
enduring commitment and love.

CONTENTS

ACKNOWLEDGMENTS

I want to thank the following people and institutions for permission to include photographs and for making available to me materials that proved invaluable to my analysis of the theoretical and practical considerations of the training received by several generations of actors: Philip N. Cronenwett, Curator of Manuscripts at the Dartmouth College Library; George Cuttingham, President and Meg McSweeney, Assistant to the President at the American Academy of Dramatic Arts in New York; Robert Fleming, Archivist of Emerson College; and Gertrude M. Webb of Curry College. As well, I am particularly indebted to David Kamara and The New York Public Library at Lincoln Center.

The greatest debt of gratitude is owed to Oscar G. Brockett, my mentor and friend throughout the years, for suggesting I undertake the task of placing American acting theory in proper perspective and to call to question long-held negative impressions and opinions regarding the significance of the schools to American theatre history, acting theory, and teaching practice.

INTRODUCTION

We have been brainwashed into thinking that significant actor training in America did not exist prior to the arrival of Stanislavsky in 1923. Nothing could be farther from the truth. During the period between 1875 and 1925, America was a hotbed of activity concerned with the elusive principles that underlie acting, how it could best be taught, and the best means of teaching it. Toward this noble goal, the professional acting schools led the way with views as diverse as the American landscape. Each contended that they possessed the antidote for America's troubled theatre and developed their own unique and comprehensive theory of acting long before Stanislavsky arrived on the scene. But the history of America's professional acting schools has been dogged by uninformed opinion. That such opinion persists is particularly unfortunate since it denies them deserved recognition as pioneers of modern acting theory and practice. This book is a modest attempt to rectify the situation.

Francis Hodge's observation is as valid today as it was in 1954 when he stated:

> The story of the first professional acting schools, important as it is, has not been set down except in isolated fragments. Like many innovations, the theatre school was lightly regarded and a victim of much buffeting during its early years. Yet as we look from the vantage point of today, its significance grows and we recognize the acting schools as one of the important links between the nineteenth century and the twentieth century theatre.[1]

The fact that only "isolated fragments" are all that have been "set down" has proved detrimental to the schools and has clouded many significant contributions to American acting theory. Further, a failure to present their positions completely and objectively has resulted in an attitude toward their acting theory and methods of approach to acting that has been tainted by ridicule and misrepresentation.[2]

Recent scholarship subscribes to the long-held view that "Acting theory was particularly neglected until 1923, when the visit of the Moscow Art Theatre *awoke a long dormant* American interest in the practice of acting."[3] The same scholar perpetuates unsubstantial opinion by claiming that America "advanced a wealth of ideas about acting . . . but never in a systematic way,"[4] and that "there is no evidence of a general theory of acting apart from Steele MacKaye's version of Delsarte" (*Ibid.*). With such statements, American professional acting schools are dismissed as advocates of obsolete theories and outmoded methods that "assigned particular meanings to various body attitudes," and offered "would-be actors a set of pre-arranged [sic] poses and vocal inflections, suitable for use in any dramatic situation" (*Ibid.*, pp. 17–18). The generally-held view of American professional acting schools is summarized in the following manner: "The actor could be sure of communicating to his audience the proper idea or emotion if he could duplicate precisely a certain gesture or vocal technique" (*Ibid.*, p. 13). Such views are mistaken and completely disregard available evidence, as a detailed investigation and analysis will demonstrate.

That acting could be taught, and taught more effectively than through older, more accepted and established means, was a bold and revolutionary idea first expressed by Steele MacKaye, an American playwright, actor, director, inventor and visionary teacher of acting. He conceived the idea and called for the establishment of an acting school in America as early as 1871, and after further experiments in 1877 and 1880, founded the Lyceum Theatre School in 1884—the first school with a formal curriculum composed of a wide range of courses taught by experts in the field. It remains the overwhelmingly predominant model for teaching acting in America today.

But even more important, MacKaye proposed from the outset that acting should be based on sound theoretical and aesthetic principles. It is undeniable that he espoused America's first prescriptive acting theory[5] fifty years prior to the arrival of Stanislavsky and the Moscow Art Theatre. These two ideas were seminal: 1) the establishment of an acting school with a variety of courses taught by experts *prior* to the actor entering the profession; and 2) that a school should be based on a firm foundation of sound acting principles which give the actor a system or method to follow. They resulted in the establishment of the professional acting school tradition and stimulated a rich diversity of acting theories, some of which are strikingly modern and explore areas previously reserved as the domain of Stanislavsky. Many were highly influential and are truly significant, despite past and present attempts to ridicule them.

Following MacKaye's bold lead, America's professional acting schools rejected the European "conservatoire" method of training as "imitative": a system in which students performed scenes followed by a demonstration by the master actor or teacher showing how the scene *should* be played, expecting the student to imitate what had been done. The schools further believed that the old stock company tradition, as it existed in the latter part of the nineteenth century, was exhausted and decadent, no longer capable of responding to the challenges of a changing theatre. The demise of the repertory stock company was a dramatic event in American theatrical history and the causes for this significant occurrence are diverse and fatally linked. But the result suggested a crisis of immense magnitude, since it threatened the life blood of the theatre: the continuity of the only reliable source of trained actors.

The history of the repertory stock company system has been well documented and does not require a detailed discussion, but certain essential features might be mentioned since it was the pattern of theatrical organization from the Renaissance and, quite probably, earlier. Its traditions spanned four hundred years by the 1850s and within its guild-like structure, aspiring actors entered the profession confident that, in time and if talented, they would move from apprentice through the various phases to an established "line of business," and eventually to "possession of parts" which they would hold for a significant portion of their professional lives. During this journey through the ranks, actors acquired skills by practicing, rehearsing and performing a wide range of gradually more demanding roles, observing experienced actors and "stars," taking the occasional supplementary class in dance or fencing, and perhaps an occasional visit to the elocutionist for study of a particular role. This was the traditional stock company "school of acting" that one might have experienced in America in the 1850s.[6]

The system fostered cohesiveness and guaranteed a consistent replenishment of trained talent to the stock company. The system brought solidity and continuity to the lives of actors and to the company as a whole. It was also, with very few exceptions, the *only* means available for entering the profession and the *only* source of actor training. The stock company "school of acting" was not without its critics, and they were at times quite severe, but it was all there was by way of gaining entrance and training for the profession—and it had proved itself and endured for over four hundred years!

It is ironic that while many of the best stock companies were organized between 1850 and 1870, the repertory system began its decline by 1875. Basic to the repertory system was the frequent change of bill, which required not only a competent company but also cheap and easy staging. The audience's demand for elaborate scenery and the "star" system soon made both conditions impossible. Already in the larger cities, plays had attracted audiences for as many as one hundred consecutive performances,[7] and the management soon realized that they could operate profitably by trying for long runs. Consequently, many theatre managers, oppressed by the expense for novel staging and the financial strain of the "star" system, began to produce plays, not on the basis of a nightly change of bill but on the long-run principle. The long-run play and the "star" system were potent forces in the disruption of the repertory system and the displacement of the resident company.

The combination system also contributed to the dissolution of the resident stock repertory company. The combination was originally a traveling company which contracted to perform mainly in cities and towns that did not have resident stock companies. At first, the combination companies presented repertory, but between 1870 and 1880 the combination presenting a single play began to appear. Thus, the single-play combination or the road-company version of the New York success competed with the resident stock repertory system. Instead of the frequent change of bill, the single-play combination performed the same play for a specific period of time or until audience attendance lessened. Then, the company traveled to the next contracted theatre and repeated the process. In the 1870s, the resident theatre managers began hiring single-play combinations and abandoned the stage to them for the length of the engagement. With this inroad into the repertory system, the combinations soon displaced the need for the resident stock company.

The rise and fall of the resident repertory stock company can be dramatically illustrated by a brief historical survey of the final seventy-five years of the nineteenth century. In 1825, there were at least thirty-five stock companies in the United States, and by 1860 there were probably more than fifty.[8] While there were still approximately fifty stock companies in operation in 1871, by 1878 the number had been reduced to twenty, and by 1880 to seven or eight (*Ibid.*, p.31). By 1887 only four companies remained, three of them in New York.[9] In that year Wallack's disbanded, and in 1893 the Boston Museum became a combination house. Palmer's New York theatre closed in 1896. A few so-called "stock companies," doing one or two plays a year, lingered until after the turn of the century, but the death of Augustin Daly, in 1899, practically meant the death of the old stock company.

As early as 1871, certain forces in the theatre were becoming aware of a need for a new type of training ground for aspiring actors. Previous to the opening of his play *Monaldi* at the St. James Theatre, James Steele MacKaye wrote a pamphlet entitled *A Plea for a Free School of Dramatic*

Art.[10] It contained a prospectus setting forth his plans to open an acting school, and there appeared for the first time a serious recommendation to remedy the "ills" of the contemporary theatre. MacKaye argued:

> There can never be a healthy vital drama until there is a safe and sure school where the dramatic aspirant may go as a student, and where he will be guaranteed the best social and moral associations, as well as the most thorough practical and aesthetic preparation for the profession. . . .
>
> As has already been announced, this theatre [the St. James Theatre] will be a school for the player and the public, having no less a purpose than the elevation of both. If dramatic art retains any of the potency which the pulpit and the press have always urged in its behalf, then this *experiment* becomes one of *social* no less than *aesthetic* importance.
>
> It now remains to be seen if the intelligent and scrupulous community will regard an effort to remedy the defects of the drama with favor. (*Ibid.*)

MacKaye's call for an acting school was slow to be heeded but he persevered in his mission and lived to see his idea flourish. The schools of acting were to prove essential in bridging the gap between the dissolution of the stock company and the new organization of theatrical management which required actors more urgently than ever before in the history of the American theatre.

The popularity of the acting school idea grew throughout the period and it was not long before schools sprang up all over New York City, Boston and Philadelphia. Soon they began to spread westward, and it was a rare city of over twenty-five thousand that could not boast a "school of acting" of some sort.

But despite their popularity, the concept of the "school" and a "system" were often fiercely attacked. The attacks were precipitated principally because much of the acting profession and some critics were deeply suspicious of the idea that acting could be taught, much less in a school. And, what was worse, that acting should be based on a "speculative" theory was untenable, unthinkable, and preposterous. Nym Crinkle

(Andrew C. Wheeler), a respected drama critic for the *World*, commented on the profession's wrath and characterized MacKaye's problem:

> If he had contemplated martyrdom, he could not have behaved with more suicidal intent than by announcing a *system*. Good system or bad, the sin is in having one. (*Ibid.*, p. 176)

The controversy endured thoughout the period between 1875 and 1925, with no resolution. But the theatre demanded actors to feed its surging growth and the schools continued to flourish as they responded to the need. The professional acting schools founded in the nineteenth century established the fact that acting could be taught successfully in a "school" setting, and reinforced the idea that a theory of acting should be the foundation.

This book investigates those theories and methods of the best known American professional acting schools during the period 1875 to 1925. Little research into the nature of acting theory and how acting was taught in American acting schools has been undertaken. I have cited two substantial articles by Francis Hodge and by Fred C. Blanchard which present the schools in a strictly historical perspective. Besides these articles, only Edythe May Renshaw's "Three Schools of Speech"[11] can be said to be a penetrating theoretical study; but she examines the schools of Curry, Emerson and Powers from the standpoint of oral interpretation and public speaking and does not attempt an examination of the relevance to acting theory or the pedagogical principles of acting. Three books, Edwin Duerr's *The Length and Depth of Acting,* Garff Bell Wilson's *History of American Acting* and Marvin Carlson's *Theories of the Theatre*[12] discuss Delsarte and MacKaye in a very brief and perfunctory way but do not examine the American acting schools, their theories or teaching methods.

The schools selected were the most highly regarded and the most written about by critics of the theatre. They also represent a cross-section of the movement, in that they show the full spectrum of purposes and methods. The specific

schools chosen for consideration are Steele MacKaye's St.
James Theatre School, The Union Square Theatre School,
and the Madison Square Theatre School and the Lyceum
Theatre School.[13] Other schools include Franklin H.
Sargent's American Academy of Dramatic Arts, The Emerson
College of Oratory, Samuel Silas Curry's School of Expres-
sion, The Leland Powers School of the Spoken Word, A. M.
Palmer's and Dion Boucicault's Madison Square Theatre
School of Instruction, the Stanhope-Wheatcroft School, and
F. F. MacKay's National Dramatic Conservatory.

The beginning date for this study is dictated by the
emergence of the idea and the formation of the first acting
school in America. The terminal date is dictated by the fact
that most of the schools under consideration had either
disappeared or had become associated with degree-granting
institutions by 1925. Also, by 1925, the vitality of the
professional acting school movement had been inherited by
universities and colleges which began competing for the right
to train actors. The force of their influence began to cut into
the position which the purely professional schools had held.
The professional acting schools were no longer unique. They
had bridged the gap that had to be crossed and the need for
them was no longer so sorely felt. Furthermore, all the
founders of the schools had died by 1925, and while many of
the schools continued to teach the theories and employ the
teaching methods of their founders, the schools changed their
character and purpose because of the necessities of the times,
the force of new leadership and the introduction of new ideas.
Some of the schools, of course, are still in existence today.
However, almost all of them are now schools of "theatre arts"
and, in addition to acting, they teach courses in playwriting,
scene design, and other arts of the theatre. By 1925, the
school devoted entirely to the teaching of acting had almost
been displaced.

This book is organized in eight chapters. The first five
chapters are devoted to schools influenced by the Delsarte
system and which were called "speculative" by their contemporaries even though they tried vainly to escape the label.

The following three chapters concern schools which were associated with more "practical" concerns and were founded by distinguished professionals who had achieved solid reputations in theatre.

Chapter I is devoted to an examination of the birth pangs that accompanied the establishment of the first schools founded by Steele MacKaye and analyzes his adaptation of the Delsarte system and the manner in which he applied the theory to practice through his teaching methods. Each of the following seven chapters is organized around two major considerations. First, the basic theoretical position of the individual school is discussed and analyzed. The function of acting and the actor is examined according to the actor's relationship to the play, the character and the audience. Characteristics of the "ideal" actor, with emphasis on the theory of imagination, emotion, intellect and technique, are considered. Finally, the theory of the relationship of art to nature is discussed. The second part of each chapter is devoted to a consideration of the teaching methods employed by the school. This includes the relationship of teacher and pupil, an examination of the curriculum, its content and how it was taught, followed by a discussion of the relationship of theory to the methods of teaching. Each chapter concludes with an examination of the coherency of the theory and the method or system devised for the actor, followed by an evaluation of the unique contributions of the school to American acting theory and practice.

In the conclusion, the theories and methods of the schools are compared so that judgments can be made concerning similarities and differences, with special consideration given to observable trends and patterns. Since Stanislavsky had such impact on acting theory near the end of the period, relevant comparisons are made of the essential and distinctive characteristics of his "system" and the theories and methods of the schools. Some discussion will be undertaken concerning the near oblivion to which the schools have been relegated and, finally, an appraisal of the significance and contributions of the schools is offered.

Steele MacKaye: Actor/Director/Playwright/Inventor, the prime mover in North America of the professional acting movement. (Photo courtesy of Dartmouth College Library)

CHAPTER I
THE ST. JAMES THEATRE SCHOOL,
UNION SQUARE THEATRE SCHOOL,
MADISON SQUARE THEATRE SCHOOL,
AND THE LYCEUM THEATRE SCHOOL

While Steele MacKaye has been frequently praised for his work as a playwright, inventor, theatre manager and innovator, relatively little attention has been paid to his contribution to acting theory or to his role in the development of acting schools in America.[1] There is little doubt that he was the most important single influence in the establishment of formal training for actors in America, but the development of acting theory and the establishment of a method of acting were his first great contribution to the theatre.

James Steele MacKaye was born in Buffalo, New York, on June 6, 1842 (*Ibid.*, I, 37). He first embarked on a career in painting, which caused Professor Samuel Silas Curry to muse about the influence of a painting career on MacKaye:

> I have deeply considered the influence of Troyon upon Steele MacKaye, who must have been among the greatest of his pupils. I never saw a sign of imitation in MacKaye's work or drawing; he was original. (*Ibid.*, I, 73)

Eventually, MacKaye gravitated toward the theatre as a career and the first sign of his interest appeared around 1861. The following schedule for a day's occupation indicated how strongly the attraction for the theatre had become.

1

Pantomime and Expression: 1861			Regulation of Time:
10:00 o'clock till	2:00 o'clock		Drawing and Painting.
2:00 "	4:00	"	Dramatic Exercises.
2:00 "	2:20	"	Exercise—Voice.
2:20 "	2:40	"	Body.
2:40 "	3:00	"	In Pantomime.
3:00 "	3:20	"	In Calisthenics.
3:20 "	3:40	"	In Emotional Expressions of Countenance.
3:40 "	4:00	"	Miscellaneous.
7:1/2 o'clock till 9:1/2 o'clock			2 Evenings in week: Speciality. (Ibid., 91)

Percy MacKaye explained the significance of the schedule as follows:

> This record of 'dramatic exercises,' in 1861, is important to a true understanding of my father's later contributions to aesthetic philosophy and to the art of the theatre. Prevented at the start, by his father's opposition, from adopting the stage itself as a career, he gave himself, during more than a decade, to intensive training in bodily and facial exercises, while his mind was constantly analysing and synthesising the whole field of aesthetic expression which underlay these. So he evolved both an aesthetic philosophy and a means for its practical embodiment through invention of innumerable co-ordination exercises. These pursuits had begun even as a boy; but here, in 1861, he had already commenced with himself an intensive regime in pantomime and aesthetic expression—*eight years before he had even heard of Delsarte.*[2]

In preparation for his career in the theatre, Steele MacKaye journeyed to Paris in 1869 with the intention of studying with Regnier[3] at the Conservatoire. At the suggestion of his father, however, MacKaye went to see François Delsarte, who had established his Cours D'Esthétique Appliquée. This fateful meeting was to have a great impact on American acting theory and the manner in which acting was taught. At their meeting in October 1869, Delsarte accepted Steele MacKaye as a pupil, and the young American remained with his master until July 1870—eight months of study (Percy MacKaye, I, 135). MacKaye's progress was so rapid that he was accepted as a coworker by Delsarte and was permitted to do a part of the teaching at the Cours. Evidently he had assimilated the principles of the system and was able to apply them with admirable success. Mrs. Steele MacKaye reported:

> So within five months of their first meeting, at Delsarte's own desire and request, Mr. MacKaye was himself lecturing and teaching in Delsarte's *Cours*, with a success which aroused as much enthusiasm as astonishment in Delsarte's lovable, loving and generous nature. On one occasion, I remember, as Mr. MacKaye finished, Delsarte rose from his chair and, putting his arm affectionately on Mr. MacKaye's shoulder, said to the listeners: '*Voila ma grande cavalerie.*' (*Ibid.*, p. 136)

There can be little doubt that Steele MacKaye was Delsarte's most brilliant pupil and that the master considered him his successor. In a letter published in Percy MacKaye's *Epoch,* Delsarte wrote, "Barely one more year of such study, my dear friend, will be sufficient to make of you *one of the first dramatic artists of the world—of the world,* do you understand? For *any other man* I should hesitate to have thus engaged my honor as a master and as an artist"(*Ibid.*, p.141. Italics Percy Mac-Kaye's). When the Franco-Prussian war began in 1871, MacKaye returned to America fired with enthusiasm for the Delsarte system and began making plans to introduce the system to America. Very shortly, however, word reached MacKaye that Delsarte was in destitute condition. Two new friends, both firm supporters of the Delsarte system, suggested to MacKaye that he give a series of lectures on Delsarte, the proceeds of which would go to Delsarte's relief (*Ibid.*). These two men, the Reverend William R. Alger and Professor Lewis B. Monroe, played an important role in the spread of the Delsarte system. Both, at this time, considered

Steele MacKaye as the person most competent to discuss the Delsarte system and philosophy.[4]

On March 21, 1871, Steele MacKaye launched his campaign to popularize Delsarte in America. On that evening he delivered at the St. James Hotel in Boston his first lecture on Delsarte. In April, the lecture was twice repeated in Boston at the Tremont Temple to large audiences and was given at Harvard University on April 12, 1871, with Henry W. Longfellow as the chairman (Percy MacKaye, *Epoch*, I, 154). Later, MacKaye lectured at Steinway Hall in New York, twice in April and several times in May. He also lectured in Brooklyn at the invitation of Henry Ward Beecher. (*Ibid.*, II, Appendix, xxi). MacKaye lectured widely in the ensuing years, and it is no overstatement to say that MacKaye's dynamic personality made a lasting impression on his audiences. The popularity of the Delsarte system in America in the 1870s and 1880s is partly explained by Samuel Silas Curry:

> One cause of its being received so popularly was no doubt the almost universal dissatisfaction with the mechanical methods. Teachers were eager for anything that might give promise of a philosophical basis for a better method. Another cause was the able lectures delivered by Delsarte's favorite pupil, Mr. Steele Mac-Kaye, in different cities of the United States.[5]

There is reasonable certainty that Steele MacKaye accepted the basic premises of the Delsarte system, and was acknowledged the person most capable of explaining it. In his biography of his father's career, Percy MacKaye clearly established the fact that Steele MacKaye accepted and was dedicated to the propagation of the Delsartian philosophy of expression. The lectures on the Delsarte method which MacKaye delivered in the spring of 1877 at the studio of Mrs. George Hall amply demonstrate that he presented the substantial essence of the philosophy of expression as taught by his master.[6] Also, MacKaye's notes, which were taken when he was a student with Delsarte, have been analyzed and clarified by Claude L. Shaver,[7] who believed that MacKaye's notes "represent the Delsarte philosophy and system at its culmination, that is, in its final form"(*Ibid.*). In 1891, Dr. Samuel Silas Curry attested to the fact that MacKaye was the one man who was able to give the world an adequate formulation of Delsarte's principles, and stated: "Mr. Steele MacKaye is thoroughly competent to give to the world an outline of the system of Delsarte"(Curry, *Province of Expression*, 337). In 1892 Edgar S. Werner wrote:

> The part Mr. Steele MacKaye has taken in developing and popularizing the Delsarte system is too well known to need any explanation or defense. He, the late Prof. Lewis B. Monroe, and the Reverend William R. Alger were the great American trio to whom the expressional arts owe an immense debt of gratitude. They are the founders of the 'new elocution,' and were in the most intimate professional and personal relations with Delsarte.[8]

It should be made clear, however, that Steele MacKaye was the only one of the three who actually studied with Delsarte. In fact, it was MacKaye who interested both the others in Delsarte and his philosophy, although Alger did study with Delsarte's son for the better part of a year. His lectures at Curry's School of Expression have also been the object of a special study,[9] and indicate that he accepted the basic premises of both the Delsarte philosophy and system. Alger's lectures validate what appears in MacKaye's notes.

The weight of evidence, then, supports the fact that MacKaye accepted the whole speculative philosophy of Delsarte, but was less profoundly religious, or at least not Catholic in religion; he was probably less interested in the philosophical implications than in the practical aspects.[10] In 1877 Steele MacKaye wrote:

> It is no exaggeration to say that Delsarte lifted expression to the level of an exact science, for he found the

fixed laws of art in nature, and advanced only such propositions as could be instantly verified by the artist himself.[11]

As Delsarte was convinced that his system and philosophy were based on "the fixed laws of nature," so, too, did MacKaye believe that his system of acting was "scientific." But, as Claude Shaver points out, "The system was . . . not a science in the modern sense of the word, but was purely philosophical and speculative."[12]

The Delsarte system has been much maligned over the years despite an attempt in recent years to reexamine its validity.[13] The generally-held opinion is that the Delsarte system as adapted by Steele MacKaye advocated the use of preconceived poses, gestures and vocal inflections which, if duplicated precisely, would evoke the appropriate thought or emotion in an audience. MacKaye dismissed such opinions and expressed his sentiments most emphatically.

> Some appear to believe . . . that I pretend to turn anyone whether they have natural ability, or not, into a first-class actor. —Nonsense!— Then they say that I number the expressions of the face to so many hundreds of thousands. —Nonsense again!(Percy MacKaye, I, 267).

It is certainly true that books written by former students leave the distinct impression of a highly artificial and mechanical system. It is also true that many teachers, also former students, misrepresented the system and incurred the wrath of the profession and critics as a result. But for MacKaye and other schools influenced by the teachings of Delsarte, such books and teachers were repugnant and a source of constant frustration.[14] Consequently, an analysis of the Delsarte system as interpreted by MacKaye may assist in arriving at an objective appraisal.

The Delsarte system attempted to reduce all phenomena to units of three.

> The basis of the Delsarte system is the philosophical conception of the trinity. Every phenomenon can be resolved into its fundamental three, and the purpose of science is to discover these underlying trinities which form the key to the divine reason of all things.[15]

Thus, the actor with a basic instrument of investigation and examination—the Delsarte system—could arrive at the "truth." MacKaye believed that "truth," or the perception of "truth," can only be achieved through careful and thorough examination, and was convinced that the imaginative act was threatened by the actor's inability to communicate expressively. He accepted Delsarte's trinitary view since it gave the actor "possession of a criterion of examination against which no fact can protest"(Ibid., 40).

Delsarte maintained that the highest form of nature is man, who is composed of two triune natures representing a duality—the spiritual reflecting heaven and God and the physical reflecting man's animalistic traits. The spiritual is called the immanent, and the physical is called the organic. Both are divided into triunes with the organic conceived as a reflection of the immanent. Thus, man's spiritual side of *life*, *mind* and *soul* is reflected in his organic being through *feeling*, *thought*, and *love*. In turn, each of these three parts of the triune is divided into other trinities.

While MacKaye believed that the function of the artist is to give his audience a perception of "truth," the actor is, in fact, giving them a glimpse of the spiritual or the immanent. "The immanent essence of life, mind, and soul are expressed through the organic acts of feeling, thought, and love, by the physical mechanisms" (*Ibid.*, 51). Since the spiritual or "truth" can only be expressed organically, MacKaye contended that the artist must become familiar with the physical mechanisms in order to discover the processes of expression. "*Life,* with its immanent acts of sensation, instinct, and sympathy, is expressed by the *vocal mechanism*; *mind,* with its accompanying immanences, judgement, induction, and conscience, is expressed by the *buccal mechanism*; *soul,* with its immanences of sentiment, intuition, and contemplation, is expressed by the *dynamic mechanism"(Ibid.* Italics mine).

The organic mechanisms (vocal, buccal, and dynamic) were also broken into triunes of three. The buccal mechanism is composed of the velum, the lips, and tongue; the vocal mechanism is composed of the lungs, the back of the mouth, and the larynx; the dynamic mechanism is composed of the head, the body, and the face. (The limbs serve as accessories in expressing the three parts of the body.) Each of these mechanisms produces its own peculiar form of expression. (1) The vocal mechanism produces inflection, the language of music; (2) the buccal mechanism produces the word, the language of logic; and (3) the dynamic mechanism produces gesture, the language of mimicry (*Ibid.,* 51–52).

It should be clear that the Delsarte system works on the basis of hierarchies. The highest expression of the spiritual is the soul and is manifested organically through the dynamic mechanism which produces gesture, the language of mimicry. The chart opposite (p. 9) should help clarify the chain-like connection or correspondences between the spiritual "truth" and the physical manifestation. The chart should also clarify why the Delsarte system became associated with gesture and pantomime. It clearly favored, in the philosophical sense, the physical manifestation of gesture as the supreme expression of the soul. It was no accident that MacKaye and American Delsartism concentrated on gesture and pantomime.

The relationship of the actor's psychology—imagination, emotion, and intellect—is explained through MacKaye's concepts of Delsartian aesthetics. He believed that, from the aesthetic point of view, man is divided into three major types: "The constitutional or natural type; the artificial or habitual type; the passional or emotional type"(Ibid., 54). From this point of view the sentiments and their significance were studied. These characteristics corresponded to the life, mind, and soul. Thus, the emotional aspect of character expressed

		FATHER	GOD SON	HOLY GHOST
TRINITY OF GOD		Function:	to purify	to enlighten	to perfect
		Postulate:	to purify	to enlighten	perfection
		SPIRITUAL AGENTS	virtues powers dominions	angels archangels principalities	thrones seraphim cherubim
IMMANENT BEING		IMMANENT ESSENCES	LIFE	MIND	SOUL
		IMMANENT ACTS	instinct sensation sympathy	judgment induction conscience	sentiment contemplation intuition
ORGANIC BEING		ORGANIC ACTS	FEELING	THOUGHT	LOVE
		ORGANIC AGENTS	VOCAL APPARATUS lungs back of mouth larynx	BUCCAL APPARATUS velum tongue lips	DYNAMIC APPARTUS torso head face
		EXPRESSION STATES	inflection language of music sensitivity state of memory	the word language of logic intellectual state of understanding	gesture language of mimicry moral state of will
		ATTAINMENT OF POSTU-LATE MAN	purity	enlightenment	perfection

(*Ibid.*, 53.)

man's soul; the habitual aspects expressed mind; and the natural aspects expressed life.

There are two aspects of the aesthetic: the aesthetic proper and the semiotic. The semiotic and the aesthetic are two ways of approaching the whole problem of expression. The aesthetic proper feels the emotion, stimulates the imagination, and expresses through certain organic movements. Aesthetics, then, is the study of the expression of the spiritual through the organic. The semiotic, on the other hand, defines the emotion *from* the organic acts. *The aesthetic proper is the outward expression of the inner state*; the semiotic is the recognition of the inner state by its outward manifestations. The aesthetic proper is inventive; the semiotic is translative. Semiotics is the foundation of aesthetics, but the aesthetic is *superior* and more difficult.

> In the Delsarte system both the semiotic and the aesthetic proper seem to be used. The semiotic is useful in analyzing expressive movement and as a method of study, but the study should be so well assimilated that the movements become *spontaneous* expression of the inner state of mind, *and thus purely aesthetic*. (*Ibid.*, 55. Italics mine)

It should be noted that most books representing the Delsarte system in America appear to be based on semiotics rather than on aesthetics. MacKaye's charts, which depict the various positions of the eye, the arm, the feet, were employed as means of observing through semiotics, while the aesthetic expressed the inner or spiritual state. Without grounding in the philosophical basis of the aesthetics of the system it is easy to understand how one could become involved in mere external manifestations. MacKaye's notes clearly indicate that *the Delsarte system advocated spontaneous creative expression which is aesthetic in nature.* The study of positions and attitudes of the agents of the body, the study of signs, was a means to an end, not an end in itself.

The study of the semiotic enabled the actor to "free" the

channels of expression so that imaginative creativity could be possible. Through the study of the semiotic, the actor exercised and learned control of the expressive instrument; the aesthetic is the spontaneous expression and the actual creation. The semiotic gives the actor a criterion and a standard of expression, while the aesthetic is the actual accomplishment. The actor must completely absorb the process of the semiotic, thus giving the creative aesthetic free rein. The semiotic is subservient to the aesthetic, and *the whole Delsarte system is primarily a method which enables the actor to achieve complete freedom of the imagination and the spontaneous expression of the emotional inner state in the truest possible manner* (Ibid., 55–56. Italics mine).

The function of the actor, MacKaye believed, is to present a reflection of "truth" or the beauty of the immanent in a manner perceivable to everyone. The imagination was considered the springboard that enabled the artist to perceive the "truth" and the organizing faculty which facilitated discovery of the best means of expressing "truth." For the actor, however, perception was not considered enough—thus, the Delsarte "system" was conceived to aid the imagination in discovering the best means of expression. In the final analysis, the "system" is the handmaiden and a codification of the laws which the actor employs in the creation of art. The Delsarte "system" can be said to be an instrument for freeing the imagination and giving it ultimate free play.

Imagination is stimulated and "fired" by memory in the Delsarte system. Of memory, he claimed that "it must possess the singular power of communicating fixity to fugitive things, permanence to instantaneousness, and *actuality* to the past."[16] Memory enabled the actor to recall not only real and actual events, and emotions, but responded to instinctual and spontaneous actions and discoveries as well. It may surprise some readers to discover that Delsarte held *instinct* above all traits for the "ideal" actor. He once called it "that marvelous instrument of divine reason," and believed that the actor must submit *his reason* to instinct.[17] For Delsarte, instinct was the result of spontaneous response to stimuli in the form of experience. One of his most famous pupils, who later taught the Delsarte method, stated:

> The actor's role arises not from intelligence but simply from instinct. *The actor identifies himself* with the person-ages he represents. He renders all their sentiments.[18]

One might presume that it is through identification with the character that the actor's instinct is awakened through en-gagement with stimuli (other actors, memory, or the environ-ment). There appears to be an interdependence in the manner in which the memory, imagination and instinct interact that is not clearly defined, but the expression that results is clearly what Delsarte would call "aesthetic." Memory would also function as an aid to the "semiotic" as the actor analyzed the appropriateness of the instinctual expression, since "he must not run the risk of frivolity" (*Ibid.*). Besides the analysis of a role, reason and intellect functioned only *before* or *after* expres-sion—never *during*. Delsarte stated, "Reason . . . recognizes itself as impotent and even absurd *a priori*."[19]

All gestures, movements, and attitudes may be classified under triune forms, and each gesture, movement, or attitude was believed to have a special significance (*Ibid.*, 60–62). The vocal apparatus is also triune: all vocal effects express life, mind, or soul, and are so classified. In addition, the Delsarte system reevaluated language according to the principle of the trinity and assigned degrees of value to the various parts of speech as well (*Ibid.*, 162). All the parts of the body are divided into zones, which in turn control other minor zones. Whether body, voice or speech, the zones and sub-zones express the inner states (soul, life, mind) in the form of attitudes which reveal themselves through movement or sound. Regardless of the acknowledged hierarchies, Delsarte was emphatic that expression was not merely a matter of assigning prearranged poses and vocal inflections in any dramatic situation, and that a duplication of "semiotic" observations would not assure success. He remarked, "Nothing is more deplorable than a gesture without a *motive*."[20]

The working relationship of all the parts of the body in the trinitary system is explained by the principle of "circumincession," which Samuel Silas Curry understood as the principle of intertwining (Curry, *Province of Expression*, 344). This principle attempts to explain the intrinsic relationships of the three essences of any trinity. A trinity is not composed of any three causal objects, but must consist of the three things definitely related in such a way that each of the three affects the other two.

> Circumincession means the reciprocal impressions of the three elements of the trinity. One of the elements is always primitive and basic to the other two.[21]

Thus, in the Delsarte system, all trinities are interrelated upward, downward, and on the same plane. Soul, life, and mind are interrelated, and in turn are related to the physical manifestation which represents them. Each essence (soul, life and mind) exerts influence on physical actions related to the other two essences as well as upon themselves. So, in movement or voice, there would be one movement that is most affected by soul, but would also have clinging to it the essences of life and mind.

> The principle of circumincession would lead to the conclusion that the controlling influences [soul, life, mind] of movements are so interwoven that any bodily expression is not only under the control of a major influence, but also is operated upon by all the influences at work on the body. Thus each movement is made through a totality of control. Inversely, every part of the body probably exerts influences on every other part of the body through its major control (*Ibid.*, 112).

This theory reflects the premise that acting is a totality of bodily action and it supplies acting with a theoretical framework which would justify the total integration of movement, voice, and speech. It also offers an explanation, however speculative, of the phenomenon known as the "ideal" actor—the actor who has completely in command the totality of the means of expression. The relationship of art to nature is clearly defined by the Delsarte-MacKaye "system" of acting. The MacKaye theory of acting, as an adaptation of Delsartism, advocated a trend toward subtle acting. "The gesture should never attempt to express fully the emotion felt by the actor, but should be restrained" (*Ibid.*, 103). Suggestion, not a literal representation, was the keystone of the theoretical position.

> The external gesture is nothing more than an echo of the internal gesture which gives it birth; the external gesture should be inferior in development and one should see through it to the soul; in a word, it is a reverberation. (*Ibid.*)

MacKaye implied that the gesture is "inférieure en développement" to the inner emotion, but that in some way it *suggests* the full intensity of the emotion.

Most actors claim that their purpose is to suggest rather than merely portray, or to suggest more than they portray. The "good actor, on the other hand, allows his gestures to reveal only a tenth part of his secret emotion which he seems to say" (*Ibid.*). The MacKaye theory of acting, then, was one which advocated suggestion, and it was probably this attitude that prompted Arthur Hobson Quinn to write:

> James Steele MacKaye (1842–94) was a pioneer, in a sense, in bringing the quiet, restrained quality of Delsarte's method of acting to the American stage.[22]

Like Delsarte, MacKaye believed that the theatre was both a *social* and an *aesthetic* experience that benefited mankind as a social critic, a spiritual guide and the strongest force available to improve mankind's state. He accepted the actor as the best instrument for implementing the theatre's purpose; and because actors are engaged in the serious business of aiding in the improvement of mankind, they must be artists above reproach. MacKaye, therefore, found it necessary to purge the stigma attached to the acting profession and began by attempting to raise the standards of the art. First, the actor must become a social asset, respected in his community. Secondly, the actor had a duty to the high calling to become proficient in the art. MacKaye believed all older systems of acting haphazard, imitative and "unscientific." He believed that he possessed a system—a system based on the laws of nature and art.[23] Trained in the Delsarte system, the actor would be furnished with a body of knowledge comparable to that of other professions.

The play, as an expression of an idea, was central to MacKaye's philosophy of the theatre. Throughout his career, his main concern was with training actors who could express the noble ideas of the playwright. The actor, therefore, was a servant to the playwright's idea. One of MacKaye's chief objectives was to create in America a great drama that offered playwrights the finest opportunities for production and monetary reward (Percy MacKaye, I, 300). MacKaye was confident, however, that only with excellent, well-trained actors could the playwright's ideas be communicated. He believed that the concern of the American theatre with spectacular scenic effects was due to the lack of good actors, and because the acting was poor, the public and managers were content with mere effect in the theatre. With good actors to express ideas, however, a favorable climate for playwrights could be created.

MacKaye's conception of the degree of identification of the actor with the character he portrayed was also influenced by the ideas of Delsarte. (Quinn, 126). The Delsarte system was conceived as a means of achieving naturalness through spontaneity. Madame Arnaud, in her book, *Delsarte System of Oratory,* insisted that Delsarte preached against artificiality.

> With this Artist there is never anything to betray *artificiality* of a situation; interpreted by him [Delsarte],

the creation, the invention, become real. From his lips a cry never seemed a studied effect. A tear seemed to come straight from the heart; his gesture was conscious of what it had to teach us; in all these applications of the 'sign to the thing' there was never an error, never a mistake. It was *truth* adorned by beauty.[24]

Madame Arnaud wrote: "Delsarte was always master of himself, however impassioned he appeared" (*Ibid.*). MacKaye offered nothing contrary to this belief held by his master. The relationship of the actor to the character was similar to the ideas of Stanislavsky—whatever the degree of passion, the actor is always in command of himself.

The actor's relationship to the audience is clearly spelled out by Delsarte, and his pronouncements appear in Mac-Kaye's notebook. In the section on acting, MacKaye's notes reveal that Delsarte distinguished between the good and bad actor by the manner in which he related to the audience. The poor actor forces himself on the audience, tries too hard, attempts to awaken interest, demonstrates exhibitionism and promises too much.

Because they say to their audience—look at me, I am going to thrill you with my point of view.[25]

The good actor, on the other hand, seems to say, "I am not going to thrill you, I am not going to win your friendship through theatrical tricks which win the moment" (*Ibid.*). The good actor should be restrained, forcing the audience to come to him (*Ibid.*, 104). "Court the audience, and she will turn on you," MacKaye wrote (*Ibid.*, 105). "If the actor wishes great success, plan so that half the audience stands without" (*Ibid.*). MacKaye desired a scrupulous public, trained in recognizing great drama brought to life through great acting. If actors courted public favor, the character and the play would suffer in the courtship. Thus, the actor was duty-bound to express the playwright's idea through the character, thereby assuring an audience interest in *what* the actor expressed. These ideas were prophetic of a modern theatre vision.

Stripped of its "speculative" trinitary concepts, the Delsarte system of expression was an amazingly modern emotion-based theory of acting. It is truly sad that many disciples taught only the semiotics of the system and thus gave Delsarte an unjustified reputation. But the fact that the fundamental principles of Delsarte were corrupted should in no way diminish the importance of the "system" as a significant contribution to acting theory. The essence of the system was "truth," spontaneity and imagination. The "truth" was applied to both the verity of feeling and the expression of emotion. Emotional honesty and a simple, natural and relaxed style of acting became the hallmark of American Delsartism as advocated and taught by Steele MacKaye. There can be little argument that the principles he advocated became America's first prescriptive theory of acting.

Returning to America after studying with Delsarte, MacKaye gave a series of lectures at Steinway Hall in New York City, and seriously undertook the opening of *a new school of dramatic art*. It was MacKaye's intention to bring Delsarte to America for the purpose of establishing here a "free school of art under the presidency of Delsarte himself, where art may be taught on scientific principles" (MacKaye, I, 157). However, Delsarte died in the summer of 1871, and MacKaye's dream of bringing him to the United States and opening a great school of art similar to the Cours in Paris died with him.

As early as the autumn of 1871, MacKaye rented a hall in New York City and renamed it the St. James Theatre. In advance of the opening of the theatre he published a prospectus[26] setting forth his plans to start an acting school in conjunction with the theatre. In stating the basic purpose of the institution, MacKaye claimed to be "the only living pupil in this country" who had studied with François Delsarte, and indicated that the Frenchman's teachings were to be followed (MacKaye, I, 164).

The St. James Theatre and School was opened in the autumn of 1871. MacKaye's play *Monaldi* was presented to the public on January 8, 1872 and closed after a three-month run. The St. James School was in operation for a maximum of six months. Little has been recorded of MacKaye's first experiment in running an acting school. At this time there was little enrollment beyond the members of the immediate acting company. As stage manager, MacKaye gave instruction while directing plays, and in addition arranged special tutoring sessions. It is clear that MacKaye accomplished something different from the conventional stage manager, however.

In the fullest sense, his project was a step toward a goal which MacKaye had hoped for in the prospectus: the founding of a Free Conservatory of Art. First, Steele MacKaye was definitely teaching a "system," in the manner of Delsarte. MacKaye lectured the cast in the principles of the philosophy of Delsarte and then demonstrated the efficacy of the principles. After first laying the groundwork, he probably set up exercises, either individually or in a group, to "teach" his actors repose and naturalness. The methods were probably similar in nature to those which MacKaye gave to Franklin Sargent ten years later in 1882. Sargent writes of one such "lesson":

> Most of the time we sat on opposite sides of the table, I taking notes and he expounding [undoubtedly Delsartian principles]. At times we would practise before a pier glass. . . . My first lesson comprised the transition of the body from one foot to the other, which I practised for one entire hour. And how grateful I have ever been, particularly for the first lesson, securing as it did the command of the very fundamental principle of the harmonic poise of the body. . . . His method in teaching was essentially scientific and mathematical. Nothing was stated ever that could not be put in the form of a scientific law.[27]

Basically, MacKaye appears to have adopted the methods employed by his master, Delsarte. Mrs. Steele MacKaye gave a good indication of the manner in which Delsarte taught.

> The first part of the morning was given to the exposition of philosophy—the explanation of some theory, or

chart. This part of the class work—during the last months—was given to Mr. MacKaye, Delsarte from his armchair putting in a word, a nod, or smile of approval, to his little audience. After the exposition came the practical part: the recitation of a fable, a scene from a play, or perhaps a song . . . rendered . . . by a pupil. . . . Again for private lessons in voice training he would choose passages with sonorous vowels for his pupils to recite. (Reprinted in *Ibid.*, I, 136–37)

The above description appears to have been the basic pattern for MacKaye's St. James Theatre School: first, the exposition of the principle, and then the practical application. This was to be MacKaye's method of teaching until he was given the freedom and money to develop fully the curriculum idea in the Lyceum Theatre School.

MacKaye was opposed to the old stock company methods of training and the results which it had achieved. In a letter to Eli Perkins, drama critic of the *Standard,* dated January 13, 1872, MacKaye clarified his intention.

Mr. Eli Perkins, Dear Sir:—One man can never thank another for such brave words of uncompromising support as you have written in behalf of the art I am aiming to learn and to teach. However, I cannot resist writing to assure you that you have given me a new supply of inspiration to fight out our little fight. . . . I have harped on one strong point only: *Let us have a school which shall teach the art and purify the artist, a conservatory not only to instruct the actor but to elevate his art and protect it from abuse.* . . . I opened this theatre to show what his [Delsarte's] system could do in a short time—and while my pupils have been praised, the system which gave them their repose and simplicity has been sneered at. I tried to make the public understand that I offered my present efforts merely as a slight promise of what might be accomplished by a four years' course of study, and hoped they would permit us to creep and walk before they would expect us to run; but we are expected not only to run but to *out run* all others.

There are many little conventional stage tricks, which

doubtless almost any utility man of the boards may
know, which we ignored. *The subtle qualities of simplicity
and naivete, of sincerity, of appropriate listening, of artistic
massing of light and shade, as well as the delicate and
truthful management of contrast and graduation in the
art—all these qualities I know are present to some degree in
our acting.* The thought and philosophy of art are there,
and, each day will become more apparent to every fair
mind that has power to perceive beyond the stereotyped
tricks of the old school. (Reprinted in *Ibid.*, 172)

The St. James Theatre and School was, then, only an
indication of what was to come. MacKaye believed that a
"four-year course of study" was necessary in order to become
a proficient actor, but one must remember that at this time
MacKaye probably did not conceive of a school with a large
and varied curriculum. Most likely, he meant a course of
study similar to Delsarte's Cours D'Esthétique Appliquée:
exposition through lecture, clarification through practice and
example.

After the venture at the St. James Theatre closed, MacKaye
again took to the lecture circuit until he decided that the best
way to prove that his ideas on acting were valid was to prove
himself as an actor. He traveled to Paris and studied with
Regnier in the autumn of 1872 (*Ibid.*, 177). After acting
successes in both France and England,[28] MacKaye returned to
America in the spring of 1874 (MacKaye, I, 197). On
February 21, 1874, he had written William Alger from
London:

> Instead of going into the world as an actor, I have retired
> into my study, impelled by a great desire to more
> perfectly prepare myself to *lay the foundations of a
> complete and radical reform of dramatic philosophy.* I have
> been investigating with the greatest ardour *the whole
> subject of Emotion.* I have been developing its facets into
> three distinct branches of study. First—physiognomy of
> Emotion. Second—The physiology of Emotion. Third—
> The poetry of Emotion. Now I hope to see a grand *corps
> of playwrights* spring up in America. . . . I shall settle

down quietly to begin the practical work of creating a corps of fine actors and dramatic authors.

I shall organize a conservatory—in little and in secret—and drill a class thoroughly from the very beginning and, when they are ready, I shall unexpectedly produce a new order of play and a higher order of talent for the stage. (Ibid., 221–23)

Three years later, MacKaye fulfilled his desires in his second theatre and school, the School of Expression at 23 Union Square (*Ibid.*, 266). A brief glimpse of MacKaye in his new setting is given in a published article reprinted in *Epoch*.

On the upper floor Mr. J. Steele MacKaye has a very pretty parlor, hung with choice engravings, etchings and oil paintings, notably a portrait of his celebrated master Francois Delsarte. The chamber is charming, picturesque, artistic to a degree. At the further end of the apartment is a well-arranged stage for his pupils. (*Ibid.*, 267)

In a pamphlet written especially to clarify the misconceptions which had begun to spring up about the young manager-teacher and his master, MacKaye attempted to state the need for an acting school and to give an indication of how his School of Expression would fulfill the needs of the American theatre. The pamphlet, *Conservatoire Aesthetique, or School of Expression,* is one of the few clear presentations of Mac-Kaye's attitude concerning the state of the theatre and what he intended to do about it. The function of the Theatre and School of Expression, MacKaye said, was to "convert the theatre into an unsectarian temple, where both high and low would be brought into sympathetic rapport; where the most opposite classes might learn to understand each other better, and to love and respect each other more" (Ibid). In order to accomplish this "rapport" among people, the theatre "must be able to command the services of a corps of artists who can, by the perfection of their art, make the finest dramatic literature fascinating to those promiscuous masses of society upon whose support the existence of the theatre depends" (*Ibid.*). It is clear that he saw the actor as the center of the theatre. Regardless of the effectiveness of a play as a work of art, MacKaye believed that it would fail to accomplish its purpose without the assistance of fine actors.

In order to raise the quality of acting, MacKaye once again asserted that the actor must be trained in the rudiments of his art.

> *Managers,* well aware of this condition, *are* gradually *giving more and more dangerous prominence to the merely spectacular portion of theatric {sic} art; and the plays which win success to-day are those which depend more upon their sensational stage attire than upon the dramatic ability of the acting company.* —Thus, the purely material side of the art threatens to out-strip the ideal and aesthetic side, and to end in dedicating the theatre to mere sensation and frivolity. . . . *Hundreds crowd to perform in public who have had no preliminary training.* —Is this right? —Would any man dare apply to the leader of an orchestra for position among his musicians, if he had not already given years of study to his special instrument? —*Is the human body, with its infinite stops—a whole orchestra of instruments in itself—less worthy of attention than a violin, a flute, a trumpet, or a drum?* It is easier to master?—Certainly not.[29]

MacKaye's answer to the ills of the theatre of his day were not at all conventional ones. The training methods of the theatrical organization of the time were being questioned. Instead of taking on apprentices and training them for specific roles, which was the custom of the time, MacKaye advocated that the aspiring actor be trained *before* applying for a position. Instead of practical "on the spot" training, he proposed to begin by training the actor in the philosophy of his art. MacKaye also claimed a "system" for accomplishing these ends.

MacKaye maintained that the actor was the basis of the theatre, but that he was less well trained in the control of his medium of expression than the musicians in *front* of him and the scenic artist *behind* him. "Why should the actor's art, which is the *centre* and *core* to which the others are merely accessory, be an exception to this rule [of excellence]?" (*Ibid.*, 268). In his second School of Expression at 23 Union Square, MacKaye decided to remedy the situation of the stage and urged the training of disciplined actors to replace the dilettantes who "threatened the deterioration of the stage." As in the St. James School, Steele MacKaye was again the sole teacher. His method of remedying the ills of the theatre was, again, his own version of the Delsarte system.

During the winter of 1878–79, while maintaining the Union Square Theatre School in New York City, Steele MacKaye spent his time profitably lecturing for the Redpath circuit and at Professor Monroe's Boston School of Oratory where he was on the faculty and listed as lecturer on Aesthetics and Dramatic Art.[30] But MacKaye was not long away from achieving one of his principal dreams. He was soon prepared to launch a new and larger project than he had ever before attempted.

On February 4, 1880, the Madison Square Theatre opened. It was to prove an unusual enterprise. Before the new theatre opened, MacKaye proclaimed:

> My idea is to open a theatre where plays reflecting the civilization of the day—its virtues and mistakes—may be rendered with a care and attention to detail characteristic of the French stage. This is my aim. I make no pretense at beginning with perfection. It is necessary, first, to get the best plays; next to secure the same hearty co-operation from the artists as the Théâtre Français in Paris. To this end, I offer all authors 25 per cent of the profits. No one, anywhere, to my knowledge, has ever before offered such terms to the dramatic author. . . . To those of my acting company who prove themselves most able and earnest I offer, in addition to their salaries, an interest in the yearly profits, amounting to 25 per cent, which will be divided among those whose conduct has won them the title of *sociétaire*. In this way I secure for my author a hearty earnestness in rehearsal rarely found on our stage, hopefully enabling me in time to build up a form of dramatic art in America, which will compare

very favorably in delicasy [*sic*], finish and sincerity with
the best dramatic art in France. (*Ibid.*, 300. Reprinted
from *Daily Graphic*)

As a modest first step, MacKaye gained the backing of the
clergy for his new enterprise. Indeed, in a clever but satirical
article, the *Daily News* reported the opening of the theatre
and commented that New York Bishop Potter invoked the
blessing for the opening of the theatre.

> He solemnly invoked blessing upon the house, and
> thereupon intoned in a loud voice: 'By virtue of my
> authority, as a Bishop of the Protestant Episcopal
> Church of America, I now proclaim this place of
> dramatic worship—formally, legally, and canonically
> opened.' (*Ibid.*, 345. Reprint from *Daily News*, February
> 5, 1880)

But the canonical invocation brought with it mixed blessings
in the form of the Mallory brothers, one of them a minister of
the Anglican Church. The financial assistance which the Mallorys offered made it possible for MacKaye to open the Madison
Square Theatre. As part payment for their aid, MacKaye signed
a financially disastrous contract which entitled the Mallorys to
all the profits from his artistic labors, even the profits from his
inventions. In return, MacKaye was paid five thousand dollars
per year. Not one to quibble over terms as yet, MacKaye
looked upon this contract as a gift from heaven. It freed him
from managing the finances of the theatre and permitted him to
concern himself with the purely artistic end of the enterprise
and the training of his pupils. All went well until MacKaye
wrote and produced *Hazel Kirke* (1880). The success of this
play made him realize what a fool he had been to contract
himself for five thousand a year. The situation became untenable. In anger and frustration, MacKaye left the Madison Square
enterprise in 1883, but only after establishing it as one of the
outstanding theatres in New York. The Mallorys and the
Madison Square were to get the profits from *Hazel Kirke* and
other of MacKaye's plays for many years.

MacKaye accomplished a great deal at the Madison Square. He brought David Belasco into the enterprise along with Gustave and Charles Frohman. His plan to open a truly separate theatre school never really developed, however. Instead, he gave young aspirants basic training as actors for the touring company. Franklin H. Sargent clearly stated that he was hired to train young actors in expression, especially those that were sent out on the road.[31] Sargent soon became plagued with applications. " 'During the past two years,' Mr. Sargent states, 'more than two hundred amateurs have applied for instruction at the Madison Square' " (MacKaye, I, 463. From *Boston Herald*, May 1884). Because of the increasing demands of the road shows, there appeared, for the first time in a hundred years, a shortage of actors. Philip G. Hubert, Jr. analyzed the problem in the following manner:

> It happened, as have been foreseen, that the supply of available actors and actresses ran low at last, and the managers of the theatre began to cast about for material out of which more useful actors and actresses might be made. Perhaps owing to the fact that the Madison Square Theatre is associated in the popular mind with a well-known New York clergyman intimately connected in its management, it came about that no theatre has been so overrun with would-be Romeos and Juliets eager to show how fiercely the sacred fire burned within them.[32]

Since the Madison Square had a real need for actors, MacKaye undertook to employ Franklin H. Sargent to train them.

> Gradually the applications in person and by letter from persons who wanted to impress the public from the stage of the Madison Square Theatre became so many that the managers resolved to make some use of the opportunity offered. Mr. Franklin H. Sargent, then an instructor in elocution and dramatic reading at Harvard, was invited to come to New York and classify the applicants for stage life. He listened to all comers, read

all letters, and encouraged the most promising applicants to begin real work, giving lessons to such as came
to New York, and advising the others by letter as to the
best course to pursue. (*Ibid.*, 485–86)

While not completely a "school" in the formal sense, the
Madison Square did teach novices a specific theory and
system of expression, besides training them in a specific style.

After withdrawing from the Madison Square Theatre
operation in 1883, MacKaye was soon drawn into one of the
most fruitful yet frustrating ventures of his life. As Percy
MacKaye stated:

We catch sight of the magnetic presence which drew to
himself groups of young men animated by interests of
psychology, art, sociology, drama, invention. With such
men as his aids, he began once more to build, and—
building with the souls of men—he builded in stuff more
plastic and permanent than stone.

Among such men, in 1883, Franklin Sargent now
rallied others and himself to Steele MacKaye's long-
maturing plans for establishing a National Conservatory
of Theatre's Art, with an experimental theatre for their
practical application. These plans began to take shape, at
first, in rather modest form of a Dramatic School for
amateur aspirants to the stage; but shortly—with my
father's increasing absorption in the scheme—the conception grew apace and became a strictly professional
undertaking, with chief emphasis centered in the theatre—once more, though in modified form, his 'dream
theatre,' to become the excelling rival of his former
playhouse on Twenty-fourth Street [the Madison
Square], in his battle with the Mallorys. (MacKaye, I,
485–486)

Thus, his son Percy claimed that it was Steele MacKaye who
first conceived the idea of the first formal "school" of
dramatic art and, in the late spring of 1884, was about to see
his plans realized. An announcement in the *Boston Herald* of
May 1884 gives the earliest indication of the plans for the new
school and theatre.

> For the first time in this country, a dramatic conserva-
> tory is to be established. This school of dramatic art will
> occupy a new, perfectly equipped *theatre, with instruc-*
> *tion in a wide range of studies from specialists in the highest*
> *rank.*—A distinguished resident of New York, Mr.
> Steele MacKaye, has been for some time nursing a
> devotion to dramatic art, which he desired to put into
> practical form. His enthusiasm infected his friends and
> pupils. They said: 'Let us build a theatre of our own, in
> which our ideas can be put into practice, with none to
> say us nay.' So a company was formed, and two lots of
> land secured on Fourth Avenue, between 23rd and 24th
> Streets, just north of the National Academy of Design.
> The work of tearing down the buildings which have
> occupied these lots was begun May 1, and the *Lyceum*
> *Theatre* will be completed by November 1. (Reprinted
> in *Ibid.*, 462. Italics mine)

"With instruction in a wide range of studies from specialists in
the highest rank"—This was, indeed, a "New School of
Dramatic Art."

A great deal of controversy has raged over the initial
conception of the "school" which was connected with the
Lyceum Theatre. While the *Boston Herald* proclaimed "For
the first time in this country, a dramatic conservatory is to be
established" (*Ibid.*), it has already been amply demonstrated
that Steele MacKaye had called for such a school as early as
1871; established the St. James School later in 1871; the
Union Square School in 1877; and the Madison Square
Theatre in 1880 "to show in his actors the result of training
according to the ideas of Delsarte."[33] According to George
Blumenthal,[34] however, Franklin H. Sargent had suggested
that a more formal school be established at the Madison
Square Theatre and that the Lyceum School was his own idea.
Arthur Edwin Krows also indicated that Sargent first conceived the organization of the Lyceum School.[35] Philip G.
Hubert, Jr., a gentleman who offered a great deal of interesting information about the formation of the Lyceum Theatre
and School at a very early date, substantiated Krows' opinion:

It was not long before capitalists were induced to invest
money in the Lyceum Theatre scheme. The theatre is to
be of the same class as the Madison Square,—devoted to
American pieces of an alleged moral character and
played, so far as possible, by native-born actors. As the
'road' business is the most money-making part of such a
scheme when once a name has been established for the
home theatre and its plays, Mr. MacKaye early began to
organize a corps from which his 'road' companies could
be drawn. *Mr. Sargent suggested the organization of a
regular dramatic school, and offered to direct such an
institution. The offer was accepted. In May last, Mr.
Sargent left the Madison Square Theatre and traveled
to Europe to study the organization and methods of stage
schools there.* (Hubert, 486) [emphasis added]

The earliest notice of the formation of the Lyceum Theatre
and School was the one printed in the *Boston Herald* in May
1884. Shortly thereafter, in the July issue of *Century Magazine,* Sargent made his first known plea for an acting school.[36]
The contention that Sargent conceived the idea for the
Lyceum School is supported by a great deal of testimony.
There is no doubt, however, as to who was the head of the
institution. Gus Frohman, as partner of both Sargent and
MacKaye categorically stated: "MacKaye runs the whole
operation and will do so next year."[37]
The strongest support for MacKaye, however, comes from
the press. The newspapers of the period give ample testimony
that MacKaye was the prime mover of the entire Lyceum
operation. The development of his other schools and his
preoccupation with discovering a practical teaching form for
the Delsarte system tend to support the contention that the
idea for the Lyceum School was Steele MacKaye's. It is difficult
to conceive that MacKaye had little influence in the organization of the staff and the classes. He was instrumental in bringing
Sargent to the Madison Square, and testimony substantiates
that it was his influence that lured Sargent to the Lyceum. It
should be remembered that MacKaye was once a tutor to
Sargent, and Sargent gives abundant praise to MacKaye for

what was taught him. Moreover, Sargent's letter in the *Century* is very little different from one appearing thirteen years earlier by Steele MacKaye titled *A Free School of Dramatic Art.* The fact remains that MacKaye was undeniably the head of the Lyceum project and it was he who gave it vital leadership and purpose. Whether or not Sargent initially conceived the idea for the organization of the school need not be settled here. The evidence for both sides seems equally strong.

If MacKaye was not the organizer of the school's curriculum, he was certainly the force behind it. If he was not responsible for formulating the structure of the Lyceum curriculum, he was certainly the molder of the idea. If he was not responsible for the specific approach to the subject matter taught in the courses, he was the formulator, along with Delsarte, of the philosophy of acting which was taught. The Lyceum Theatre School, then, can be said to be the fullest expression of Steele MacKaye's contribution to the American acting school.

TEACHING METHODS

The contributions of Steele MacKaye to the development of acting schools in America were not only in the theoretical realm, but in the practical realm as well. MacKaye gave meaning to the speculative philosophy of Delsarte, but it was in his teaching methods that MacKaye demonstrated the practicality of the theory and added some refinements that were to have great impact on the American theatre.

Until the Lyceum Theatre School, Steele MacKaye had generally followed the practice of lecturing and of teaching acting through individual and group tutoring. His teaching practices differed from many contemporary tutorial methods, however, because MacKaye was not preparing his pupils for individual roles, but was teaching them a whole new aesthetic philosophy as well as a method applicable to *any* role. The St.

Frequently maligned, Delsarte had immense influence on North American acting theory. (Photo courtesy of Dartmouth College Library)

James and The Union Square operations were schools of acting in which MacKaye was the sole teacher of Delsarte principles. The Madison Square Theatre School, under MacKaye's direction, hired Franklin Sargent who also taught students by means of a fully cultivated "system" which was to set the mode for the Lyceum School.

MacKaye's methods of teaching appear to have been diametrically opposed to the "imitative" and elocutionary methods which were current at the time. Pupils were encouraged to discover the best form of acting through their own natural development after being presented with the theory. Imitation of the teacher was frowned upon; instead, individual expression and spontaneity were advocated. Thus, it was believed that everyone to whom the Delsartian philosophy had been presented possessed the essential elements necessary for fine acting. The degree to which one took advantage of this knowledge depended upon the ability to convert theory into practice.

The relationship between the teacher and the pupil was quite intimate and informal. As in Delsarte's Cours Aesthétique, MacKaye availed himself of the lecture method to explicate the philosophy. Next, he appears to have employed a series of "exercises" which demonstrated the practicality of the method. Thus, MacKaye was first a teacher in the academic sense when explaining the philosophy; and a working practitioner when demonstrating the workability of the method. Once students grasped the essential philosophy, they were given "exercises" for practice, relaxation and control. If these were successful, the teacher encouraged the development of the imagination and spontaneity as students achieved truthful aesthetic expression.

MacKaye's chief addition to the Delsarte system was his method of making the theory practicable for the actor. In doing so, his major contributions appear to have been what he termed "Aesthetic" or "Harmonic Gymnastics," and "Gamuts of Expression." These exercises were the most objective and the most easily grasped feature of the whole system and

Madison Square Theatre: A uniquely innovative theatre for more reasons than the elevator stage. (Photo courtesy of Dartmouth College Library)

appear to be what the charlatans seized upon—and what led, more than anything else, to the misapplication and ridicule of Delsartian principles and practice. The central element of MacKaye's method of teaching lay in "Harmonic Gymnastics," a series of exercises of which relaxation or "decomposing" seemed to be the primary purpose. It is difficult to determine whether these exercises were a part of the system as taught by Delsarte or whether they were added wholly by MacKaye. In one of his frequent lectures MacKaye credited Delsarte with a system of exercises:

> Delsarte has an adequate background for the basis of his system. His long study enables him to extend to the student of art three gifts, (1) a simple but philosophical and effective method for the treatment and study of his subject, (2) a profound knowledge of aesthetics, elements and principles of his art, and (3) a system of significant exercises which will develop to the utmost his executive power and give him the greatest command of his instrument. (Morris, 44–45)

In 1892, however, MacKaye clarified the extent of his contribution to the system. In an article which appeared in the July issue of *Werner's Voice Magazine,* MacKaye's wife, acting on her husband's instructions, wrote: "The whole system of aesthetic or harmonic gymnastics is, from the first word to the last, Mr. MacKaye's invention."[38] MacKaye had urged his wife to clarify the situation in a letter to her dated April 11, 1892, which reads in part:

> I enclose your thoughtful page, with the questions answered. In relation to Harmonic—or, as I first called them, Aesthetic Gymnastics,—they are, in philosophy as well as in form, absolutely my own alone, though founded, in part, upon some of the principles formulated by Delsarte.—In the beginning of my teaching I never dreamed of separating my work from his, for it was done in the same spirit as his, and I cared not for the letter, nor the fame.—It is only now, when others are

teaching so much nonsense in his name, and basing it
upon truths stolen from me, that I am forced to do this.
It is not done to detract from the desert of Delsarte, but
to defend us both from the frauds who trade upon and
obscure—by an irrational and sentimental presentation
of inconvertible truths—our philosophy as well as our
names. (MacKaye, II, 270)

Supporting MacKaye's statement was the daughter of
Delsarte. While on a tour of the United States, Mme. Geraldy
was beset with questions concerning her father and the
relations he had with Steele MacKaye. Concerning Mac-
Kaye's claim that he had originated "Harmonic Gymnastics,"
Mme. Geraldy stated: "My father taught expression . . . he did
not teach gymnastics. I do not say your relaxing exercises . . .
are not valuable, for I believe they may be for certain
purposes; but I say that my father did not teach them."[39] Mrs.
Steele MacKaye also quoted M. Alfred Giraudet, a pupil of
Delsarte, as having said: "With the exception of two or three
exercises for the development of suppleness of the arms,
Delsarte paid no attention to gymnastics in general" (Mac-
Kaye, I, 187). The weight of evidence seems to support
MacKaye in his claims of having formulated "Harmonic
Gymnastics" and the "Gamuts of Expression" for the purpose
of relaxation and control of the body as an expressive
instrument.

Genevieve Stebbins, a pupil of MacKaye's at the Union
Square Theatre and School, wrote *The Delsarte System of
Expression*[40] which is regarded as conforming, externally at
least, to MacKaye's theory and practice. She received her
knowledge of Delsarte from MacKaye, and her book, with its
application of "Harmonic Gymnastics" and "Gamuts of Expression," gives valuable insight into his methods. Stebbins
defined "Harmonic Gymnastics" as movements which "free the
channels of expression, and the current of nervous force can
thus rush through them as a stream of water rushes through a
channel, unclogged by obstacles"(*Ibid.*, 11). The "decomposing" exercises appear to have been limbering-up exercises and

Even more revolutionary than the Madison Square Theatre, the Lyceum seated only 614 patrons, an unheard-of number for the time (1884). There is little doubt that MacKaye's vision of acting style resulted in this choice, despite the financial consequences. It is interesting that playwright August Strindberg called for the same sort of intimate theatre some eighteen years later. The Lyceum Theatre also housed the classrooms for The Lyceum Theatre School. (Photo courtesy of Dartmouth College Library)

based on the assumption that a relaxed body will free both body and mind. The concept is similar in idea to certain modern acting theories which claim that physical and mental relaxation are intimately related and essential to good acting.[41]

After the first phase, or "decomposing exercises," "Harmonic Gymnastics" extended to the various expressive organs of the body. Delsarte's fundamental positions of the head, arms, legs, hands, etc. were used as the basis for these movements. In this way the student could study and experience the relationship of emotion to its expression, exercise and gain control of all parts of the body employed in expression. The following chart (p. 36) which explicates MacKaye's analysis of the positions of the attitudes of the

	NORMAL	ECCENTRIC	CONCENTRIC
N O R M A L	Normo-normal. Weakness, respect, attention. Feet parallel, equal weight.	Normo-eccentric. Transitory: preparing to step aside. One foot bearing weight, other free.	Normo-concentric. Strength in repose; quiet force. One foot drawn back. Weight on rear foot. Front foot free and knee bent.
	1	2	3
E C C E N T R I C	Eccentro-normal. Confidence; vertigo; absolute repose. Feet parallel and wide apart. Equal weight.	Eccentro-eccentric. Violence; vehemence. One foot far advanced. Weight on front foot. Rear foot free.	Eccentro-concentric. Defiance. One foot drawn back. Weight on rear foot. Front foot free and extended.
	4	5	6
C O N C E N T R I C	Concentro-normal. Hesitation. One foot drawn back, the other advanced equal weight.	Concentro-eccentric. Pomp or ceremony. One foot crossed behind. Weight on rear foot. Front foot free.	Concentro-concentric. Weakness succeeding violence, one foot drawn far back. Weight entirely on rear foot. Front foot free.
	7	8	9

ATTITUDES OF THE FEET.

(Stebbins, 177)

feet, may clarify this point. As already clearly established, no gesture, movement or vocal expression was permitted without a clear *motive*.

Following the study of the nine basic positions of the individual organs, MacKaye probably gave more elaborate exercises. Miss Stebbins describes the next step as demanding more complicated movement which included exercises for Back Full, Front Full, Kneeling, Pivoting, Bowing, Rising from Sitting, Rising from Kneeling, etc. (Stebbins, 83–85). The progress of the pupil, then, began with simple exercise of the arm or leg, *and culminated in* a complete unit of action. Suggestions for situations, or circumstances, were given which would require the action of "Kneeling," and the student would determine a motive, refer to the emotional attitude, and then examine the appropriate expression as laid out in the nine basic attitudes of the organs involved.

After the students mastered the "Harmonic Gymnastics," they were assigned a "Gamut of Expression in Pantomime" to reproduce.[42] An example of an exercise is given by Stebbins. The student was told, "You are standing idly in a room; a step on the stairs attracts your attention. The door opens to admit a person for whom you have an affection. You greet this person in delighted surprise."[43] After the "situation" was given the student, suggested movements appropriate to the emotional and physical action as indicated by Delsartian "attitudes," "gestures," and "inflections" were offered. Stebbins is again helpful, because she reprints several of these exercises in complete form. Using the situation suggested above, the student was given the exact movements of the body necessary to reproduce the scene.

> Assume attitude of legs con. ex.; right leg strong. Attention called to the noise on right, you lift your right ear, eyes turning left in opposition. Door opens. Eyes turn right toward object entering. Head follows in rotary motion leveling gaze on object. Face assumes an expression of delighted surprise. Titillation of eyelids. Head lowers slightly toward object in tenderness, con.-

con.; shoulders rising in opposition. Movement creeps
down upper arm and turns eye of elbow toward object
thus asserting tenderness. This movement has slightly
bent forearm as it hangs from elbow decomposed. Now
unbend forearm. Rotary movement of wrist turns hand
into relative attitude con.-ex. Hand then expands in
conditional attitude ex.-nor., affection. During action of
arm head has been rising in its proportionate arc; it
finishes in attitude con.-ex., abandonment to affection.
(*Ibid.*, 177–78)

This description, from the pen of one of MacKaye's pupils at
the Union Square, presents a curious blend of Delsarte's
basic positions for the body and of MacKaye's "Gamuts of
Expression." It also illustrates how far the idea of "spontaneity," the keystone of MacKaye's acting theory, had been
mechanized.

The conception of "Harmonic Gymnastics" and "Gamuts
of Expression" can be traced to MacKaye's desire to improve
the instrument of the actor. Unfortunately, his ideas and
practices were corrupted by those who were not aware of
their significance and the purpose for which they were
intended. Clearly, the idea of *motive* behind every gesture or
utterance was crucial. Moreover, the motive was recognized
by both Delsarte and MacKaye as originating in the student!
Through her husband, Mrs. MacKaye clarified many of the
problems attendant upon the teaching of the "Harmonic
Gymnastics" and "Gamuts."

These notes [MacKaye's notes from which he lectured
and instructed] are useful only as reminders, to the
pupil, of the exercises which have been given previously
by the teacher, and which have already been done by the
pupil under the teacher's eye. As reminders, therefore,
they are most valuable, but as directions to be followed
from a written page and without a competent guide,
they are of little benefit, as the subtleties of movement
are the distinguishing characteristics of these exercises.
. . . So he [MacKaye] has preferred to keep his notes in
manuscript, until such time as he was prepared to

> present them in a completed and permanent form, for
> the use of well-trained teachers.—Many of Mr. Mac-
> Kaye's notes, however, have been published far and
> wide, without his consent, and the books containing
> them are fast increasing in number. . . . As these notes
> were not arranged for publication, and as these exercises
> were always given to meet the special requirements of
> the pupil, it follows that only in rare cases, even in the
> direct copies from his manuscript, is there given an
> arrangement of the exercises of which Mr. MacKaye
> could approve; while, in the perversion and exaggera-
> tions so frequently met with, the true meaning and value
> of the exercises are wholly lost. . . . (MacKaye, I, 187)

Two things emerge as having great significance: (1) Mac-
Kaye was working on a system of exercise designed to aid in
relaxing the "total" actor, and (2) he was developing a form of
controlled improvisation. The suggestions given by Stebbins
in her book, *The Delsarte System of Expression,* seem totally
mechanical with their specific suggestions concerning what to
do and exactly how it should be done. MacKaye, on the other
hand, appears to have hit upon the creation of imaginary
scenes which could serve as stimulation to the actor. He did
not appear to employ "scenes" from plays, but rather situations which could happen in *any* play. The purpose, it is
assumed, was to study the reactions of a person in *any*
situation. MacKaye did *not* employ "Harmonic Gymnastics"
and "Gamuts of Expression" as mechanical exercises. They
were intended to stimulate the actor to possibilities, test the
refinement of control, attain relaxation and, finally, arouse
the imagination and instinct to individual spontaneity and true
aesthetic expression. The degree of control which the
"Delsarte" positions placed on a given exercise might be
debated, but it must be remembered that MacKaye and
Delsarte insisted on instinct and spontaneity.

The basic positions of Delsarte, called "attitudes," were *not*
considered as limiting or prescribing the *exact* form of
expression. On the contrary, MacKaye intended them as
observations which presented a working frame of reference

and exercise for the actor. Indeed, besides the nine basic "attitudes" of the head, there were literally hundreds of "inflections" in units of three and nine. These "inflections" were even subtler variations or combinations of the physical manifestation of emotion.[44] MacKaye believed that the actor would be adequately "free" for spontaneous expression only when *complete* control of the body was mastered. When the actor spontaneously synthesized thought, feeling, and expression, it could be said that he was truly operating in the realm of the aesthetic. MacKaye's position is not so far from the principles underlying Tai Chi, so popular in modern training methods.

It is interesting to note that as recently as 1972, E. T. Kirby commented: "This is to suggest that the Delsarte method, now long forgotten, may still contain clues that could direct us toward that which is presently lacking in training and toward new forms of theatre."[45] Kirby investigated the various techniques advocated by Delsarte and concluded: "This same orientation to the objective expression in terms of signs—a conscious technique—is a means of exposing the spiritual process of the actor" (*Ibid.*, 68). Further, Kirby recognized that conscious technique liberated the actor and quotes Jerzy Grotowski, who said, "And we find that artificial composition not only does not limit the spiritual but actually leads to it" (*Ibid.*). (It should be added that Grotowski acknowledged Delsarte as being one of the principal influences on his theory of acting.) Kirby also recognized what is difficult for many to grasp: the so-called Delsarte method's system of signs was merely the semiotic translation of physical expression of emotion and physical states, and not a prescription for imitative practice. Delsarte is quoted as saying, "The semiotic is a science, the aesthetic an act of genius" (*Ibid.*, 69). Kirby concludes by recognizing that the final leap for the actor who studies the Delsarte method is the "fourth frontier, the aesthetic, which is inherent in Delsarte's method" (*Ibid.*).

In the hands of Steele MacKaye, the Delsarte system became an active force in generating a new acting style and a whole new concept of acting. MacKaye developed a new generation of young actors and actresses, and had trained a nucleus of teachers who were to carry on the philosophy of Delsarte and the idea of the acting school. The St. James Theatre and School lasted about five or six months and MacKaye taught only the immediate cast of his play, *Monaldi*. Of this group, Ada Griswold was the best known.

The Union Square School was in operation intermittently for nearly three years. It is not possible to determine the exact number of students at this school, but Blanche Meda, Ida Grey, Genevieve Stebbins (stage name Agnes Loring), and C. W. Couldock were among the outstanding graduates. Certainly the most famous actor who credited MacKaye as his teacher was the well known actor, John McCullough. Samuel Silas Curry and Franklin H. Sargent were also students under MacKaye at the Union Square.

MacKaye's influence and teaching at the Madison Square Theatre and School must have affected literally hundreds of aspiring actors and actresses. Harrison Grey Fiske, drama critic for the *New York Dramatic Mirror*, wrote of MacKaye and the school:

> He was a genius. He demonstrated this at the Madison Square, of which every detail was as practical as it was original. . . . Yet I think he is best of all as a teacher of the art of acting. He made the Madison Square a school for actors. He had this idea in his brain when he built that theatre, which lived upon his ideas long after he had been turned out of it. He created a new school of acting—the Hazel Kirke school.[46]

MacKaye cannot be credited as being the only teacher of the one hundred pupils who registered for instruction at the Lyceum Theatre school in 1884. However, he did work with a great number of them in the theatre's first production, *Dakolar*. Among those students were such aspiring actors as Lincoln A. Wagenhals, Robert Tabor, Dorothy Dorr, Wilfred Buckland, George Fawcett, Alice Fisher, Emma Sheridan,

Blanche Walsh, Harriet Ford, Grace Kimball, Cora Maynard and a host of other luminaries. The list of MacKaye's pupils is impressive in both numbers and in the quality of talent. It is quite likely that the powerful personality of Steele MacKaye helped to shape both the style and approach to acting of many of them.

MacKaye's contributions to both theory and the practice of teaching acting were unique. He was dedicated to raising the perceived "status" of the theatre as an art form and the actor as the principal servant of the institution. Toward that end he accepted Delsarte's view that the theatre was an instrument that benefited mankind, served a social and spiritual purpose, and was the strongest force in the improvement of the quality of life. Consequently, he believed that acting should have underlying principles common to other arts and professions.

Many of the theoretical principles espoused by the Mac-Kaye-Delsarte system form the core of modern theory and method. It called for identification with the character and insisted that the actor must have a motive behind each character's movement, gesture and utterance. This view suggests that an objective is pursued which concentrates the actor's attention and organizes the totality of thought, feeling and means of expression. The MacKaye-Delsarte system also seems to be the first prescriptive acting theory to consider in depth the emotional base of expression. Instinct and "emotional memory" play a critical role in a system which encouraged the actor to draw upon these sources as the wellspring and foundation of truthful acting. Also, the idea that the imagination held an important role in actor training was prophetic; that it could be developed and cultivated was revolutionary. MacKaye was convinced that once physical freedom was reached through relaxation, and once control of the medium of expression was attained, the imagination could be liberated and true spontaneity achieved. He contributed a series of exercises designed to relax the body and to free the channels of expression, and introduced improvisational elements into the exercises by suggesting imaginary scenes and situations out of context with any play, anticipating modern training techniques. And, finally, he was the first to call for and found a school of acting as we know it today. Steele MacKaye took the training of actors out of the theatre proper, taught them a specific theory and gave them the means to achieve the practical application of the theory.

MacKaye was one of the pioneers in the area of acting—modern acting. Many years before Stanislavsky, he admonished the first class of the Lyceum School, "When you can forget yourself in your art you will have lost your worst enemy."[47] As one of the first Americans who called for an acting school where actors could learn their craft he cautioned: "Don't be afraid of time. . . . Bear in mind that upon you rests the dignity of the beginning, with us, a movement which we believe will do more to ennoble art, and secure for it a place over all the other arts and institutions in the civilized world, than any movement that has thus far been initiated" (*Ibid.*). Indeed, he did found "A New School of Dramatic Art."

Franklin H. Sargent's leadership and vision resulted in the oldest and longest lasting professional acting school in North America, The American Academy of Dramatic Arts.

CHAPTER II
THE AMERICAN ACADEMY
OF DRAMATIC ARTS

When Steele MacKaye opened his Lyceum Theatre and School of Acting in October, 1884, his principal assistant in the project was Franklin H. Sargent. A year later, and after a good deal of quarreling, charges and countercharges, Mac-Kaye severed his connection with the theatre, while Sargent continued as head of the acting school. Renaming it the New York School of Acting in 1885 and finally, The American Academy of Dramatic Arts in 1892, Sargent remained president of the institution for thirty-eight years until his death in 1924.

Sargent was an able and enthusiastic pupil of MacKaye's. He said of the association in 1923,

> On coming to the Madison Square Theatre, I immediately became a pupil of Steele MacKaye and was daily under his tutelage. Meanwhile, I have studied under some of the most famous experts in England, Germany, Paris and in this country; but I am quite content to-day to speak of Steele MacKaye as my principal master, whose teachings mean more to me than all the rest combined.[1]

Sargent, however, did not adhere completely to the Mac-Kaye-Delsarte theory of acting and his departures reflect interesting changes. He appears to have been able to make the transition to the practical and avoided the stigma of being too "mechanical" or too speculative. Because he was able to formulate the principles of acting and synthesize them effectively into a method of teaching, Sargent deserves to be ranked among the outstanding contributors to the development of American acting theory and teaching of acting. Following MacKaye's basic idea, Sargent carried through the organization of a unique "school of acting" that brought together a faculty of specialists in their field to teach aspiring actors a specific theory and technique of acting in formal classes. The "school of acting," which was inspired by MacKaye and organized by Sargent, was the *first* of its kind.

Spurred on by MacKaye's idea for "A New School of Dramatic Art," Sargent wrote an article in 1884 that was prophetic of what was to come. Titled "Conservatoire, Shall We Have One?" the Sargent article maintained:

> The theatre of America has no 'traditions' such as have nourished the Théâtre Français. Our theatre has little of the artistic surroundings that have proved so helpful to the Meiningen company and Henry Irving. Where, then, lies the hope of our theatre?
>
> The revival of the 'stock company' system and all the necessary reforms of the American stage can be sought for in a cultivation of the art spirit in the people (in place of the speculative mania), in the erection *here* of a standard of taste.
>
> Must we go to France for our dramatic instruction? The professors of the Conservatoire are also the principal actors of the Théâtre Français. Teaching and acting are two allied professions, but based on different modes of mental discipline. The actor is an artist, the teacher should be a scientist. The *empirical and imitative method of 'coaching'* for the stage has given way in this country especially to the methods of scientific training.
>
> Surely a little attuning of the instruments, body and voice, a little philosophy, a little study of the history of the human heart, would round many a mechanic or amateur of the stage into an artist.
>
> Whatever reforms are needed for the stage can be easily and quickly brought about by means of a good training school.[2]

When the Lyceum Theatre School, under MacKaye's directorship, opened in October 1884, there were "twenty-nine chairs for professors, not including the business staff,"[3] reported David Belasco in an interview with the *New York Dramatic Mirror*. By February 28, 1885, however, the staff had dwindled to nine, not counting MacKaye. They were:

> Misses Wickham, Whinnery, Serven, Brace and Thompson, and Messers Belasco, Fred. Williams, Franklin Sargent and Steele MacKaye. Belasco and Williams . . . , Stage Managers. (*Ibid.*)

The cause for the dwindling of the staff from the original twenty-nine to nine presents a fairly clear picture of the direction in which Sargent was moving. Sargent appears to have taken the school in hand and administered its policies to his liking. The *New York Dramatic Mirror* reported that by January, Mrs. George Vandenhoff, Max Freeman, Professor Alfred Ayres, William Seymour and Madame Ivan C. Michels had either been dismissed or had chosen to leave the school. The sundry reasons for their departures add to our knowledge of the type of teaching and the philosophy of acting which Sargent opposed. Madame Michels stated that Sargent dismissed her because, "I was not Delsartian and my method didn't suit."[4] Sargent replied in print:

> She did not suit the School. Her style is old fashioned and entirely at variance with our policy. . . . Professor Ayres was a similar case. He belongs to the old school. (*Ibid.*)

Professor Ayres was a little more specific about the nature of their differences. "After the first lecture I was told I should not be wanted any longer, because my system was elocutionary rather than pantomimic."[5] Sargent stated the philosophy of the school quite clearly:

> The Delsarte system was the foundation, and no departure will be recognized.[6]

While Sargent's theory emphasized pantomimic dramatization over vocal instruction, it was not opposed to thorough training in both voice and speech. Quite probably, Sargent objected to the imitative and elocutionary methods of teaching which Ayres and Madame Michels epitomized. (Both taught privately and advertised in competition with the Lyceum School after they left.)

In April 1885, the Lyceum Theatre went through a crisis that resulted in MacKaye's leaving. He was occupied with rehearsals of his play, *Dakolar,* and was literally barricaded inside the theatre until his show opened. It was hoped that the *Dakolar* would solve the financial ills of the Lyceum project. The students rebelled, supposedly because of displeasure with the teaching methods; Gus Frohman was accused of taking $33,000 in tuition money from the schools for the production of *Dakolar,* and the rest of the faculty, including David Belasco, were preparing to leave the enterprise for lack of pay. The play had a two-month run and MacKaye took it on the road. He awoke on June 6, 1885 to discover that he was no longer connected with the school and that "the School authorities [meaning Sargent] are now repudiating MacKaye and his methods."[7] Harrison Grey Fiske quoted Sargent as saying:

> In order to disassociate the name of the Lyceum School from the Lyceum Theatre in name as well as in fact, the former will be known as the New York School of Acting. Mr. MacKaye has no connection in the future with the Lyceum School. (*Ibid.*)

Master and pupil had come to a parting of the way, even though Sargent conceded the debt he owed MacKaye. While Sargent accepted certain of the basic tenets of the MacKaye-Delsarte system, he modified them to conform with his own concept of acting and how it should be taught.

The New York School of Acting opened its doors in October 1885 with the following personnel:

> Instructors—First Term: David Belasco, Stage Manager; Abbie Whinnery, Voice; M. P. Brace, Reading; Ida

Serven, Pantomime; Carla Malvena, Dancing; Ada
Ward, Orthoepy; Franklin H. Sargent, Pantomime;
Lysander Thompson, Makeup.[8]

Since Sargent, for all practical purposes, had been running the
Lyceum School in much his own way, an article by P. G.
Hubert which appeared in *Lippincott's Magazine* of May 1885
is of particular interest. It is the only article concerned with
more than superficial detail of the early period of Sargent's
acting theory and teaching methods.

> Mr. Sargent was engaged in giving his class a drill in the
> expression of emotion by action. *Mr. Sargent, though
> not so enthusiastic a follower of Delsarte as Mr. Mac-
> Kaye, is sufficiently imbued with his ideas to believe that the
> bodily and facial expression of emotion is subject to well-
> defined laws, and even that shades of emotion may be
> conveyed without speech.* He does not believe at all,
> however, in the attempt of Delsarte's disciples to fit
> every emotion and shade of emotion, no matter how
> complex, with its proper facial or muscular expression,
> and to portray grief, for instance, after a fixed model,
> following inflexible rules. . . . *Mr. Sargent agrees with
> Delsarte's critics that to expect a man or woman to act by rule
> is fatal.* Another objection he admits is that, while
> Delsarte's definition of the proper muscular and facial
> accompaniment to certain emotions may be perfectly in
> keeping with a Frenchman, it might be absurd in a
> German or American. . . . But there are some ideas of
> Delsarte which may find recognition in an American
> school for actors. *He believed, for instance, that, while the
> average man has all the requisite means or machinery for the
> expression of emotion, the machinery is rusty.* The merest
> tyro in acting may be able to say to the servant, 'Put
> some coal on the fire,' with the most perfect accent and
> action in the world, because these are words and
> gestures of everyday life. But if he has to say, 'Let the
> wretch be torn limb from limb,' that is quite a different
> matter. *He is not accustomed to give orders of that kind every
> day of his life, and though he may have some notion of how
> the facial and bodily machinery ought to work at the
> moment, it is likely to be rusty. Delsarte's exercises in this*

way of expressing strong emotion are designed to keep this machinery of emotion well oiled and in order for use. And while a husband whose wife has just eloped may not be able to indicate by expression the fact that his wife was young and lovely instead of old and ugly, or that she is rich instead of poor, *there are certain rudimentary emotions the language of which is to some extent the same to all people.* Grief, joy, defiance, anger, supplication, command, etc. have certain recognized forms of expression. It was with great interest that I watched Mr. Sargent's class portray in rapid succession all these emotions. Mr. Sargent's aim is to bring into play positions and expressions which do not occur in every-day life: he does not give these exercises as instruction in acting, but as tending to facilitate acting.[9]

Sargent was quite clear about the need for a "school of acting." He frankly stated:

The stock company form of training was a necessary product of American theatrical history. The stock company of today differs from the old-time organization in both purpose and accomplishment. . . . In response to the changing theatrical conditions the educational needs of the theatre have been met exactly as the needs of life in general, by the evolution from the unsystematic mode of the stock company guild to the organized institution for the education of actors as paralleled by every other art or science.[10]

Sargent regarded the stock company methods as imitative and claimed that the acting school "evolved a deeper and more comprehensive education for the actor's physical instruments, for the instincts, imagination and dramatic powers of the mind, and conceptive and emotional faculties than is possible in the present day theatre" (*Ibid.*). Sargent's idea of the function of the school was that it aided creative growth by enabling the actor to overcome weaknesses and gain eventual command of the expressive instrument. He maintained that "The best teaching throws all on the pupil," and believed the function of the school is "the training of the pupil's mind, cultivation of the right principles of investigation. It is merely a primary department for the higher studies which are never ending in the actor's professional career."[11]

Over the years, certain positions regarding acting changed and new methods of teaching displaced the old. In an interview in 1914 Sargent remarked:

> Many years have been spent in shaping our *modus operandi*. No system should be a mould to which a student should conform, but a corrective influence exerted upon the individual case. Individual teaching [suiting the teacher to the pupil, not the pupil to the teacher], as far as possible, is always the most successful. It is accomplished here with each teacher a specialist in his line. . . . With all its experience to supplement the early knowledge, I feel safe in saying to-day we are nearer the truth.[12]

What was the "truth" to the American Academy of Dramatic Arts? Sargent's theory of acting emphasized original creativeness through the cultivation of imagination and feeling. His Academy of Dramatic Arts, therefore, aimed "to develop the originality of the student, not to impose certain fixed conceptions of character" (*Annual Catalogue*: 1939–40). Before an actor can understand a character, however, "he must know himself." He must "make his body strong and healthy, his voice clear and resonant, and his speech incisive and articulate." Only then will his physical being "respond perfectly to his mind, imagination, and feelings."[13]

One of the primary functions of the actor, then, was to discover, through training, the best way to free, yet control, the three basic elements of his being. Although the American Academy of Dramatic Arts was practical in its interests toward the theatre, it still recognized that the actor was a creator first. In the broad, general sense, then, his function was to create through his imagination, intellect, and feeling "a character, a living human being."[14]

One of the first prerequisites of the Academy-trained actor

was that he must learn to accept "the play as a truth and not a fiction" (D'Angelo, 6). Acting, then, was considered as "living in terms of the theatre," with the playwright dictating the terms. Acting was defined "as that process whereby the actor conceives the character and reveals him before the audience. Conception and revelation—the whole art can be summed up in those two words" (*Ibid.*, 3–4). The actor must accept the imaginative truth of the character unreservedly and unqualifiedly, but his imaginative conjuring must have its roots imbedded firmly in the play (*Ibid.*, 6). Charles Jehlinger, who was in the first graduating class of the Academy and subsequently taught there for nearly forty years, emphasized the fact that the play was supreme and that the playwright was the final arbiter of the character. "The minute you go contrary to the author's instructions, you defeat yourself" (*Jehlinger in Rehearsal*, 9).

Once the actor is firmly convinced of the "truth" of the play, he is able, says the Academy, to believe in the reality of the character he is portraying. In 1918, Jehlinger emphasized, "The character you portray must be you. But it isn't just you. It is you as the character in the situation created by the author. This is acting—and artistry" (*Ibid.*). The Academy is clear concerning the relationship of the actor to the character. "Every character has a heart, brain, and soul. You are the servant of the character; the character is not your servant. The biggest mistake you can make is to divide your brain by using it partly for yourself, partly for the character" (*Ibid.*, 1). At the Academy, the beginning actor was warned again and again about the tenuous relationship of the actor to his character. He was warned, "Your development is nipped in the bud if you do not develop a sensitive response to the character" (*Ibid.*, 2). One dictum that appeared in the *Catalogue* and was taught the actors in the classrooms was "*live* your characters. . . . You must live with them, study their attitude towards the various other characters in the play, their habit of thinking and living" (*Ibid.*, 3). The main source of knowledge of the character sprang from the script. "You must take your text

Charles Jehlinger: A renowned teacher of acting, Jehlinger taught at The American Academy of Dramatic Arts for nearly four decades. A graduate of the Academy, he led the acting program until his death in 1951.

and *study* it (*Ibid.*). The actor's art was based on "The great lesson: eliminate self; to serve gloriously, freely and gladly" (*Ibid.*).

The most pressing question concerning the actor's desire and ability to "lose himself in the character" and to "eliminate self" was the manner in which this transubstantiation took place. Jehlinger and the Academy solved this problem by introducing the "Magic If" long before the phrase was popularized by Stanislavsky. He said to his students:

> Stop and ask yourself. What would happen here in real life? I would do a thing this way—but how am I different from the character that I am portraying? So—how would the character react to this? (*Ibid.*, 7).

The beginning actor was admonished, "Let the character run things, don't dictate to it" (Ibid., 5). The actor, then, does not control the character in the play. "The secret of the whole thing is this: Yield to the character and let it take control of affairs" (*Ibid.*). One of the best ways to eliminate self and to let the character "control" affairs is, of course, to become familiar with the character as the playwright created him. Another dictum which was drummed into the heads of the Academy students was "Don't bring in subject matter that the character wouldn't. She's not thinking about stage business or mechanics. The thought of them is death to the character" (*Ibid.*, 5).

Once the "Magic If" is accepted, the actor wholeheartedly enters into the realm of the imaginative and sheds the world of reality. Yet, the actor cannot foreswear reality completely. The actor, then, works in the realm of imaginative reality, and attempts to reconstruct the human nature of another person—the character. "If acting is not founded on nature, it will never reach the realm of art. All great things are simple and natural" (*Ibid.*, 1). In this way, the Academy would say, actors are shown the common humanity, the universal human traits in characters, and are taught to identify sympathetically with them. The Academy *Catalogue* explained:

> Attention is drawn to the psychological nature which exists in all of us in a greater or lesser degree of intensity—the feelings and passions which, when fully or abnormally developed, bring about those dramatic situations of life which the playwright endeavors to present in a vivid, condensed and classified form. (*Annual Catalogue*, 30).

The actor, then, must create not only the external signs of reality, but the inner manifestations as well. "Establish the age of your character, his nationality, profession, social standing, temperament; his physical, emotional and mental qualities" (*Jehlinger in Rehearsal*, 10).

The final step in the creation of the character was the maintenance of the character throughout the duration of the play. The character must be consistent throughout. "Stay in the scene," remonstrated the Academy teachers. "Never break illusion" (*Ibid.*, 4–5). The whole point of acting, said Sargent, is to "Get under the skin of your character, into the habit of his mind, the habit of his action" (*Ibid.*, 12). Thorough understanding of the nature of the character enables the actor to concentrate, to "Focus your mind on the exact point of thought to be conveyed" (*Ibid.*, 11). For the actor's beginning steps in character, "Concentration is the first great mental state in preparation" (*Ibid.*). From the power of concentration, the focusing of thought and feeling on one point, the actor is able to make the imaginative leap into the world of the theatre. The initial stages of Academy training were devoted to conception only. In the first step, the actor studies the complete script with the attitude that "the play is a truth and not a fiction." In the second, the actor investigates the character to be portrayed, reconstructing every detail of the character's life, looks, mannerisms, physical and mental makeup. Finally, the actor concentrates *as* the character through the "Magic If," focusing thought and feeling and directing them toward the object of attention. This view constitutes a well-conceived and distinctly modern approach to acting prior to the Stanislavsky "system" and its introduction in America!

The actor's relationship to the audience was based on one fundamental precept: "You cannot win an audience by untruth" (Ibid., 3). The basis of this position appears to be grounded firmly on the assumption that the play is a situation occurring in the lives of the characters in which the audience is an unobtrusive onlooker. "How can you be human beings conversing in a *four-walled room* when your brain is handicapped by self thoughts?" (*Ibid*, 5. Italics mine). It appears that the Academy accepted the position that the theatre was illusionary and that the audience was viewing a "slice of life." Instead of awareness of the audience, the actor was asked to concentrate on the character in the "lifelike" situation of the play. This appears to be a concept that is similar to that suggested in Steele MacKaye's notes on Delsarte: Do not curry the favor of the audience; make them come to you. It also brings to mind another Stanislavskian view: public solitude.

Yet the Academy students were not urged to forget absolutely the existence of the audience. Always a pragmatic institution, the Academy recognized that it was, after all, training actors to act before an audience. Thus, a great deal of emphasis was placed upon the actor's ability to "guide" the audience. Aristide D'Angelo, a former student and instructor at the Academy, stated the problem as follows:

> It is the actor's duty to make the audience behave as the character demands. 'The actor's mind must always be quicker than that of the audience,' says Jehlinger. (D'Angelo, 27)

In essence the Academy regarded even the performance situation as a training ground wherein the actor "gets the feel" of the audience. While the Academy admitted that the audience frequently dictates the "taste, proportion, and propriety. . . . This does not mean, of course, that the actor should not strive to steer the audience in its reactions" (*Ibid*.). This is but another way of saying that the actor must cause the audience to believe in the reality of the play and the character.

The basic philosophy of the American Academy of Dramatic Arts was admirably summed up by Sargent in 1896 when he said: "The dramatic school idea is something more than the putting on of plays. It is the training of the pupil's mind, cultivation of his body and the inculcation of the right principles of investigation. It is merely a primary department for the higher studies which are never ending in the actor's professional career."[15] The Academy, then, proposed not merely to teach stage deportment and business, but to develop the "total actor." In this endeavor, Sargent conceived that two major faculties had to be developed: "imagination, which is creative, and interpretation which is realistic" (*Annual Catalogue*, 29). The *Annual Catalogue* further claimed that the work of the Sargent system "cultivated not only the intellectual and physical faculties and functions, but the powers of personality itself—the inner and deeper natures— . . . the temperamental and imaginative, instinctive, and conceptively original powers of feeling" (*Ibid.*, 9).

In an attempt to develop actors through its own particular methods, the Academy conceived acting to be a twofold process of *conception* and *revelation*. In the conceptive part of instruction, the teachers attempted to help the aspiring actors cultivate imagination, intellect and feeling. In the revelatory aspect of their training, the actors worked on technique; *i. e.*, voice, speech, and movement. It should be noted, however, that the classifications *conception* and *revelation* were not treated as being separate; on the contrary, they were seen frequently as interdependent. For instance, when training the voice, the actor was not asked merely to produce sounds for technical effects such as inflection, tone color, grouping, tempo, etc., but to make technique subordinate to mind and imagination. D'Angelo voiced this belief of the Academy tradition when he said: "Keeping the thought alive, fresh, and new will insure correct word stress" (D'Angelo, 49). This view is deeply ingrained in the American acting school tradition and is associated with the MacKaye-Delsarte tradition. Essentially, it amounts to the "think the thought" school of acting similar in outline to Stanislavsky and subscribed to by Strasberg.

The basis of the Academy's theory was the cultivation of the imagination, mind and feeling, and its theory was firmly rooted in the premise that imagination, like principles of technique, could be enhanced. The fundamental principle from which all acting begins, the Academy taught, was that the actor must accept the imaginative truth of the play, surrender to the play, and see it through the character. Belief and acceptance were the keys to the Academy's theory of the imagination. "Imagination may be the mirror in which the raw material of life is reflected" (*Ibid.*, 60), wrote D'Angelo. But, "Life conceived in the imagination is beautiful as compared with life in the raw or life imprinted on memory" (*Ibid.*, 59). The imagination appears to be regarded as a filter through which the actor sees life. The imaginative act, said D'Angelo, occurs "When the individual creates a life of his own making . . . drawing upon his memory of experiences and reshaping them in newer combinations" (*Ibid.*, 58). Imagination, then, was considered to be the power to "recall" vividly, and the faculty which "reshapes" the recollection.

The springboard of the imagination is the memory. "Definite feeling reactions follow the recollection of experiences because our senses react to the memory of them" (*Ibid.*), wrote D'Angelo. The intensity of the memory feeling will depend on the vividness of the reconstructed experience (*Ibid.*). Following the principle of the "Magic If," the actor is asked to eliminate himself and identify with the character. "From this new imaginative life the individual gets definite feeling reactions because his senses work in the imagination. *The nature of his imaginings determine the nature of his feeling reactions—reactions born directly from his imaginative creations but indirectly from his memory of life experiences*" (*Ibid.*, 59. Italics mine). Explaining this complex phenomenon further, D'Angelo said, "The actor's feelings are in a sense real [since they are derived indirectly from memory of life experiences], but imaginatively real, and spring from the selected and perfected life of the stage" (*Ibid.*, 62). D'Angelo may here be influenced by Boleslavsky and the Stanislavsky "system." Writing in 1939, he could have absorbed and integrated many ideas since *Acting: The First Six Lessons* was published in 1933, and before that in a series of articles published by *Theatre Arts Magazine* in 1923–1931. But many of the MacKaye-Delsarte influenced schools embraced similar ideas as early as the 1890s. Drawing on memory of life experience as a source for imaginative feeling was, therefore, an American view long before Stanislavsky appeared on the scene.

The will is nowhere discussed, even though it is evident that the actor "wills" the initial "belief" in the reality of the play and the character he is to portray. How the "belief" is reinforced is not explained, except through the nebulous use of the word "concentration." The Academy is adamant, however, in its conviction that such a process of total acceptance and belief is possible, and once having secured belief, the actor is ready to operate in the realm of the imaginative. Following this course, the actor then employs, indirectly, his own memory of life experiences, and through total identification with the character, reshapes the emotional memory and organizes it to serve the character. In an abstract sense, the actor *is* the character, and the character is merely making use of the actor's life experiences.

The operation of emotion or feeling within the framework of the theory of the American Academy of Dramatic Arts is quite pervasive. The entire concept of acting springs from the feelings which are conjured through the imaginative situation. Given a specific character, the actor was asked to identify *feelingly* with the character, to understand the character's feelings, and to project them. The imaginative act eliminated the actor as a person with an identity; in theory, at least, the actor *is* the character, feeling as the character might feel in the same situation. The *Annual Catalogue* is quite clear in its stand concerning the emotional demands placed upon the actor.

> It does not suffice to indicate emotion; the actor himself must learn to feel . . . he must feel ever more deeply, until he becomes lost in his emotions and all sense of personal limitation vanishes before the anger, the sorrow, the love, the pain or the joy that is stirring within him. (*Annual Catalogue, 33*)

The Academy seems firmly on the side of those who support the contention that the actor must "feel" the emotions which he is portraying.

As indicated in the section concerning the imagination, the Academy accepted the idea that the actor employs his own emotions and places them at the disposal of the character in the imaginative situation. Consequently, feeling or emotion in the theatre should be considered as being "imaginative feeling."

> Imaginative feeling—not feeling derived from direct contact with life or memory—comes closest to the theatric. The play, its characters and the incidents are themselves products of imagination. Artistic feeling comes when the actor is in complete, imaginative *rapport* with the character. It is this artistic or theatric feeling that stirs the actor to physical and vocal expression. (D'Angelo, 59)

There is, then, a distinct difference between the feeling reactions prompted from memory and life experiences and those derived from the imaginative situation. "Imagination may be the mirror in which the raw material of life is reflected, but the reflection itself is beautiful to behold" (*Ibid.,* 60). The Academy maintained that "Because the raw material has changed in this reflection [imagination], it follows that the feelings derived from concentration on this new reflected life have correspondingly changed. They become crystal clear, living, as they do, in a world of imagination" (*Ibid.*).

The manner in which the imagination "reflects" life experiences is not explained in any Academy publication. One is forced either to accept the speculative position merely on faith or to reject it. In some way the imagination "beautifies" the feeling derived from life experiences without sacrificing its intensity or spontaneity. The Academy is adamant, however, about the manner in which the actor draws upon his feeling drawn from life through emotional recall, or what Stanislavsky labeled "affective memory."

> In the light of this analysis one can readily see how false and shallow is the feeling of many actors on the stage. Their characterizations suffer because they will not make characters and incidents their source of study and inspiration. *Many of them will throw their own personal feelings upon the character* to a point where the character is never fully or even partially realized. The actor's personal feelings and the character's imaginative feelings seldom, if ever, blend consciously. But *subconsciously* the richness of the actor's personal feelings born of full living will subtly nourish the character's feelings provided the actor will create and obey the character as shaped in the imagination. (*Ibid.*, 61. Italics mine)

The criterion against which all feeling is measured, then, is the imaginative character in an imaginative situation. "Everything on the stage is imaginative. The feelings, therefore, spring from this imaginative life" (Ibid., 62). Feeling in the theatre must abide by the laws of the theatre—laws based on the fact that the actor is living a character other than his own, in an imaginative realm, on a stage, in a theatre, and before an audience.

The consistency of the concept of feeling and emotion appears to have its origins in the Sargent-Jehlinger period. In 1918, Jehlinger wrote, "Every part must have passion behind it" (*Jehlinger in Rehearsal*, 12). Another of Jehlinger's dicta which became familiar to Academy students concerned the intellect, but it also had an application to emotion. "Your brain [and feelings] no longer belongs to you when you are creating. It is the character's. You have no right to it (*Ibid.*, 5). The short, hard-hitting phrases of Jehlinger were driven home again and again and there was always the same tune: the actor is the servant of the character, and the actor's feelings must correspond with those of the character he is portraying.

Once the actor bridges the gap between reality and imagination, real feeling becomes imaginative feeling which is just as genuine. It is at this point, in a state of imaginative feeling, that the Academy believed creation takes place. How is the creative act stimulated? "Obey your impulses," said Jehlinger. "It is better to be crude by overdoing than to be negative. Obey your impulses at any cost. Don't fear mistakes. Be *fearless*! Yield! Obey!" (*Ibid.*). Repeating an oft-spoken dictum, Jehlinger urged: "The secret of the whole affair is this: Yield to the character and let it take control of affairs" (*Ibid.*). And again, "The emotion will handle itself if you just give in" (*Ibid.*, 4). The Academy obviously was convinced that if the actor was in a state of imaginative animation he was incapable of being untrue in his emotional feeling. This state, of course, was dependent upon the actor's ability to "know" the character's background and to "surrender" completely to the demands of the character. Jehlinger admonished his students, "Trust your instinct, your impulse first, then control it" (*Ibid.*, 11). Artistic or imaginative feeling was considered to be fresh and spontaneous—unencumbered by contemplation. Imaginative feeling was the result of, first, the belief in the character and the incidents; and second, the imaginative creation of the character in a situation through concentration upon what he does in the play which in turn results in instinctive, artistic feeling.

If the actor should intrude his own attitudes and feelings, he is no longer in the realm of the imaginative and, technically, destroys the artistry of his performance. The feelings must be real, but imaginatively real. In this sense, the

Academy differentiates the two modes by indicating the feeling of the actor as opposed to the feelings of the character. Only the latter can attain the realm of true imaginative feeling. Through acceptance of the character, the actor surrenders himself and permits the character to "run things" (*Ibid.*, 4). This surrender of control is, in every way, to be considered impulsive. The actor is now in a complete state of "free play," permitting the character free rein. Jehlinger urged, "Yield. Give in" (*Ibid.*). "Fine feeling is a solvent. It permeates the body, makes it plastic and responsive" (*Ibid.*, 13). The American Academy of Dramatic Arts held the view that instinct guided by imagination will always be right. Again, this position is the basis of the "think the thought" school of acting and a distinctly American tradition.

The function of the intellect is really twofold. First, the actor employs his intellect as an investigative and analytic tool; secondly, the intellect functions as the mind of the character, not as the mind of the actor. Jehlinger's succinct phrases sum up the point admirably. "Use your brain not as your brain, but as 'A' brain, then your brain is usable" (*Ibid.*, 3). Jehlinger made the point more emphatic when he asserted, "You can't do two things at once with your brain; it's hopeless, idiotic" (*Ibid.*, 4). It was believed, then, that the function of the intellect as a critical and investigative faculty halted at the moment of creativity. D'Angelo, in quoting Jehlinger, amplified this Academy point of view.

> The actor should give the character free rein. 'You cannot be critic and creator at the same time,' says Jehlinger. *The critical faculty may work before or after but never during the creative moment.*[16]

Concentration on the object of attention through focusing *all* the actor's resources *as* the character brings about this *total* surrender to the imaginative reality of the moment and permits impulsive and instinctual freedom that will be true and real.

It should be clear from the material already presented concerning the emotion, that imagination and feeling were the prime movers of the Academy's acting theory. Intelligence was certainly not slighted, but it was considered primarily a critical tool to be employed before and after, but *never* during creation. During the moment of creation, the mind or intellect functioned as the character thought. One might say that the character "borrowed" the mind of the actor. Sargent, Jehlinger, and D'Angelo were quite clear about one thing. "Give in to your instincts. Instinct must rule in the performance, not judgement."[17] The worst sin of the actor, according to the Academy, was to be a purely intellectual actor—one who, like Diderot's opinion of Garrick, acted without emotional involvement with the character. "The devil of the theatre is the personification of intellect without feeling. The most beautiful thing in acting is feeling intelligently expressed. That is art."[18]

In this sense, the Academy conceived that intelligence was the logical consistency of the character. This is what Jehlinger meant when he urged, "Use your God-given intelligence in a perfectly simple, natural way" (*Ibid.*, 6). The intelligence of which he spoke was the intelligence of investigation and analysis *before* creation, and the logical behavioral pattern of the character in performance. In performance, the actor uses the brain in terms of the character's needs, never for an instant thinks a thought except as the character would think and react. Any thought or idea which intrudes itself other than in the manner the character would think was considered a breach of good acting. This concept, like so many others we have examined, bears a strong resemblance to the Stanislavsky "system." It appears, however, to have been an organic and practical approach that constitutes a viable prescriptive acting theory, years before Stanislavsky's influence appeared on the scene.

Any institution devoted to the training of actors must, in

some way, supply those aspirants with an adequate means of expressing the imaginative feelings of the characters they are to portray. The American Academy of Dramatic Arts was such an institution. The expressive instruments, the actor's voice, speech, and body were considered the channels of expression through which the playwright's ideas were conveyed. Consequently, the first step in the actor's preparation for his profession was the perfection of his channels of expression. Even before the aspiring actor was given an opportunity to train his imaginative powers, rigorous training was pursued which was intended to free him vocally and physically. The deeper powers of human nature, it was believed, can assert themselves in acting only when the voice and body of the player are free, flexible, and under perfect control. Before an actor can understand a dramatic character "he must know himself," wrote D'Angelo, echoing former teachers. He must "make his body strong and healthy, his voice clear and resonant, and his speech incisive and articulate." Only then will his physical being "respond perfectly to his mind, imagination, and feelings" (D'Angelo, 5). Jehlinger stated the same position. "Only when your body is free and naturally relaxed can the brain function normally, and only when the brain functions normally can work be done."[19] This was also a keystone of Stanislavsky's and Lee Strasberg's views on acting and actor training.

Training of the actor's voice and body, then, were given special consideration by the Academy. The entire basis of the actor's success was the assumption that he was physically free so that he might be creatively free. In the theoretical position and in the methods employed in teaching the techniques required of the actor the Academy tended, from its beginnings, to elevate pantomimic over vocal expression. This apparently stemmed from the early influence of Steele MacKaye and Delsarte. However, the Academy also appears to have found a theoretical position which it conceived as justifying this attitude. "Pantomime is the universal lan-

guage," wrote D'Angelo. "Speech is the result of civilization.
. . . Spoken language, therefore, is conventional and local."[20]
In theory, however, the total physical equipment of the actor
was developed, with each element given sufficient consideration.

The basic training in technique at the American Academy
included exercises for the voice and the body. These physical
exercises were (a) corrective, to remedy bad habits into which
the actor may have fallen, and (b) formative, to "organize the
various parts of the body and to render every movement
definite" (*Annual Catalogue*: 24). Jehlinger stated the general
method of the Academy quite succinctly: "Your whole
motive must be that of genuinely acquiring, of genuinely
improving,—of discovering your weaknesses and turning
them into your strengths" (*Jehlinger in Rehearsal*, 2). Again,
Jehlinger asserted that the whole process of training actors
was one of discovering "weaknesses in order to remedy them"
(*Ibid*).

The Academy recognized the need for good technique in
the theatre and found both practical and theoretical proof to
support its contention. Theoretically, the body and voice had
to be free in order that the mind might be free from dwelling
on the "mechanics" of acting. Practically, the Academy was
aware of the need for a good voice and a body that was
flexible, graceful and free. Consequently, Sargent advocated
a position which was based on the premise that actors must
first rid themselves of the bad habits they have acquired—this
was corrective. Next, the bad habits are supplanted with
constructive training—this was formative, giving the actor the
confidence that engenders relaxation of tension.

In all technical training, the Academy eschewed the mechanical approach. When developing the voice and body
"thought must be dominant" (*Annual Catalogue*, 25). It was
always urged that training in technique should never be
performed in "a perfunctory manner, as in an ordinary
gymnasium." Rather, all training, regardless of the obvious

mechanical nature of it, must be accompanied by an "appropriate feeling" and a "motive." Even the Delsartian exercises in the teaching of pantomime were regarded as secondary, since the student "is concentrated in the emotion which causes the action" (*Ibid.*). This theory of training in technique was consistently supported by Sargent, Jehlinger, and D'Angelo. Technique was regarded as a means to an end, not an end in itself. It was regarded as necessary for good expression, since the body and voice are the means of expression. Therefore, complete mastery of the physical equipment of the actor was the goal, since only complete mastery could produce the freedom necessary to imaginative acting.

One other point must be considered concerning the Academy's theoretical position regarding technique. It was believed that bodily movement and vocal utterance were not separate items. True, they are different channels through which the thought, feeling, and desire of a character are made manifest. They may be different means of communication "but they must both communicate the same thing at the same time. . . . There should always be a balanced harmony between gesture and voice, the one supplementing the other according to which is more important at the moment" (D'Angelo, 52–53). The technical side of acting must have the same feeling of wholeness that is necessary to the imaginative, emotive and intellectual side. In the final analysis, the Academy regarded acting as an expression of the "total" man—the union of imagination, mind, feeling and technique. Technique is the servant and the channel. It is the outward expression of the inner state.

The relationship of art to nature was a source of constant investigation at the Academy. Courses in Life Study were established so that the students might perfect their ability to examine the minute details of life. However, one must ultimately regard their position concerning the matter as being somewhat eclectic. The playwright was considered the dictator of the relationship of art to nature. Respecting the playwright's right by entering into the imaginative reality of his play, the actor was urged to adapt his view of life and reality to the playwright's. If the playwright regarded life as composed of minute details, the actor was expected, after accepting the imaginative reality of the play, to express these details. On the other hand, the playwright might see life only in its broadest and most significant aspects. The actor was, again, asked to comply with the proper expression.

It should not be assumed, however, that the Academy took no definite stand concerning the relationship of art to nature. Art is selective and, therefore, "Don't blur your canvas with too many details" (*Jehlinger in Rehearsal*, 7), said Jehlinger. The Academy was aware that the theatre involved imaginative expression, and not merely a direct representation of life. Jehlinger urged the student to "emphasize more on the stage than you do in real life" (*Ibid.*, 11). D'Angelo reiterated the basic position of the Academy when he said:

> However much we contradict it, we come sooner or later to the inevitable conclusion that a play is a cross section of life filtered through the imagination of the artist. As a result of that filtration process, characters and situation and their expression in form are necessarily condensed. (D'Angelo, 33)

The Academy, then, never taught that the theatre is a direct representation of life. "Everything in the play, every minute detail, even down to that which may appear casual, is significant. Insofar as it lacks significance in any of its parts, the play is deficient and can be entered on the debit side of the artistic ledger" (*Ibid.*, 32). Sargent, too, conceived that the theatre was selective and, in many ways conventional. This, it is imagined, is the reason for his maintaining the validity of some of Delsarte's and MacKaye's ideas concerning "certain rudimentary emotions the language of which is to some extent the same to all people."[21] The Academy recognized that a play, after all, was performed before an audience, and that it must be heard and seen. These requirements, it was believed, produced certain accepted conventions. While the Academy warned against clichés in acting and demanded that the actor abhor imitation, it appeared to accept that, especially in pantomime, there are certain fundamental attitudes and expressions which, if produced through concentrated imaginative thought, are recognizable by all mankind.

The contributions of the American Academy of Dramatic Arts as it evolved from the Lyceum Theatre School and the New York School of Acting were many. As Bronson Howard, noted American playwright, remarked:

> We [Americans] have been the first in the world to establish a fully organized school for the training of young men and women for the stage, with a large corps of teachers (twenty-four) for the various branches of the art, with additional lectures, and with special exercises in each requirement, physical and intellectual, and a graded curriculum, regular classes, and all such details as belong to other academic institutions.[22]

Besides the unique organizational structure of the American Academy of Dramatic Arts, the school also contributed to the body of American acting theory. MacKaye's earlier attempts must be considered the endeavors of a single man dedicated to the propagation of a specific acting theory. Here, for the first time, one encounters a similar but more developed acting theory, broken up into branches of specialization and taught by numerous instructors.

It is critical to recognize the fact that The American Academy of Dramatic Arts developed from the MacKaye-Delsarte tradition. That is not to say that the Academy contributed nothing new to acting theory. On the contrary, it built on the tradition, embellished and brought it to its fullest development. Further, under Charles Jehlinger a new and extended version of the MacKaye-Delsarte tradition clarified acting theory, made it accessible and developed a coherent, prescriptive theory that could be used by actors in the practical world of the theatre.

TEACHING METHODS

The basic position of the teacher-pupil relationship at the American Academy of Dramatic Arts has not changed since its inception. Sargent and the Academy were adamant about one major concept.

> No teaching can give anything—it can only draw out and encourage or discourage tendencies in the pupil.[23]

This method of indirection, of the slow process of attempting to draw out the latent talent of the individual actor, was critical. Sargent was dismayed at the difficulty of obtaining good teachers.

> The greatest difficulty I have to contend with is the almost absolute ignorance on the part of the dramatic profession of what the proper educational policy and processes really are. . . . At once there comes the question—not who can be the pupils of such an institution so much as who can be the teachers, and this is really a serious difficulty, for there are very few trained teachers except in the mechanical branches of the art. While efficient instruction can be found in dancing, fencing, singing, and the like, it is quite difficult to find those who, without imitative methods, can develop the pupil's needs. There are many who can illustrate and train by imitation; there are many who coach, but such instructors have no real educational method and do not bring out the best in the pupil. (*Ibid.*)

Sargent conceived the ideal relationship in every classroom to be that association enjoyed between the director and actor. "Every stage manager is or should be a teacher," he said, and "every actor is a pupil under the direction of a stage manager" (*Ibid.*). Sargent reiterated this same point of view fifteen years later.[24]

The teacher at the Academy was conceived as a "guide" and the purpose was to teach the actor "to use his tools before he

TOP: The teacher at the far left is May Robsen who taught at the Academy before going to Hollywood to gain late-in-life fame playing character roles.

"HAIL, KING THAT SHALL BE !"
Pupils rehearsing the spectre scene from "Macbeth."

makes his house suffer while he learns by experience. The guide says 'That is the way.' The student may take his word for it or he may climb a tree for a perspective of his own, and perhaps find a shorter cut. That is the value of initiative to the student. Let him verify what he is told" (Krows, 3. Quoting Sargent). The basis of the teacher-pupil relationship, then, consisted of the independent investigation by the pupil under the helpful supervision of the teacher. "Best teaching throws all on the pupil. A teacher is a pair of eyes, a pair of ears, and a warning brain, not making actors, but helping and criticising them through the early stages" (*Ibid.*). Nothing could be clearer than this explanation. Sargent wanted the actor to grow and be encouraged through constructive criticism. The growth and initiative were always upon the actor. Imitation was frowned upon. The teacher merely provided the stimulus and the prodding to challenge the actor to improve and to grow.

The Academy appears to have been intimately concerned with the well-being of the students, and Sargent seemed always sincere in his attempt to provide the student with the best teachers and the most challenging and varied curriculum possible. Early in the student's career at the Academy, he was tested and retested in order to reveal more about temperament and talent. The purpose of these tests was to supply the teacher with information which would help in developing the individual student. Sargent explained the process as follows:

> The first problem is to find the nature of the individual pupil. Much is learned from the entrance examinations, which are calculated to bring out the salient features of the candidate's experience and manner of thinking, his imagination, temperamental nature. From the answers and elaborate practical tests, each instructor gets data that has bearing upon his department, and in his own line finds the specific needs of the pupil. After some weeks, during which these views have become more or

less adjusted, the faculty meets to discuss each case and deal with it harmoniously. Much of the earliest part of the curriculum is devoted to this gradual accommodation of teacher and student. Each pupil, having almost unconsciously betrayed his habit of mind, is taken in his own way, so that he is not confused by having unfamiliar tools thrust into his grasp for the performance of unaccustomed work. (*Ibid.*)

The practice of testing prospective students has been a policy of the Academy since its founding. Indeed, Sargent's first duty upon his coming to the Lyceum School was to screen the more than four hundred applicants who applied for admission in the Summer and Fall of 1884. In 1885, Philip G. Hubert reported, "Before the School was opened, preliminary examinations were held, and some persons physically or mentally unfit for work were kindly advised to save their money and time" (Hubert, 486). In 1896, Ernest P. Stevenson was the interviewer. A brief description of the nature of the testing process makes it amply clear that, from the beginning through 1914, the testing procedures had not changed.

Each student is required to pass an entrance examination, the first process of the kind ever introduced in stage work. This examination is in charge of Ernest P. Stevenson, an expert who devotes his entire time to it. It includes a thorough investigation by questions and answers, of matters of past environments, education and experience, previous occupation, state of health, age, etc. All the physical conditions applicable to a stage career, aims and ambitions and tastes, voice, and action are thoroughly tested by reading and acting at sight, and the pupil is required to recite or present extracts from plays which he or she has previously prepared without coaching. The powers of imagination, temperament, instinct, versatility and qualities which must be inborn are sought for, and a thorough diagnosis is made.[25]

The series of examinations designed to discover the potential talents of aspiring actors is still practiced by the Academy to this day.

While the curriculum and the methods of teaching at the American Academy of Dramatic Arts constantly changed, the changes were not the result of a shift in theoretical position. On the contrary, the theory of the Academy remained, in general, constant throughout the period 1885–1925. Curriculum revisions were essentially a reflection of response to conditions and needs of the students in an ever-changing theatrical environment. Also, the Academy appears to have been quite willing to experiment and to perfect its basic methods of teaching. Sargent conceived his school as a phenomenon that was constantly evolving, and the evolution was always toward the ideal of perfection of the methods employed by the Academy. As a result of this attitude which was well disposed toward change, the Academy curriculum reflected an ever-widening variety of courses throughout the years. The basic philosophy of training the imagination, mind, and physical apparatus of the actor, however, remained constant. The changes involved improved methods and techniques of working on imaginative exercises and synthesizing the various parts of the actor into a whole.

When the Academy opened as the Lyceum School in October 1884, course work included "training of the voice, the art of vocal expression, the art of imitation or mimicry, the study and understanding of plays and dramatic situations and effects, the study of character, and practical lessons in acting [business and stage deportment]."[26] In May 1885, Philip P. Hubert visited the Academy and reported that voice and speech, pantomime and action, makeup, dance and fencing, and practical acting were being taught (Hubert, 483–488). Hubert specifically commented on the manner in which Sargent and Belasco conducted their classes. While he indicated that Sargent rejected a great deal of the MacKaye-Delsarte system, he mentioned that Sargent did accept the basic premises. Hubert also related how Sargent taught the class:

> It was with great interest that I watched Mr. Sargent's class [in pantomime] portray in rapid succession all these emotions ['Grief, joy, defiance, anger, supplication, command, etc., which have certain recognized forms of expression.']. Mr. Sargent's aim is to bring into play positions and expressions which do not occur in every-day life. He does not give these exercises as instruction in acting, but as tending to facilitate acting. (*Ibid.*, 488)

The class in pantomime that Sargent taught appears to have employed the "Gamuts of Expression" which MacKaye invented. The nature of the course was apparently designed both to "free the channels of expression" and to introduce the actor to the fundamental positions and expressions laid down by MacKaye and Delsarte.

Belasco's class in stage deportment and business must have been a rare opportunity for the aspiring actors. The thoroughness of his methods must have been of great benefit in training them in the rudiments of practical stage movement. Hubert described the class as follows:

> Mr. Belasco's class were [*sic*] rehearsing a scene from an emotional drama of his own. A husband who has been deeply wronged visits his home for the last time to demand his child. The scene between husband and wife is short, but Mr. Belasco, who sat in front of the stage, watching his pupils as a cat watches mice, was so particular about every detail that the young woman who personated the wife, and who is required to enter to slow music, clutching the furniture for support, had to make her entrance eleven times and to make seventeen attempts to sit down in a chair before Mr. Belasco was satisfied. (*Ibid.*)

It should also be noted that the students were given the opportunity to act in the Lyceum Theatre production of

The ever-practical American Academy of Dramatic Arts was probably the first school to have formal classes in make-up.

Dakolar which MacKaye directed, and they were also employed in Lawrence Barrett's production of *Julius Caesar* in May 1885. Thus, along with the class work which the students received, the Lyceum School gave them the opportunity to act in several plays in the professional theatre. In later years, the school provided them with matinees which were opened to the public. This practice afforded the students the "practical experience" for which they were being trained. The

Senior students in a playette when The American Academy of Dramatic Arts was then called The New York School of Acting and was associated with The Empire Theatre founded by Charles Frohman.

integration of theory and practice was one of the strong points of the Academy's history of training actors.

In October 1885, the Lyceum School changed its name to The New York School of Acting, with Franklin H. Sargent firmly at the helm of the operation. The personnel were the same as those who finished the first year except that Fred

Williams and Mrs. Wickham were dropped and Ada Ward and Carla Malvena were added to teach Orthoepy (a class in phonetics and pronunciation) and Dance respectively.[27]

By 1887, the school appeared to be a flourishing enterprise. However, unrest within the student body over the lack of thorough vocal training must lead one to conclude that pantomime was elevated over vocal training. On May 27, 1887, a letter appeared in the *New York Dramatic Mirror* which was signed by several of the female students of the School.

> In the Prompt Book of the school is an imposing array of instructors. One of the best we had but *once* during the school, and two others were taken from us at Christmas vacation. . . . The interest seemed to wane as the year progressed, and at the close of school many who had been deluded by specious promises, or praise of their talents, were suddenly undeceived by their cards, which contained the first intimation of their actual standing. *Pantomime and its accompaniment of Delsartian gymnastics, is taught quite thoroughly, but the voice work is of the most rudimentary description, the voice-teaching not being allowed sufficient time. One-half hour a week was all the vocal training* we received during the greater part of the school year.[28] [emphasis added]

In the same article, Sargent denied all the accusations concerning the promises his School was said to have made to the aspiring actors, most of which was supposed to have been about future employment in companies.

Fortunately, the unrest of the students caused the whole situation to be aired at great length, with the result that a good deal of information concerning the amount of time spent on specific subjects in the classes at the Academy became available. On June 4, 1887, the pros and cons of the New York School of Acting were aired in the *Mirror*. In attempting to justify his position, Sargent really justified the complaints of the students. In reality, there was four to five times as much time spent on pantomime as on voice and speech. Sargent offered a breakdown of the "average number of hours of instruction per week for each instructor." It was as follows:

	First Term	Second Term[29]
Stage Business and Rehearsal	4	3
Pantomime	4	4
Education	2	3
Dancing	2	1
Fencing	2	2
Character Pantomime	0	3
Voice	1	$1/2$
Make-up	0	1
French	$1/2$	0
Lectures	1	1

Sargent argued that "These total 16-1/2 hours the first term and 18-1/2 hours per week per pupil the second. The class in voice averaged six members each" (*Ibid.*). The fact remains that the students were correct in their claim that voice was slighted. The whole pattern of course offerings indicates that movement was stressed far in excess of voice. It would appear that the Delsartian influence was still quite strong at this period in the development of the Academy. The mention of "Delsartian gymnastics" would appear to validate this assumption.

Sargent also presented, in his defense, an even more elaborate breakdown of the amount of teaching at the Academy in a "Summary of the amount of instruction given by each teacher" (*Ibid.*). This valuable report gives insight into the nature of the classes and the importance of the various members of the staff to the operation of the school. Also, the titles of the lectures indicate the practical nature of the approach to acting by the Academy. The Summary of the amount of instruction given by each teacher for the year follows:

Mr. Belasco (in stage bus. and rehearsal) . . . . 312 hrs.
F. H. Sargent (in pantomime, elocution, lectures) . . 230   "
May Cameron (in voice) 114   "
W. C. Bellows (in character pantomime) 100   "
M. de Chadenedes (in fencing) 82   "
M. de Chadenedes (in French) 6   "
Carla Malvena (in dancing) 71   "
Ada Ward (in orthoepy) 47   "
Mrs. Georgen (in pantomime and recitation) 45   "
Maria P. Brace (in elocution) 40   "
W. A. Backland (in make-up) 15   "

Special Lectures
Mme. Rah, "The French Theatre"
Thomas Gossman, "Stage Mechanics" (1)
Emma Sheridan, "Practical Stage Hints" (1)
J. D. Gaillard, "The French Language" 12 hrs.
A. P. Burbank, "The Study of a Play"
Roger Foster, "Legal Relations of Actors"
Horace Townsend, "Costume"
C. Wiley Presbrey, "Color in Stage Effect"
Total number of hours taught. 1074[30]

Again, the hours spent on course work indicate that panto-mimic work was far more developed in the curriculum than vocal training. The fact that Sargent was especially interested in pantomime and that it was his field of specialization undoubtedly explains why it was given such prominence. However, David Belasco's 312 hours in stage business and rehearsal points out the emphasis given to the practical side of the students' training.

In the early nineties, Sargent appears to have changed drastically the curriculum of the Academy. The program of study involved two terms of six months each, with the first comprising technical training in all basic essentials, and the second, advanced classroom study and the production of plays.[31] First term work covered three major areas: Action, Diction, and Stage Work. Training in Action consisted of Physical Training, Dancing, Fencing, Pantomime, and Life Studies. Diction instruction included the special subjects of Vocal Training, Phonetics, Elements of Vocal Expression, English Language, and Dramatic Literature. Completing the

Junior, or first term courses was Stage Work, which introduced the student to Stage Mechanics, Makeup, Costuming and Art Decoration, Stage Business, Stage Rehearsals, and Complete Performances. It is clear that the curriculum for the Junior years was decidedly slanted toward introductory classes. The aim was to limber up the voice and body and gradually present progressively more difficult and demanding work. This follows Sargent's concept of "natural growth."

Course work in the area of Action began with classes in pantomime. All pantomimic work consisted of two parts: the corrective and the formative. The first part, called "bodily action," "physical training," or "physical culture," was a series of limbering exercises which appears to have been a holdover from the "decomposing" exercises of MacKaye. These exercises were intended to bring about relaxation, to correct bad habits, and to replace them with good ones. Algernon Tassin, a graduate, and later a teacher at the Academy, explained the process and purpose of the training in bodily action:

> Acting means the use of muscles as well as of voice and mind. In the gymnasium, however, there is no apparatus other than a piano, for the object is not muscular development, but suppleness and harmony of action. Every part of the body must be free and responsive, auxiliary and subordinate. The exercises are arranged with this in mind and are consequently practiced to rhythm. Wrong physical habits are corrected and right ones are established; and when this result is accomplished, gymnastics are more or less supplanted by dancing and fencing.[32]

The *Annual Catalogue* was quick to emphasize that these exercises are not performed in a "perfunctory manner, as in an ordinary gymnasium" (*Annual Catalogue*: 1899, 25). Rather, each must be accompanied by an "appropriate feeling" and "motive." They lead directly into simple pantomimic scenes in which action is secondary and the student "is concentrated in the emotion which causes the action" (*Ibid.*).

Bronson Howard also explained some aspects of the methods employed and their significance to the actor.

> The classes in physical culture, also, are particularly important. Physical weakness means awkwardness, on or off the stage; and many strange uses of the body, for man or woman, in various plays—falling is one of them—call for persistent cultivation of nearly all the muscles. One who has been through the exercises of a regular gymnasium would be astonished at the new and unexpected motions he would be called upon to make in the physical-culture class of a histrionic school.
>
> Here again, we have the 'seeming' to provide for, and not the real thing: the seeming to fall when you do not fall, but sink down in section; the seeming to trip lightly up-stairs, when you are straining every nerve to reach the top with enough breath left to speak another line; the seeming to rush across the room with all the strength of sudden desperation, when you are carefully avoiding a lady's train; seeming to spring savagely upon a man with a single bound, when you must interpolate a few intermediate steps, like grace-notes in music to reach him at all. (Howard, 32)

In the formative part of the actor's bodily training the Academy taught two distinct forms of pantomime: natural and artificial. They are described by Howard as follows:

> The art of pantomime in its two great divisions has its distinct place in the histrionic curriculum: the pantomime common to all the race, expressing the various human emotions by movements; and also that artificial language of pantomime, with its vocabulary of signs, almost with a grammar, that has grown up on the theatrical art of the Latin races. The 'natural pantomime,' so called, is of very great value in all acting; and the conventional pantomime of the Italians and the French is a thing to be studied, just as one may study the meter and rhyme of their poetry, as an accomplishment, and to quicken the intelligence. This exquisite art, too, enhances the physical grace. (*Ibid.*)

In the division of pantomimic study at the Academy there was still, in the early twentieth century, a strong trace of the MacKaye-Delsarte tradition. Pantomime was called "the purest expression of emotion," and each part of the body was said to have "its own peculiar significance." The students were taught that people in real life exhibited various characteristics by using certain expressions of the body, and they were urged to acquire a "vocabulary of pantomime" to match their vocabulary of words. Sargent appears to have seen real value in the exercise of the body for the purpose of relaxation, correction, and formative development. However, lest the use of any collection of gestures might become mechanical, the students were warned that they must feel the states and moods they were illustrating. They must "surrender themselves to the feeling aroused." "The great task of the instructor," stated the *Catalogue,* "is to start the spark of feeling and to see that its expression is kept sincere. It does not suffice to indicate or describe emotion; the actor himself must learn to feel" (*Annual Catalogue*: 1899, 3).

As early as 1891, Sargent appears to have introduced improvisation into the curriculum of pantomimic expression. Mariana McCann wrote about a visit to the Academy:

> Mr. Sargent frequently gets the best results from pantomimic work not supplemented by lines. Half a dozen pupils are given a dramatic situation, and are sent up stage to carry it out to the best of their ability and unguided conception. Not a word, laugh, or sigh is heard, but the story is told by pantomime alone.[33]

The course was an experiment that was unique in its time, and it was not popularized until the advent of the Stanislavsky system. Yet, the Academy had employed this technique of improvisation to stimulate the imagination as early as 1891!

Life Studies was an advanced course in the area of Action, and was specifically in the realm of pantomimic and dramatic action. The course was instituted around 1893,[34] and appears to have changed throughout the period. Its primary purpose was to emphasize the importance of "going to life" for material to use in creating a realistic representation. The Academy posed the question: If the author drew from life, "should not the actor study that life also, that he may the more justly portray it?" (*Ibid.*). Observing the Life Studies class in operation in 1900, Bronson Howard commented:

> All the students belong to this class. They are expected to observe their fellow human beings and afterwards to illustrate their actions and speech on a platform in the school: beginning with mere movement of the hand, or head, or other parts of the body, under the various circumstances of every-day life; then constructing little scenes for themselves, based on their observation, even bits of unwritten plays, after they have become suffi-ciently skilled in the minor work. (Howard, 32)

Algernon Tassin wrote of the Life Studies class in 1907:

> Sometimes the students bring in their pantomime stud-ied from life. This is an invention of Mr. Sargent's aiming to teach observation and reproduction. . . . The importance of such training to make students to see quickly and embody truthfully is inestimable. It makes them scour the streets for characters; for instance, during her season as a student, Ida Conquest brought about a dozen newsboys as studies in the life class. Again, in pantomime, the same scene is illustrated one after another by each member or scenes are performed in couples or in groups. (Tassin, 161)

The department of Action at the Academy was always headed by Sargent. He composed the Action curriculum in a manner that was to lead the novice through a series of courses designed to aid him in "natural growth." First, the process of "freeing the channels of expression" was accomplished in the Physical Training of Bodily Movement class, a class based on MacKaye-Delsarte principles, but with the admonition that all gestures be accompanied by thought and feeling. This part of the course was primarily corrective, but as the academic year progressed it became formative. The course in Bodily Training naturally evolved into Pantomime, which was almost entirely formative in its desire to teach the student to "express" feeling through the use of his body. Pantomime led naturally to the introduction of Life Studies with its emphasis on observation, selection, and improvisation. In addition, Dancing and Fencing were taken to improve the student's bearing and grace. The entire program of Action was based on pantomime and pantomimic dramatization. Sargent's great contribution to the methods of teaching acting are nowhere more vividly apparent than in the improvement of techniques in Action.

The Junior term also found the idea of "natural growth" applied to voice training in the Department of Diction. The general philosophy was that, as in Action, it was first necessary to correct bad habits of voice and speech, and then to implant good habits. The general method, again, was corrective and formative. First, voice was treated.

> The visitor may hear a class of young men and women going through the elemental sounds. It has a comic effect; but the teacher is always very earnest. The pupils are learning not only to utter sounds clearly, but to breathe properly as they talk—a mechanical process, just as the young blacksmith must learn to work the bellows to keep a steady flame. In the higher classes of the same department the niceties of tone are taught— purity, resonance, flexibility, these things and many more, before they come to expression. With that, of course, comes in the great art of elocution, but not until these children have gone back to their babyhood and relearned how to talk. (Howard, 34)

After the voice was corrected and developed, the student went through classes in Phonetics and Elements of Vocal Expression. The latter course was conducted in much the same manner as a present-day course in Oral Interpretation. It was under the general heading "elocution" at the Academy.

Tassin is quite helpful in describing the manner in which it
was taught:

> Here the words are analyzed step by step with due
> regard to the character who utters them, and this
> conception is embodied by reading aloud. Then it is that
> the good effect of that training in fundamental sounds
> and combinations, which to the visitor sounded at first
> so fantastic, is apparent in the purity of diction and the
> ease and variety of delivery. But from one to the other
> is by no means an immediate step. Such training
> provided only the material, not the means of expression.
> These—inflection, color, phrasing—must previously all
> have been studied by application to short extracts in
> ordinary prose and poetry. This intermediate stage of
> vocal expression has only gradually grown into the
> interpretation of dramatic writing, the basis of which is
> characterization. (Tassin, 158)

In this way, Sargent continued the practice of what he
regarded as "natural growth." In the Diction department, the
student was led through the fundamental course work of
voice, phonetics, and finally to a course in oral reading. The
basis of the course in Elements of Vocal Expression was the
reading and interpreting of short extracts which would
eventually lead to the interpretation of dramatic literature
with emphasis on character.

In general, Dramatic Literature was considered to be a
course which operated in the middle-ground of the students'
development and which fell into the category of analysis. Its
aim was to cultivate "creative imagination" through the
analysis of character and situation; the motto of the course
was "conception, analysis, expression." Students were taught
to know and understand the great characters of literature.
They were "shown the common humanity, the universal
human traits in all these characters and taught to identify
themselves sympathetically with them" (*Annual Catalogue*:
1899, 30). As the *Catalogue* explained: "Attention is drawn to
that psychological nature which exists in all of us in a greater

or lesser degree of intensity—the feelings and passions which, when fully or abnormally developed, bring about those dramatic situations of life which the playwright endeavors to present in vivid, condensed and classified form" (*Ibid.*).

Diction, then, was the complete study of spoken and written language. Its eventual conclusion was embodied in a class of analysis of literature designed for the benefit of understanding character. D'Angelo summarizes the position of the study of voice quite well.

> Insofar as the actor identifies himself with the past, present, and imaginative life of the character and is sensitized toward everything that falls within the aura of his concentration on the stage, the quality of his voice will bear the stamp of truth. (D'Angelo, 46).

Study in voice, speech, and literature, then, were regarded as a means to an end, not an end in themselves. The reason for this treatment of Diction appears to lie in the "think the thought" philosophy, which tended to maintain the position that if the thought is correct the expression will naturally follow, providing the channels of expression are free. D'Angelo voiced the belief of the Sargent tradition of vocal training when he wrote: "Keeping the thought alive, fresh, and new will insure correct word stress" (*Ibid.*, 49).

The final category of work which was given in the Junior term was Stage Mechanics, Makeup, Costuming, Art Decoration (what to wear, what colors, etc.), Stage Business, Stage Rehearsals, and Complete Performances. This aspect of study is quite self-explanatory. It consisted of work on short scenes and slow progression to a full performance at the end of the Junior term. Fortunately, Eleanor Cody Gould transcribed copious notes from her classes with Jehlinger and Sargent in 1918 and 1919. These notes, which have already been quoted profusely, indicate that the classes in Stage Rehearsals involved the teacher as *supportive critic and guide* of the actor's attempts at characterization. Jehlinger's device of the short, terse comment gives every indication that he was employing suggestion

A later, more elaborate production which was most likely staged for the graduating class as the culminating experience of their student careers.

An early production of Molière's *Tartuffe*, shortly after The New York School of Acting evolved into The American Academy of Dramatic Arts.

and not teaching the course through imitation. His method was always intended to get the actor to "think for himself." The main contention, which permeates all the work in the class as he taught it, was "never change thought, theme or mood until something occurs to cause that change" (*Jehlinger in Rehearsal*, Introductory Notes, 2). The implications are that the course was handled in a completely informal manner and that it was basically a course which taught the actor to sustain the character in the situation *and to think independently*. Tassin, writing in 1907, indicated that the methods of teaching the class changed little from the time of its inception at the Academy to the end of the period under investigation. Tassin wrote:

> Then at last the student is ready for stage rehearsals. When a pupil is cast for a play he finds his 'call' posted on the bulletin board just as in the regular theatre. The rehearsals are conducted in the same professional manner. He has a few days in which to go through his part book in hand, and then comes the announcement, 'letter perfect.' The stage manager sits in front and directs, and all things are conducted as on the professional stage—with one important exception. *The student is never told how to speak his lines—the stage manager is there to correct, to suggest, to steer his conception of the part into the right channel—but that he must do for himself.* (Tassin, 161). [emphasis added]

The class in Rehearsal was run in a manner similar to that of other classes. In Rehearsal, the dramatic "thought" was the most important thing. Jehlinger urged his students: "Avoid all thoughts of cues and stage business as you would avoid poison" when rehearsing or acting a play (*Jehlinger in Rehearsal*, 8). The learning process, then, appears to be similar to that of Stanislavsky: Learn the fundamentals of the profession so well that they become second nature and need no reflective thought. Jehlinger also warned his students: "You must never allow yourself to go through a rehearsal mechanically. You must give everything you have to every rehearsal or you cannot grow in your part" (*Ibid.*, 9). This practice was a far cry from the rehearsal conditions which most actors encountered in the late nineteenth and early twentieth centuries. While Daly and others had improved rehearsal techniques and the time given to the play, a slipshod attitude was still prevalent. Daly, MacKaye, Belasco, Sargent and Jehlinger contributed a great deal toward improving rehearsal practices and creating an "independent" actor. The Academy carried on the tradition in the best sense of the word and gave a generation of Americans an approach to acting that Stanislavsky would have admired and approved.

At the end of the Junior term the students' training culminated in the course titled Complete Performances. However, even the final performance was regarded by the Academy as a mere step in the development of actors. Earlier, Sargent had said that a dramatic school was "more than the putting on of plays." In 1918, Jehlinger reaffirmed that position:

> A performance is merely an incident in your develop-
> ment, a means of showing up your weaknesses in order
> to remedy them, merely an experience to give you the
> 'feel' of an audience. (*Ibid.*, 2)

Seen in this light, the Academy regarded the performance of the play not as a momentous event, but as merely the final filling out of the form. It was regarded as the essential adjunct to the school's philosophy of "natural growth." Performance was considered no more important than any other facet in the growth of the aspiring actor.

Before entering the Senior term and the Academy Stock Company, the student had to pass a comprehensive examination. Once over this hurdle, he continued class study in several areas, although the primary emphasis was placed on the study of roles and on performance. Among the important courses that continued during the two-term period was Life Study, with its emphasis on observation and improvisation in pantomime, and Rehearsal, which was in the nature of criticism, reinforcing the method of approaching the role, and the movement toward independence.

The main current of criticism, by some, of the Academy's training during the period under investigation was that while it trained the actor in movement and pantomimic dramatization, thorough vocal training was sorely lacking.[35] From the beginning of the institution, this criticism was sometimes violent, but as Sargent slowly collected the people he wanted to teach in his institution, the criticism seemed to abate.[36] In any event, the Academy turned out hundreds of aspiring actors in the period being covered, many of whom joined the ranks of the professional theatre. The stigma attached to the "acting school" was apparently mitigated by the sheer impact of such numbers. For example, in 1896 Sargent announced, "The graduates now number nearly 400."[37] In 1902, the graduates of the American Academy of Dramatic Arts numbered 704[38] and by 1925, a total of 1,836 students had received diplomas.[39] Of the nearly two thousand students who graduated from the Academy between 1886 and 1925, almost two hundred achieved "stardom." The honor roll of successful graduates who won fame in the American theatre is too long to mention here, but the school proudly lists the names of famous alumni in its catalogues and other publications. It can safely be said that no other professional acting school has contributed as many outstanding actors and actresses to the American theatre as the American Academy of Dramatic Arts. It seems highly probable that the Academy had won its argument, that acting schools could supplant the old stock system of training.

One outstanding contribution to the practice of teaching made by the American Academy of Dramatic Arts was embodied in the nature of its organization. Sargent applied the idea of "natural growth" in the classroom, and apparently made it work within the framework of theatre training. Still more important was Sargent's aversion to imitation and his acceptance of the concept of "throwing all on the student." As far as can be determined, the instructors were faithful to

Sargent's theory maintaining the necessity of permitting the student to develop in his own way. In the area of specific course work, certainly the most outstanding contribution was the origination of the Life Studies course. Within its structure, Sargent introduced improvisation as a means to stimulate the imagination. Finally, and perhaps the greatest contribution, was Sargent's concept of training the "total actor." The entire organization of the school was built around the needs of the actor. The curriculum was specifically divided into Action, Diction, and Stage Work departments to accommodate those needs and, within the departments and classes, the concept of natural growth was implemented by progressively more challenging class work.

The relationship of theory to the practice of teaching at the American Academy of Dramatic Arts was well integrated and consistent. Perhaps the greatest success of the Academy was that Sargent was able to succeed where MacKaye failed—he bridged the great gap that existed between speculation and practicality. The evolution of the Academy was, in great part, the story of constant searching for the correct methods of applying theory to practice.

The American Academy of Dramatic Art and the writings of Stanislavsky have many points of similarity. The Academy preached that the actor must accept the reality of a play as a "truth" and an "imaginative fiction"; that the actor was an artist and must be committed to the art of the theatre and to its serious purpose. The Academy actor was taught to trust instinct, cultivate imagination, focus on the character's motive and objective, concentrate, and to think *as* the character. Further, the Academy recognized acting as emotionally based: it was the intensity of the emotional memory of experiences that aroused true feeling. The imagination was cultivated, exercised and developed; and the Academy asked actors to regard a play as a private experience, not unlike Stanislavsky's "public solitude." Also, acting was considered an organic process which moved from the internal to external expression.

Recognizing that acting demanded far more than the development of an "inner" technique, the Academy demanded that the beginning actor "free the channels of expression" through breaking habitual behavior and acquiring mastery over the physical and vocal apparatus. This, it was believed, would release tension and permit instinct, imagination and feeling to flow naturally. Given this success, the elements of conception, analysis and revelation (expression) came into play. Conception was not merely intellectual but also instinctive. Also, analysis brought into play the imagination and a grasp of the intensity of feeling. Finally, conception and analysis were liberating to the mind as physical freedom was to the body. The revelation of the character was considered a natural outgrowth of the preparatory work brought into play. Actors were told repeatedly that if all the groundwork was well developed, they could literally think and feel *as* the character and the right external expression would occur without need of conscious direction. This very idea is found not only among Stanislavsky's principles, but in Lee Strasberg's as well (Quoted in Friedman, 51). The principle of "think the thought" was well known in American acting theory, and it was the keystone of all the schools that descended from the MacKaye-Delsarte tradition.[40] While their paths may be divergent, many of the conclusions about acting were shared by Stanislavsky and the Academy.

The impact of the American Academy of Dramatic Arts continues to the present day. It offered *an integrated and practical* prescriptive acting theory long before the ascendancy of Stanislavsky, and one that proved worthy and effective. The American Academy of Dramatic Arts was a pioneer and its long endurance alone is ample evidence of its importance and lasting contributions to the American theatre.

Charles Wesley Emerson, founder of the Emerson College of Oratory (1880), which evolved into the present-day Emerson College in Boston. (Photo courtesy of Emerson College Archives)

CHAPTER III
EMERSON COLLEGE OF ORATORY

To include the theories and methods of teaching of the Emerson College of Oratory may, perhaps, seem to be wandering far afield from the study of acting theory as taught by the acting schools in America from 1875 to 1925. Actually, however, the schools of expression, of which the Emerson College of Oratory was one, contributed substantially to the development of acting theory in America. Emerson College of Oratory formulated theories of expression which affected literally thousands of its graduates, both in the profession of acting and in teaching of speech and dramatics in colleges across America.[1] The basic seven or eight books written by Charles Wesley Emerson, Henry Laurence Southwick and his wife Jessie Eldridge Southwick, enjoyed enormous circulation during the period and undoubtedly influenced thousands more to adopt the Emerson theories of expression. While the purpose of the school was not specifically oriented to the teaching of acting as a discipline since formal courses were not introduced until 1893, its theories are decidedly applicable to the study of acting.[2] Emerson's contributions to acting theory in America and to expression in general were unique and in many ways prophetic of certain modern ideas concerning acting.

Charles Wesley Emerson founded the school first known as the Boston College of Oratory in 1880, and the following year renamed the institution the Monroe Conservatory of Oratory in honor of his former teacher Lewis B. Monroe. By 1886, the conservatory was incorporated as the Monroe College of Oratory and had a faculty of a dozen teachers. In

1890, the name was again changed, this time to Emerson College of Oratory, the name by which it was known throughout the rest of the period under investigation. The college gradually moved in the direction of formal academic recognition; and a four-year course was established in 1913. The right to confer the degree of Bachelor of Literary Interpretation was granted by the Massachusetts legislature in 1919. In 1936, the institution acquired the name Emerson College and was granted the privilege of awarding the B.A. degree; the M.A. degree was added in 1941. Emerson College still exists today, with a significant reputation as a theatre school.

The title of the school, The Emerson College of Oratory, is actually quite misleading to those uninitiated in Emersonian principles. In reality, the teaching of oratory was only one purpose of the institution. Emerson employed "oratory" as the generic term for the study of literature in the broadest possible sense of the word. By the study of literature, "Emerson meant the study and practice of oral interpretation of literature whether the selection was a poem, a speech, a story, or a play."[3] Other synonyms which Emerson used for "oratory" were: rendering, reading, vocal interpretation, literary interpretation, and dramatic interpretation. "Oratory," then, was the study of literature and the various forms in which literature could be communicated, whether by the reader, impersonator, or actor. The voice and body were the necessary means of expression, and the platform artist needed control of the means of expression no less than the actor. Regardless of the name used and irrespective of the form of expression, the same elements are emphasized in all official publications. Understanding, active thinking, and communication were the points stressed by Emerson and other teachers in his school when they explained the aims of the oral interpretation of literature.

Concerning the function of the actor,[4] Emerson emphasized that he must respond to the author's thought as to his own. At the same time he must be inspired with the desire to give the thought to others.[5] The aim of the actor, furthermore, must be to interpret truthfully to others the meaning of the best literature.[6] The actor tries to experience in active form the vision of the author. He tries to realize the motives and the original creative impulse which caused the author to write.[7] Jessie E. Southwick, long associated as a teacher with the Emerson College of Oratory, and whose husband became president of the institution shortly after the retirement of Emerson, best explained the function of acting. As she phrased it, literary interpretation is "taking up onto the imagination in terms of experience the meaning which the author expressed in literary form to the minds and hearts of those who listen" (*Ibid.*). Literal understanding and exact repetition, she insisted, are not enough; those actions are not interpreting or acting. The author's facts and motives should be illuminated by the actor's sympathy and imagination. "To do this," she continued, "requires personality capable of experience, a mind capable of focusing the experience in terms of clear vision, and the body and the voice to be trained to instant response to the imagination" (*Ibid.*).

The actor's relationship to the author's script was in the closest possible terms. The actor, while a creative agent who brings an added dimension to the author's ideas, must be faithful to every idea and motive suggested by the author in the script. Emerson and his colleagues conceived the author's ideas as so important that they insisted that the actor recreate the *exact* feelings and mental activity of the author at the time of his creation of the play. With the class as the audience, the student was "required at every step . . . to depend . . . on his mental activity at the moment of speech. *He must make his hearers think, feel and act.*"[8] The students were taught that the greatest actor should go even farther.

[He] must not only think the thought, experience the feeling, see the picture and realize the purpose of the

> author, but he must reproduce the author's process at
> the moment of delivery. The creation of the [actor] is a
> re-creation of the author's creation. (*Ibid.*)

The relationship of the actor to the character involved a
thorough understanding of Emerson's philosophy and psychology of expression which will be considered at a later time;
however, it should be amply clear that Emerson wanted
complete identification with the character as the playwright
conceived him. Emerson's overriding conviction was that
acting, to be effective, was predicated on the actor's ability to
communicate the playwright's intentions; and since Emerson
believed that only feeling and thinking as the character could
produce effective delivery, it would appear that the relationship between the actor and the character would be quite
intimate.

Emerson acknowledged the didactic purposes of acting as
well as of all "oratory." A major point in the Emersonian
doctrine was that if the actor is to become a creative artist, he
must love the theme of the play and he must be filled with
great love for those whom he seeks to serve—the audience
(Emerson, *Evolution of Expression*, IV, 10–11). The audience,
Emerson claimed, assisted the actor at the moment of
expression because it was the object of communication.
Emerson believed that repeated attempts to impress ideas, as
a character, on the minds of the audience would enable the
actor to see his ideas more vividly. Here, according to
Emerson, lies one of the most helpful means of cultivating the
imagination. The attempt on the part of the actor "to make
listeners put themselves in the place of another, see through
the eyes from the point of view of . . . Shakespeare, quickens
his own imagination, broadens his sympathies, and develops
his intellect as nothing else can" (*Ibid*, II, 60). In addition,
Emerson believed that successful communication of feelings
and thoughts produced a corresponding activity in the audience (*Ibid.*, IV, 11). Elevating the audience to creative and
constructive thought through the stimulus provided by the

playwright's character benefited the actor by expanding his own resources.

Because Emerson believed that acting, as one part of "oratory," was an instrument for the good of mankind, it follows that only the "good" was suitable for the stage. The criterion for choosing good plays was provided by his philosophy of education, which held that contemplation of worthy objects of thought will naturally facilitate evolution of the mind (of both actor and audience), a necessary phenomenon if man is to progress (*Ibid.*, I, 12–13). Thus, only plays of high moral tone were considered suitable for expression by the actor and worthy of contemplation by the audience (a commonly held opinion in the nineteenth century).

In summary, then, the actor was the servant and the interpreter of the character's thoughts and feelings. The actor could expand those ideas, but only to animate the audience's imagination, and then within the limits of the playwright's intent. The actor must completely identify with the character; he must feel, think, and act the character as the playwright conceived him. Nothing less than complete surrender of self to the character could satisfy Emersonian beliefs. The actor must never acknowledge the audience; instead, he must create the belief in the audience that he is someone else, so that they might completely empathize with the feelings, thoughts, and actions of the character. It was through surrender of self and complete concentration, through love of the idea and a desire to communicate that idea to the audience, that the actor was truly creative.

Like Delsarte, Emerson saw in life the correspondence between the finite mind and the infinite mind. Man, like the Divine Mind, possesses a threefold nature: intellect, sensibility, and will. These activities (which Emerson called faculties) make men sensitive to the truth because they are related to the Infinite. Just as the soul must learn the truth, so too must the body. Even though the body has the power to act upon the mind, nature has decreed that it should be subservient. All education of the body, Emerson held, should be directed toward rendering the body a flexible instrument for the mind.[9] The primary purpose of training for the actor was, consequently, the freeing of the body so that it might be the interpreter and instrument of the mind.

Emerson's idea of evolution as a general principle undoubtedly came from Charles Darwin and his aesthetics from Hegel. Also, Emerson appears to have adapted William James's psychological principles to evolutionary theories.[10] In evolution, Emerson saw a law of natural growth which could be utilized by education. He believed that man's mind had reached its present stage of development by a process of gradual upward growth.

> Therefore, the race, in its march from savagery to civilization may be considered as one man, showing first, animation; next, manifesting his objects of attraction; third, displaying his purposes; and finally, putting forth his wisdom in obedience to the true, the beautiful, and the good. (Emerson, *Evolution of Expression*, I, 16)

In his consideration of the "ideal" actor, Emerson conceived that the intellect was the generating factor in all expression. The component faculties of the mind were given by Emerson as intellect, sensibility or feeling, and will. "It is when these activities are concentrated—when the intellect has been held upon a subject until emotion and will respond—that man is powerful."[11] For the actor, then, intellectual concentration produces response from the other faculties.

Emerson cautioned that feeling is dangerous unless controlled by thought. While sensibility can sharpen discernment, feelings unguided by thought may be misleading (Emerson, *Evolution of Expression*, II, 9). The feeling of the actor may be the path over which knowledge comes to intellect, but intellect must interpret and give form to feeling.[12] It is apparent that Emerson considered emotion and intellect as being closely related in mutual interaction. Just as concentration of the intellect upon a proper object can stimulate feeling, so too could feeling be a means to knowledge. That this concept of interaction was taught in the classes is evident because the same views are set forth in a student-written, faculty-sponsored essay on one phase of college work.[13] Furthermore, Emerson once stated that "the laws of the mind are such that feeling will follow the mental seeing always; there can never be an exception to this law."[14] Emerson also explained that the work in the *Evolution of Expression* was based on the fact that *thinking brings feeling, and feeling brings choice (Ibid., 24)*.

Emerson's theories of the interaction of the faculties of intellect, feeling, and the will present for the actor a clear method of approach to the character in a play. Employing the principles of evolution and natural growth and following the normal operation of the mind as indicated by Emerson, the actor was believed able to stimulate the imagination and approach the ideal through suggestiveness: (1) By focusing one's intellect on the whole, the actor is energized; (2) through feeling, which results from intellectual contemplation, the actor is attracted to the parts and immersed in them without relation to the whole; (3) next, feeling operates as a stimulant to intellect, which examines the relationship of the parts to the whole and permits the will to select the proper manifestation; (4) finally, as all the faculties are in operation and have perceived the progressive relationship of the separate parts of the playwright's intent, the actor's imagination is stimulated to express the ideas in idealized form.

One of the distinguishing features of Emerson's work was said to be his training of the imagination under control of the will. Imagination and will, according to Emerson's point of view, were fundamental and could not be imparted. However, it was held that imagination and will could be developed.[15] Before any consideration of the manner in which the Emerson College of Oratory went about its training of the imagination, however, it seems appropriate to discuss what Emerson conceived to be the nature of the "creative" faculty.

From a combination of statements concerning the imagination, a compact definition of that faculty can be obtained. One of the early Emerson explanations is that imagination is the power by which the mind creates an image of its own concepts.[16] At another time, according to a former student, Emerson defined imagination as *the power which enables man to feel and see as others do.*[17] On still another occasion, Emerson defined imagination as that power of the mind which will seize upon all or any of the powers of the individual and expand them indefinitely.[18] The concepts of the imagination which Emerson accepted appear to be quite applicable to the actor, especially his definition of the imagination as a faculty which enables the actor to feel and see as others do. The imagination appears to be the power of the actor to identify through empathic response, to conceive the character, and to instinctually create through expression.

Emerson believed that one of the best means of developing the imagination (as well as the intellect) was to impress ideas on the audience. In doing so, the actor sharpened his own perception. However, where the imagination fitted into the pattern of intellect, feeling, and will is not clear. Emerson repeatedly stated that there were but three general faculties, though in actuality the three were one.[19] Emerson said that "the imagination is the eye of the intellect—the basis of all sympathy" (Emerson, *Evolution of Expression*, II, 11). By this statement, he may have intended to imply that imagination is a link between intellect and sensibility. Imagination was held to be the basis of sympathy (*Ibid.*). "Sympathy . . . comes from studying others," and "from imagining their relation to their environment."[20] Sympathy, however, must be turned into useful action or it becomes an emotional intoxication.[21] The power of sympathy should be carried on, the students were told, "Until by the slightest communication, you can feel what another feels as well as see what he sees."[22] Hence, sympathy must be intellectual, emotional, and imaginative. Emerson appears to believe that while the activities are combined in endless variety, all action of the mind may be traced to the three distinct activities of the mind: intellect, sensibility, and will. Imagination and sympathy, the sub-activities of the mind, appear to be parts of the endless varieties of interaction.

As he described the mind's activities, it seems to have something of the nature of both these faculties, but it fills a function that belongs precisely to neither. While not entirely successful, Emerson is one of the first acting theorists to come to grips with imagination as a concept as well as giving it a specific function. Sympathy was an outgrowth of intellect, feeling, and imagination. Its place in the basic outline is even less clear than imagination's.

In theory, at least, Emerson conceived that the "ideal" actor should have cultivated the intellect, sensibilities, will, imagination, and sympathy by means of natural growth through the evolutionary process. Each faculty was believed to be capable of development, and as each one evolved, it acted upon the faculty following it in the hierarchy of "activities." Thus, as the mind evolves, feeling becomes more acute and in turn affects the will. Somewhere in the process, probably between sensibility and the will, imagination and sympathy come into play. Finally, the will, which has been perfected through concentration of the intellect and feeling, selects the appropriate results of imagination and sympathy, and determines the appropriate form of the expression. While the analysis appears mechanical in its exposition, Emerson conceived it to be spontaneous and creative in its actual operation. Emerson's theories of the cultivation of the imagination were unique in that the method employed was his evolutionary process. It cannot be said, however, that Emerson was original in his contention that the imagination could be developed.

The voice and body were regarded by Emerson as servants of the soul. They must be trained to give spontaneous expression to the activities of the soul at the instant of utterance. Emerson believed that the mind or soul is supreme; it affects the body and is affected in turn.[23] It was accepted by Emerson that the outer expression in voice, bearing, and movement was the direct outflowing of the inner state of being.[24] Consequently, any consideration of the "ideal" actor would be incomplete if it did not include an analysis of Emerson's theories pertaining to technique of expression.

The view that the voice naturally grows as the mind evolves *did not* presume that the voice needed no cultivation. Mrs. Southwick observed that those who postulate a "perfectly natural voice" either presuppose a condition of innate perfection or assume that the simple wish to speak well was sufficient to overcome wrong habits and conditions.[25] It was generally assumed, then, that if the mind was well concentrated and if the faculties of expression functioned properly, the result would be perfect vocal expression—provided the voice was completely free from wrong habits. Emerson recognized that poor training and habit made additional training necessary if the voice was to be a "free channel of expression."

Emerson's idea of the relation of the voice to the mind is distinctly similar to the "think the thought" school of expression. Study of the physical mechanism of the voice is good, said Emerson, but the most important factor is the "proper state of mind." "There must be a *state of mind* which shall cause these organs to properly adjust themselves."[26] Naturally, Emerson believed that voice should be taught according to the principles of evolution. However, no matter how accomplished the actor was in his ability to technically or mechanically produce voice and speech, Emerson was still adamant concerning his first principle of vocal expression.

> If I were writing a teacher's manual, I would tell the teacher . . . to induce in the pupil the proper states of mind.[27]

Continued concentration upon the object of the character's thoughts and feelings for the purpose of communicating will cause the tones of the voice, under the repetition of drill, gradually to improve, declared Emerson in discussing the second stage of vocal evolution. To get this improvement,

Emerson admitted that he had formerly used a physiological approach, but had abandoned it when he found that psychological direction would develop evenness of support (*Ibid.*, 105). The whole approach to the voice, then, was devoted to concentration on the "idea" of a selection. It then progressed along lines of evolution. If the sounds of speech and tones of the voice were imperfect, the attempts were regarded as failures in the proper state of mind.

Following his general philosophy that thought creates form, Emerson arrived at what he called a natural law concerning gesture: "When the mind is cultivated to responsiveness, the right mental activity will create the right gesture" (Emerson, *Expressive Physical Culture*, 17). The secret of his system, as Emerson unfolded it, was teaching from the conviction that "Mind is power, and that it creates its own manifestations." Further, *the principle was that the right thought would create the right gesture and the actor need not know anything about it.*[28] Emerson did not want gesture to be the object of thought while acting. *It should be clearly noted that no course in the MacKaye-Delsarte manner was taught at Emerson College of Oratory until after Emerson's retirement.*

There was a distinct difference, then, between voice and gesture training in the Emerson view of expression. While there were definite standards for voice and speech, gesture was conceived as being totally dependent upon thought for its expression. Instead of practicing appropriate forms of gesture which supposedly signified an appropriate emotional state, Emerson advocated physical culture. Physical culture, as Emerson conceived it, had two purposes:

1. *External*—Free body through exercise. Learn to control movement—*Vitalize*—*Break habits*.
2. *Internal*—Think thought. Teacher must help student have right objects of thought in his mind until his animation takes definite form.[29]

Thus, it is clear that Emerson's philosophy of physical expression was devoted only to "freeing the channels." The appropriate gesture was conceived as being expressed *only* through the proper state of mind.

Emerson naturally approached movement through the evolutionary process. "Freeing" and "thought" exercises were believed to require four years of daily practice to achieve their purpose in accordance with the four steps of evolution. By the time the aspiring actor completed the evolutionary process, it was held that gestures would be natural. Gestures suggest only form; the audience imagines the full thought. The actor should become a sculptor whose art is found in gestures which are thought carved in the air. (*Ibid.*, 98–99). In the final period of evolution Emerson asserted that the gesture "born of imagination is awakened by purpose at the instant, that a person who is deaf shall see visions of the truth you are uttering" (*Ibid.*, 99–100).

Emerson maintained that when the actor's mind perceived the relation between the parts in literature being interpreted (the final step in evolution), the actor should not employ gestures in a literal way. It is the suggestive power of gestures which causes people to think. In fact, Emerson declared that the most effective gestures are made *unconsciously* by the actor and are unobserved by the listener (Emerson, *Expressive Physical Culture*, 27–30). Nor must the actor forget that each fresh thought creates fresh form. Each time a person thinks about a subject there is a shade of difference in the thought. That shade of difference naturally produces a difference in the form of expression (*Ibid.*, 23–24). After having observed Salvini's playing of Othello a number of times, Emerson declared that the great actor never repeated a gesture. Each time there was a spontaneous, though slight, change (Emerson, "The Emerson Philosophy of Gesture," 98). Such responsiveness should be the actor's ideal.

Technique was a necessary concomitant of expression in Emerson's philosophical position, but it was not an external technique. Voice, speech, and movement were dependent upon the state of mind of the actor at the time of expression. The entire function of the physical instruments of the actor was to act as the interpreters of the soul. Complete freedom from constriction and inhibition was demanded and technique was not conceived as technique in the conventional sense. The actor was expected to be so completely in control of his voice and body that he could literally "forget" them at the time of the actual performance. Emerson's entire purpose was to make voice, speech, and movement spontaneous and unconscious.

TEACHING METHODS

The function Emerson delegated to teachers was that they should serve as a kind of husbandman for the growing process (Robb, 172). Consequently, several outstanding characteristics emerge as typical of the teaching methods of the Emerson College of Oratory. (1) All teaching was conducted along the lines of the evolutionary process; (2) an element of "free play" was permitted the student; (3) the teacher guided the student in keeping his mind fixed on the ideal; and (4) the pupil was never made conscious of his faults.

Emerson indicated that the teacher could foster a more rapid evolutionary process by wise selection of material for study and exercise, and he must take care to keep the pupil's mind fixed on an ideal appropriate to the stage of development. The material must, therefore, be presented in accordance with the four stages of growth.[30] It is a mistake in teaching, Emerson contended, to present the next step beyond the one occupied by the pupil. The first thing should be to find the truth already possessed by the student and dwell upon it until it expands and carries the student to the next step. Emerson perceived that the evolutionary process was not the same in all students. He also recognized that for full fruition, the student must experience total development in one step before he is hastened on to the next. Consequently, the function of the teacher was to permit the student

The first classroom, 13 Pemberton Square (1880–1886). Notice the stage platform, decor, and footlights. (Photo courtesy of Emerson College Archives).

to discover, under guidance, the true unfolding process for himself.

Emerson enumerated the duties of the teacher in broad outline in an article published in 1894.[31] He maintained that the teacher should not only present the right objects of thought, surrounded by the right atmosphere, but make the student's mind act. He can do that, Emerson said, by means of clear statements and suggestion. All things do not need to be explained. Sometimes, when a pupil is reading, he has almost expressed the thought. Then the teacher can, by a look, a word, a tone, a gesture, suggest the thing the student has not said and would not achieve at that reading without some suggestion. The teacher may even read for his classes. He should not say, "Now I will read this passage, and I want you to read it as I do." Mimicry, in itself, is not educational. But the teacher may read to illustrate a principle. The attention of the class should always be on the principle involved. *Imitation can thus be used educationally.* He further justified the use of imitation by declaring that people do not learn rapidly in any art until they have seen some exhibition of that art. It is not necessary that every person rediscover familiar processes.

Perhaps the most salutary effect of Emerson's methods of teaching was the pupil-teacher relationship. In order to hasten progress, Emerson taught that the teacher should be constantly seeking a new aspect in the old material, and thus maintain the student's intense interest.[32] The student will learn best when he is spontaneously active. Since Emerson believed it important to stimulate and not repress growth, he urged that sufficient time always be allowed for each student to develop. Furthermore, since self-consciousness handicaps spontaneous outgrowth, the student should never be made conscious of his faults.[33] The criticism should be constructive and never severe if the student is making an honest effort. All encouragement, however, should rest on truth. While Emerson advocated that teachers practice the habit of telling students the excellent things they do, he also maintained that the teacher must be sincere.[34]

It is certain that one of the Emerson system's leading exponents advocated free play for the development of the individual's power. Henry Laurence Southwick, when dean of the college, declared that teachers in the past were regulators who suppressed, but "today we are beginning to see that glad following is productive of higher results than forced repression."[35] Without the recognition that the creative spirit must have free play for its expression, Southwick held, teaching tends to harden into formalism. Officious regulation is substituted for helpfulness. In studying expression, therefore, both student and teacher, he believed, must be free of the critical attitude. The free play mood is the parent of initiative; it is the antithesis of the critical attitude. An attitude of positive creativeness combined with helpfulness, avowed Southwick, will secure the ideal condition of inward enrichment and outward usefulness (*Ibid.*, 9–19).

It should be clear from this outline of the general principles upon which all teaching was based at the Emerson College of Oratory, that the climate there was dedicated to aiding the student. The Emerson College of Oratory was progressive in its ideas toward education of the student of expression. Individual consideration, helpfulness, and a creative environment were conceived necessary for full development of the powers of the aspiring actor.

The methods of teaching the individual courses at the Emerson College of Oratory followed the basic principles as enunciated by Emerson. Good voice training, Emerson insisted, depended on teaching the mind to conceive the right tone. Consequently, the first step in the education of the voice was to teach the pupil to think in sounds (Emerson, *Psycho Vox*, 4). Emerson held that this principle was true for teaching all aspects of the voice. Not only was the mind trained to perceive beautiful vocal sounds, it also must be trained to concentrate constantly and exclusively upon these ideal tones (*Ibid.*). Emerson believed that it was the cultivated voice that set its listeners thinking of the thousand relationships between what the actor said and the other things in his mind. These subtle, rich relationships, Emerson maintained, are conveyed not by words, but by tones.[36]

Elementary voice practice was supposed to achieve four results. It should have established freedom by means of right direction of tone. It should have perfected the elements in polished articulation. In addition, it should have developed facile handling of voice in combining elements. And last, it should have produced a certain degree of responsiveness in practice of various musical qualities (J.E. Southwick, *Expressive Voice Culture*, 16–17). In accordance with Emerson's stages of growth, voice work was divided into four parts. In the first phase the teacher helped the student to develop freedom, support, openness, and correct speech sounds.

Again, it should be noted that the process of teaching was not concerned with mechanical perfection of voice and speech sounds, but with maintaining the correct states of mind which were believed to lead to good voice and speech sounds. Here, work began on syllables and sounds which, in turn, stimulated the mind to create the correct sounds. In the second stage there were exercises for two kinds of inflections and for what Emerson called "elasticity" or "flexibility," and for power. In these two stages Emerson intended to show the relationship of physiology to the voice. Like all work at the Emerson school, voice was first perfected through external or relaxive and freeing exercises; and then, internal work, or exercises to achieve responsiveness to mental states (Emerson, *Psycho Vox,* 100).

Bodily expression was recognized as a part of the natural language of the actor. Emerson recognized the need for training the body and instituted aesthetic or expressive physical culture to hasten the student's evolution. The exercises were not entirely original—a fact he freely acknowledged. Part of the exercises were adapted from the systems of Ling, Delsarte, and Monroe, while some, Emerson believed to be new. Altogether, the system of aesthetic or physical culture consisted of three hundred movements, some being repetitions. Four years of daily practice were required to develop sufficient control for free expression (Emerson, *Expressive Physical Culture,* 1–17). These drills, quite reminiscent of Steele MacKaye's "Harmonic" or "Aesthetic Gymnastics," were designed to "free the channels" of expression. The course in Physical Culture was primarily devoted to relaxive and "decomposing" exercises, and then progressed to the responsive drills. The movements in the responsive drill began with voluntary action but achieved results largely by involuntary or reflex action (Emerson, "The Emerson Philosophy of Gesture," 84).

As stated earlier, Emerson was opposed to any form of gesture training for the actor. His courses in Physical Culture and Responsive Drill should not, therefore, be confused with courses in pantomimic training. It was Emerson's contention that if the thought was right, the gesture would naturally follow. The courses in Physical Culture and Responsive Drill included training only in the freeing of the body. They were not concerned with instilling "right" gestures for the students. After the Physical Culture course, the student was considered ready for the responsive drills which consisted of making gestures and movements which were the result of thought. *No attempt was made to introduce any form of mechanical gesture pattern.* If the gesture appeared inappropriate to the thought the student attempted to express, the corrective measures were devoted to the thought, not the gesture. This method of body training remained the only mode of physical training in the Emerson College of Oratory until Emerson retired in 1903. After 1903, however, it was decided by Southwick, then dean of the college, that a third kind of instruction would be offered, and during the scholastic year 1903-1904 systematic work, which Southwick described as teaching of typical gestures based on the laws and charts of Delsarte, was introduced in classes at The Emerson College of Oratory.[37]

The Southwicks went to great lengths to justify the departure from the fundamental principle of Emerson that gesture should only be taught as a natural expression of a state of mind. In defense of teaching gesture, Mrs. Southwick granted that it was true that if the mind was properly concentrated on an ideal, the proper gesture would result. But, she added, any faculty of the human organism is susceptible to culture. Therefore, beauty and freedom of the body could only be hastened in its perfection by increased practice of exercises and attitudes that emphasize characteristic patterns.[38]

In advocating specific training in gesture, however, Mrs. Southwick warned against indicating precisely what gesture was to be used in a particular place. She preferred, like her husband, to believe that there existed certain "typical" gestures of which all others are modifications. Consequently, the "typical" gestures represented only general foundations.

> I believe it is not desirable to prescribe too closely with
> reference to the expression of any particular thought
> just what gesture a person should make, but the criteria
> of gesture should be understood and applied in criticism
> and correction of what the person does when striving to
> realize the best expression of his thought. (*Ibid.*, 208)

The apparent desertion of one of Emerson's basic principles
was modified by Mrs. Southwick's total acceptance of another
of Emerson's precepts.

> The only suggestion I will make at this point to guard
> the student against mistakes is this: Fix the thought
> clearly before the mind; invite through expectancy,
> some expression; criticize that expression by means of
> love of the right ideal and strive to feel its significance.
> If you can do this, you will not be in danger of falling
> into that slavish and mechanical imitation which all true
> artists and lovers of natural expression would desire to
> avoid. (*Ibid.*, 209)

It appears that Mrs. Southwick was looking for a semiotic
standard against which the teacher could gauge the success of
the spontaneous system in order to give it greater validity. It
was justified on the basis that the mind controlled and affected
the nervous system in such a way as to force it to respond to
thought correctly (*Ibid.*). Consequently, Delsarte's classified
criteria were employed as "scientific" observations of the
external signs which were incited by correct thought; thus, the
teaching of specific gesture became a valid means of improving
expression.

The method of teaching the beginning course in gesture in
1909 was described by Mrs. Southwick as giving the simple
outlines of fundamental types of expression.[39] Along with
practice in these simple types, there was insistence upon the
expectant attitude which was thought to call forth spontaneous unity of the body. The subtle difference in motive caused
by the expectant attitude, Mrs. Southwick looked on as
providing the distinction between freedom of expressive
response and the mechanical practice of calculated arrange-

ment of the various agents of the body. A reconciliation of Emerson's method of stimulating natural growth and a more effective way of teaching Delsarte's artistic responses was thus believed to have been achieved.[40]

Emerson's "system of progressive steps through which the pupil may be led to realization of himself" (Emerson, *Evolution of Expression*, I, 7) is detailed in his four-volume *Evolution of Expression,* which constituted the basic textbook of Emerson College of Oratory (Renshaw, "Three Schools of Speech," 40). "Its principles were applied to all forms of oral interpretation, as well as to voice training, and gesture" (*Ibid.*), and the methods of evolution which were applied can be of great use to the actor. In an article for the official school organ, Agnes Smith, one of the graduates, developed the theme that intelligent conception was the first essential of acting.

> According to Smith's method, the teacher . . . should at first scarcely let a single passage by unchallenged. The challenging questions asked were said to bring about two very satisfying results. In trying to answer specific questions . . . , the student gains a better grasp of the author's thoughts because he had been stimulated to express these ideas in his own words. In the second place, the questions also stimulate the student to visualize . . . so he can describe it and feel every emotion so that, for the time being, he can forget his own identity. When the teacher is sure that the practice of ascertaining the whole meaning has become general, he can vary his method. (*Ibid.*, 74)

The methods of teaching appear to have been quite consistent among the various faculty. Edythe May Renshaw, in her study, "Three Schools of Speech," asserts that the material in the three major sources of information—the Southwicks' lectures, articles, and books; Emerson's lectures, articles, and books; and student notebooks—"does not differ greatly" (*Ibid,.* 156). The basic methods reflect Emerson's basic theoretical position of evolutionary development.

The emergence of acting as a discrete subject at the

Emerson College of Oratory is intimately involved with the evolution of the institution. From 1886 to 1892 the *Annual Catalogue* gives no indication of a formal acting course. Instead, Literary Interpretation, a course intended to train the student in *all* of the expressional arts, was considered sufficient for the development of the actor.[41] By 1893, however, training in acting was integrated into the curriculum through two classes: Public Presentation of the Plays of Shakespeare and Sheridan, a course taught by William J. Rolphe, and Dramatic Interpretation, a course under the direction of Laurence and Jessie Southwick and Walter Bradley Trip (*Annual Catalogue*: 1893, 11). The plays studied in these classes were presented under the auspices of the Southwick Literary Society and were a featured part of the meetings of that organization.

Of the courses taught in 1893, Dramatic Interpretation was most closely allied to a formal acting class, but only Seniors and Post-Graduates were eligible to take it. Training in acting appears to have been quite extensive, but it should be noted that the course was listed under the general heading of Literary Interpretation and taught according to Emerson's principles of evolution. The work in Dramatic Interpretation included:

> 1. Applications of the steps of the Evolution of Expressions and the criticism of the Perfective Laws of dramatic forms. Drill work in the interpretation of the plays of Hamlet and Macbeth.

> 2. Study of Dramatic Attitudes and Criticism. Bearing. Dramatic Action. "Stage Business." Criticism. Presentation of scenes from the plays of Hamlet, Macbeth, Othello, Merchant of Venice.

> 3. Interpretation of the comedies of Sheridan. Presentation of scenes from The Rivals. Criticism.

> Of the above courses, No. 1 is given four periods per week throughout the second year; No. 2 is given six

periods per week during the third year; No. 3 is given once a week as a post-graduate study. (*Annual Catalogue*: 1894, 18)

In 1898–99, "setting of plays" was added to No. 2 (*Annual Catalogue*: 1898–99, 18).

The *Annual Catalogue* for 1899–1900 indicates that while course work in acting was extremely popular, the school still permitted only Seniors and Post-Graduates to take specialties. The Emerson College of Oratory still remained dedicated to its founder's contention that his system was applicable to *all* expressional arts, and that the student must be firmly grounded in the fundamentals of expression before he engaged in specialized training. After Emerson's retirement, however, the curriculum evidenced a greater interest in acting and theatre courses.

In 1903, a new course called Practical Theatric Training was announced in the *Annual Catalogue*. It was taught by "four instructors, two of whom have had thorough schooling and the widest experience. One has served an apprenticeship in the companies of John McCullough and William H. Crane, and one under the management of the late Augustin Daly" (*Annual Catalogue*: 1903, 12). The instructors were listed as the Southwicks, Charles T. Grilley, and Clayton D. Gilbert (*Ibid.*). The course in Practical Theatric Training included: "Life study, costumed pantomimes, grouping and tableaus; criticism of standard plays; make-up and costume; lighting and color scheme; stage management; rehearsal and performance" (*Ibid.*). In the same year, George P. Baker was listed as lecturer on "The London of Shakespeare" (*Ibid.*), and in 1905, one-act plays were presented regularly once a week by the Senior students (*Annual Catalogue*: 1905, 18).

By 1907, the work in the general area of Literary Interpretation was dominated by courses in acting and theatre arts. The school announced that it was "especially interested in theatric training" (*Annual Catalogue*: 1907, 16), but still stated that its aim was the development of all the expressional arts. As early as 1909, the Emerson College of Oratory had begun training students in what today is called "theatre arts."

> Pupils are not only given practical stage training [in acting] but are taught how to produce plays and entertainments of all kinds. The annual public presentation of plays provides special training and further advantages for many students. (*Annual Catalogue*: 1909, 19)

The theory and practice of makeup achieved full course status by 1914 (*Annual Catalogue*: 1914), playwriting by 1917 (*Annual Catalogue*: 1917), and children's theatre in 1921 (*Annual Catalogue*: 1921). As the school developed, the entire range of theatre courses were added to the curriculum.

The Emerson College of Oratory graduated 2,561 students[42] in the period between 1880 and 1925. Twenty per cent of the graduates were awarded professional degrees in Interpretation (both acting and platform reading) and, of these, eighty-five per cent entered the professional theatre as actors or platform readers.[43] Many other graduates entered the teaching profession and founded their own schools. Still others entered teaching at the high school and college level and were quite influential in introducing course work in acting and theatrical production. While the Emerson College of Oratory contributed several hundred actors to the American theatre and many teachers, its most important contribution has been the development of a unique approach to acting.

Stripped of Darwinism and Hegelian "evolutionism," Emerson and the Southwicks taught that the actor had a social responsibility to the audience which served a reciprocal purpose by actually participating in the improvement of the actor's aesthetic. Further, like other contemporary acting theories, Emerson believed that relaxation and mastery of technique were necessary components for liberating emotional expression. Above all, he advocated that the right thought would create the right gesture and vocal expression and that the actor need not be concerned at the moment of

The fourth location of Emerson College of Oratory, Chickering Hall on Huntington Avenue. Notice the expansion over only twenty-one years (1901–1911). (Photo courtesy of Emerson College Archives)

delivery. Emerson's canon of theory is aimed at the evolutionary development of the actor that reinforces the intellectual, emotional and imaginative resources. His view that intellectual perceptions enhance the sympathetic or emotional identification is as important as his view that the imagination is the result of and interacts with the other faculties.

The Emerson system of creating natural expression and the methods of teaching it contained several departures from the contemporary methods of the day. First, the evolutionary process became the criterion for the teaching of all course work. Second, the attitude toward the student and toward criticism were decidedly ahead of their time. Emerson was a leader among the teachers who advocated the best possible critical environment for the pupil. "Free play" in the classroom was considered a necessity to the encouragement of creativity, and in the following several decades was to become a practice among many schools that taught acting. The Emerson system of creating natural expression may seem complex and difficult. Still, it must be admitted that Emerson perceived the chief dangers and the weaknesses in a corrupted Delsarte system and other mechanical methods, and took steps toward remedying them. He showed that true expression cannot be stimulated from the outside but should come from within; that it flows spontaneously from genuine emotion which the actor can induce through his own creative imagination. Emerson supplied the actor with a method of inducing creativity that was found to be workable in an institution which produced several thousand actors, platform readers, and teachers. In stressing his principle of "Creative Evolution" and maintaining that all expression comes from within and moves outward, Emerson made his chief contribution to modern acting theory.

TOP: Samuel Silas Curry, prolific writer on the subject of expression and of acting in particular; and BOTTOM: his wife, Anna Baright Curry, a highly respected teacher who, along with Curry, guided the destiny of The School of Expression, now Curry College, a liberal arts college in Milton, Mass. (Photo courtesy of Curry College)

CHAPTER IV
THE SCHOOL OF EXPRESSION

When Franklin H. Sargent opened his New York School of Acting after his break with Steele MacKaye, he advertised in the *New York Dramatic Mirror*. Beside Sargent's advertisement appeared a similar announcement for Samuel Silas Curry's Boston School of Acting, an adjunct of his School of Expression. This advertisement in the *New York Dramatic Mirror*[1] gave notice to the professional theatre world that the "schools of expression" were prepared to offer competition to the more "practical" theatre schools for the right to train actors.

Curry maintained this competition throughout the duration of his life. He refused to accept the view that "practical" training in acting had any value unless the aspiring actor was firmly grounded in the principles of his art. Curry's position was similar to that offered by elocutionist Alfred Ayres, who advertised: "No stage with which to amuse the pupil and squander his time. Begin with rehearsals when the trees begin to grow at the top; when architects begin with the house and follow with the foundation." Like Curry, Ayres warned, "He that begins with rehearsals never gets far," and "Essentials are never taught by those who do not themselves know them."[2] Ayres' statement contains the essence of the position concerning the teaching of acting which the "schools of expression" maintained.

Like Emerson, Curry studied under Lewis B. Monroe at Boston University. When Monroe died in 1879, Curry, who had completed his Master's degree the year before, was asked to carry on the work. In 1880 the university conferred a

Ph.D. degree upon him, and in 1883 he was made Snow
Professor of Oratory. His assumption of this post and his
organization of private classes may be said to comprise the
informal founding of the School of Expression.

> The School of Expression was organized from private
> classes in the spring of the year 1885 by the now
> Professor of Elocution and Oratory, Boston University,
> with the permission of the trustees to carry on the work
> of the University School of Oratory, discontinued in
> 1879 at the death of the lamented Dean Monroe. The
> work of the school [School of Expression] has so grown
> that it has been incorporated as a school entirely
> separate from the University.[3]

In 1886, Curry married Anna Baright, who had also studied
with Monroe and was conducting her own School of Elocution and Expression. Their classes were merged and a prospectus was issued the next year. Curry continued to hold his
position at Boston University until 1888, and from that time
until his death in 1921 he was the head of the School of
Expression. Like Emerson's institution, the School of Expression became a degree-granting institution (1939) and was
permitted by the Massachusetts Legislature to award Bachelor of Science and Master of Science degrees in Oratory. The
name was changed to Curry School, and in 1943 it was
renamed Curry College. The school is still in existence.

By 1891, the School of Acting was as important as the
School of Expression.

> The School of Acting purports to be a branch of the
> School of Expression; but even a casual visitor at the
> school would be quick to see that the so-called 'branch'
> school rivals in importance and vitality the parent
> school.[4]

It should be clearly understood, however, that the School of
Acting and the School of Expression were in no way separate
institutions. They both availed themselves of the same build-

ing, the same faculty and, with the exception of two or three courses, the same curriculum. In every way, the Curry School of Acting was a part of the parent institution and merely offered additional courses in specialized delivery. As Marianna McCann suggested, The School of Acting represented an important role in Curry's School of Expression but it was organized along the lines of Curry's philosophy of expression in general, and his theories and methods of training actors in particular. Consequently, before specialized work in acting was started, "The School of Expression, or of elocution and aesthetic gymnastics . . . supplies the rudimentary work for more artistic study" (*Ibid.*).

True expression, Curry said, manifests the soul of man through reproducing the processes of nature. In another place, he asserted that permanency was not the most important criterion of art.

> But if art is the revelation of the human soul, then the most direct and powerful manifestation through the living voice, the living body of the most profound experience is art.[5]

Curry maintained that "Vocal expression is the freest art"[6] but that expression through the voice *and* body was the highest form of art and "dramatic art has ever led the way."

> Histrionic art is the most direct means of expressing the emotions and conditions of the human soul. . . . When histrionic art . . . is elevated to the highest standard, universal art is ennobled and refined; for this is the most direct means of stimulating the imagination and awakening ideals in the mass of the people.[7]

While the School of Expression has always been associated with what is now called Oral Interpretation, it should be noted that acting, in its highest form, was recognized by Curry as one of the most powerful forces in society. Curry's feelings about acting, however, did not diminish the primary function of the school—the cultivation of *all* the expressional arts.

Expression, as defined by Curry, is "the effect of the possession of an idea by the mind, or of the mind being dominated by an ideal or passion" (*Ibid.*, 207). As a part of expression, therefore, acting is the result, not of physical, but of psychic action at the moment of delivery (*Ibid.*, xi, 214). All faults of the voice and body, all faults of acting, can be traced directly or indirectly to wrong actions of the mind (*Ibid.*, 216). If the proper action of the mind, proper cooperation of all the faculties of the soul and coordination of thought and emotion by will are secured, Curry contended, acting will tend to be right and natural (*Ibid.*, 222). In this sense, Curry was a firm advocate of the "think the thought" school of acting.

The function of acting, as of all expression, is that it "endeavors to influence the human mind" (*Ibid*, 27). In a much narrower sense, however, acting "aims to awaken the same faculties in another mind which are active in the mind of the artist [actor]" (*Ibid.*). The means by which acting achieves its purpose is through the voice, speech and body of the actor. Curry would also add to this list of "means" the imagination, feelings, and thoughts of the actor. Thus, acting was conceived as being the revelation of the playwright's ideas through the psychic and physical being of the actor. However, Curry saw the actor's function as more than merely recreating the playwright's idea. "He must think and feel with *greater intensity* than the writer. By him the ideas of the writer are made salient, their movement more natural, their realization more vivid" (*Ibid.*, 20. Italics mine). The objective of the actor "is to make truth more vivid; to give it the life of personality; to bring unity out of diversity; to change abstractions into living moving creations" (*Ibid.*, 21). Curry demanded that the actor bring to the play his imagination, which would enable him to expand the playwright's ideas. The actor, then, was in every sense a creative artist. He was not the mere servant of the playwright, but an artist who brought the play to its fullest fruition through the art of acting.

The relationship of the actor to the character is partially

explained by Curry's insistence that acting is the truthful revelation of the soul. Through revelation of the soul the actor leads men to recognize truth and Nature. Consequently, Curry maintained:

> There must be insight not only into truth and Nature, but into men. The . . . actor must have a quick and instinctive insight into character. He must see as others see, and feel as others feel. He must have that sympathy which will enable him to identify himself with all situations. (*Ibid.*, 20)

The power of the actor to place himself in the situation of another person, feel his feelings, and think his thoughts was considered absolutely necessary. The actor must be able to accomplish identification through the workings of the imagination, but the emotions are no less the actor's. Curry believed that feeling was essential for natural expression. He contended:

> If the mind really sees each scene, and feels the movement of the events and situations, voice and body are freely and naturally modulated. Thus the real cause of genuine experience in . . . dramatic expression, is the identification [of the actor] with the thought or situation. Unless the expression is meant to be cold and mechanical, or mere imitation, sympathetic identification . . . with the scene must cause the experience. (*Ibid.*, 199)

It should be clear from the above that Curry was not only in the "think the thought" school but in the "feel the feeling" school as well. Not only did he believe that the actor needed great insight into the ideas of the playwright and into the character he portrayed, but he demanded a complete identification which aroused passion as well. Of course, Curry recognized that the emotions of the actor must be disciplined as thoroughly as the body and voice, but the feelings expressed were no less real. The actor's feelings vivified the playwright's characters.

The relationship of the actor to the audience, as presented by Curry, appears to be similar to that professed by Sargent and his school. That is, the manner in which the playwright presents his ideas dictates the manner of presentation. Curry strongly admired those actors who created the illusion of another life and another place on the stage. His favorite actors were Jefferson, Booth and the elder Salvini. Curry dreaded exhibitionism on the stage. "Dramatic art is directly antagonistic to show or theatrical display," he said. "It is not exhibition, but is a revelation of the mind, of spiritual force and life and movement" (*Ibid.*, 340). Curry also advocated that the actor be a good listener.

> Accordingly, the true actor is known for his capacity for listening rather than by his speaking. The secret of acting consists mainly in the power to give attention to the ideas uttered by the interlocutor, and his 'action' is the response of imagination, feeling, and body to his ideas. But while this is true, the actor must speak as well as listen; he must have the power to change from the attitude of hearer and become a speaker. . . . He is best . . . who is able to give subjective attention to his own thought. Each successive picture, each stage in the process of his thought, must cause a sensitive response. (*Ibid.*, 322)

The actor wins the audience's attention through creating the belief in the audience that he is someone else; and wins the audience through indirection. Curry asked the actor to ignore the audience except for the underlying feeling of love for them and the desire to communicate to them. He insisted, however, that this be accomplished subtly and through the audience's acceptance of the "truth" of the situation on the stage.

Curry accepted the position that "The art of acting is an indispensable adjunct of the dramatic arts" (*Ibid.*, 238). He appears to have accepted the position of A. W. Ward, whom Curry quoted as saying, "The dramatic and histrionic arts are to him 'really inseparable from one another. Properly speaking, no drama is such until it is acted' " (*Ibid.*). The actor, therefore, was an indispensable agent in what Curry considered the highest form of expression. The training of the actor was of great importance to Curry and he undertook to train the actor in the best possible manner: from *within outward* according to the processes of Nature (Curry, *Province of Expression*, 171–72).

In Curry's consideration of the "ideal" actor, one basic idea is constantly repeated: "The highest activity of the soul is imagination" (*Ibid.*, 185). Since acting was believed to be the revelation of the soul of man, it followed that the best acting is imaginative acting. As stated earlier, Curry disagreed with the position that "thought and imagination belong only to the author" (*Ibid.*, 19). He opposed the belief that the actor "must not interpose his mental action between the author and the auditor: he must present correctly the form of the author's words" (*Ibid.*). Curry contended that true acting was interpretation and, therefore, must be the actor's "thought and emotion as suggested by the language of words, and manifesting these by means of the other co-ordinate languages or modulations of voice and body" (*Ibid.*). He did not deny the right of the playwright to a fair hearing, but was firmly convinced that the actor should bring his own thoughts, feelings, and imagination to the play in order to expand and vivify the playwright's ideas. Indeed, Curry asserted that it was the only way a play could be acted. He insisted on this idea because he recognized that true dramatic art was imaginative and that a play was not, in fact, a play until it was acted. Since all expression depended on imagination, dramatic expression was thought to be based on the imagination also.

In order to understand more fully Curry's concept of imagination and its relation to acting, one must first recognize that Curry considered imagination the major factor in all creativity. In one discussion of imagination, Curry stated that the imagination can unite a general idea to an individual conception. Imagination may evolve a general idea or a universal in a way which is exactly the opposite of the process of abstraction. The imagination, instead of eliminating the specific and concrete, penetrates beneath accidents and fixes attention on the essential elements. By vivid realization and by getting at the heart of objects, the imagination chooses such a mode of expression that a specific and concrete fact becomes a suggestion of universal truth. In so doing, the imagination unites a specific and definite image with all the marks of intension and gives it in such a way as to suggest extension. The imagination, Curry concluded, is thus a power that can unite intension and extension in conception (*Ibid.*, 67).

Another elemental action attributed to the imagination is the transforming of abstractions into vivid pictures. Imagination could also elevate or idealize simple objects, scenes, or events (*Ibid.*). In still another discussion, Curry listed the powers of the imagination as: providing the basis of insight and sympathy; placing every idea in some relationship to life; bringing all elements into unity; comparing object with object; identifying the unknown with the known; creating the new whole. In short, Curry maintained that the imagination is the faculty of creative power.[8]

The process of the imagination is stimulated by thought or conception. From the moment the actor conceives an idea through analysis, he enters into the world of the imaginative. Conception, however, should not be confused with imagination. "In general," said Curry, "conception has reference to single objects or ideas: imagination to their relation. An idea to be conceived is more or less isolated" (Curry, *Imagination and Dramatic Instinct,* 25). Conception was conceived as the power of the intellect, and primarily an analytical tool which made inductions from observed phenomena. "Conception may be vivid, and imagination dim; for conception deals with distinct features, with things which lie on the plane of sense" (*Ibid.*). Memory operated as an aid to conception. "Memory recalls specific facts and objects; but imagination supplies situations and living relations. Imagination takes facts, and gives them vital kinship to other facts" (*Ibid.*, 38). Intellect and memory, then, appear to be the fuel for logical conceptions, which in turn are the fuel for imaginative conception.

> In order to . . . [act a play] well, we analyze it, we study all possible references, we look up facts regarding places mentioned, we refer to events of history, we study the lives of any historical characters which may be referred to; all this knowledge is so assimilated that it furnishes only a background or material for imaginative conception. (*Ibid.*)

In another place, Curry warned that dependence on the intellect alone was futile in acting. "We can analyze . . . [a play] so as to destroy all its poetry" (*Ibid.*, 25). Again, warning against mere intellectual conception, Curry claimed:

> The reason may pre-judge, may mechanically compare, may be unreceptive and unresponsive; but not so with the imagination. Intellectual or commonplace attention may dwell upon accidents, but imagination looks to the heart. Imagination is the spontaneous result of sympathetic contemplative attention. (*Ibid.*, 34)

The basic point which Curry attempted to bring across to his students was that ideal relations of conceptions must be given as well as their logical relations. In order to penetrate the consciousness of the audience and maintain responsiveness, "Each conception must be presented as part of a situation, each thought with a background" (*Ibid.*, 192). Intellect and its helpmate, memory, were clearly relegated to a place of secondary importance in Curry's estimate of the needs of the "ideal" actor. Imagination appears to be the end toward which all the faculties contribute in the process of acting. "Conceptions alone, however vivid, do not result in perfect expression," Curry stressed (*Ibid.*, 191).

The imagination, then, is the fountainhead from which all great acting springs. Imagination not only synthesizes and expands conceptions, the imaginative realization of a situation, said Curry, is also the true source of emotion in acting.

As he explained emotion, feeling results from vivid understanding of relations or associations. *Imagination arouses
feeling by vividly conceiving ideas as present realities*; the distant
is made near, the past made present. By means of the
imagination, the actor is brought into sympathy with the race.
It gives the power to create and to understand and feel the
message of the art of every age" (*Ibid.*, 89–94). "Feeling is
often eliminated by abstract thinking, but it can always be
aroused by sympathetic, contemplative, imaginative thought"
(Curry, *Foundations of Expression*, 149).

"Emotion in life," said Curry, "is often independent of
thought and will" (Curry, *Province of Expression*, 87). The
emotions which imagination stimulates, however, can be
more easily controlled than emotion which is awakened by a
real object; its cause is mental, and we can control that cause,
Curry emphasized. "But for this reason, the emotion is none
the less genuine."[9] Even when feeling is evoked by conscious,
deliberate attention to the individual concepts, it is still truly
spontaneous because it springs originally from the mind of
the actor. In his enthusiasm for the spontaneous power of the
imagination, Curry asserted that the imagination cannot be
governed or guided in any deliberate manner. But he stated
elsewhere that the imaginative responses result from deliberately holding attention on ideas (Curry, *Imagination and
Dramatic Instinct*, 101–102). A certain indirect control is
clearly implied. Furthermore, insofar as he maintained that
the imaginative results from feeling induced by deliberate
conscious attention (Curry, *Foundations of Expression*, 137),
there must be a kind of control over imagination. Curry
ultimately decided that spontaneous actions "may be regu-
lated or awakened and consciously united to voluntary
elements without interfering with their spontaneous up-
springing" (*Ibid.*, 137–138). Belief in this theory led Curry to
base many of his principles for development of natural
expression upon these two elements: imagination and feeling.

Imagination also functioned as the motivating factor in
sympathy, insight, assimilation, and dramatic instinct. Imagi-

nation, Curry claimed, is the source of sympathy; and sympathy he defined as "the power to realize a thought or situation with its appropriate feeling or the identification of one individual with the point of view and spirit of another" (*Ibid.*, 260). "Imagination is also the faculty which gives us insight, but we can never have insight without sympathy."[10] Quite plainly, Curry believed that the imagination was the source of the actor's fundamental powers. He asserted that assimilation is founded on imagination, but it is more than imagination. Assimilation manifests the effect of sympathetic observation (Curry, *Imagination and Dramatic Instinct*, 223). Imagination causes insight, but sympathy causes identification and participation. To achieve assimilation, Curry insisted that a thorough understanding of the ideas beneath the words was imperative (*Ibid.*, 149) and that every successive idea must be fully realized. "The best method of securing assimilation," he declared, "is the development of the imagination and dramatic instinct" (*Ibid.*, 315). In the book *Imagination and Dramatic Instinct*, Curry explained that dramatic instinct means the spontaneous realization of ideas in living relations and of the motives and manifestations of character. This instinct, he pointed out, has two elements—imagination, which gives insight into another's point of view, and sympathy, which enables us to identify ourselves with this point of view (*Ibid.*, 235). Another book gives approximately the same definition.

> Dramatic instinct contains two elements—imaginative insight into relations of a fact to human life and character, and sympathy or the power to identify one's self with such a character or situation. (Curry, *Foundations of Expression*, 245)

Curry defined the nature of "instinct" as the spontaneous action of all the faculties in their unity, as consciousness recognizing results but not the process, and as unconscious action toward unconscious purpose. The chief significance of instinct is that "The use of such a term implies the fact that all true expression is traced to the action of the mind and that there is ever an unconscious element in all true delivery" (Curry, *Province of Expression*, 226). It is in connection with the spontaneous emotional and imaginative elements that the actor's instinct seemed important to Curry.

That the characteristics of nature present in all forms of art are also present in acting, Curry believed to be self-evident. All through Curry's books the fundamental characteristic of nature to which he constantly referred is the process of growth or unfoldment *from within outward*. In one place he declared that for lack of a better name, this characteristic could be called spontaneity. Or it could be called originality, since everything that obeys this law has a character distinct from everything else.[11] In showing its relationship to other qualities of art, Curry pointed out that spontaneity "underlies other qualities, such as freedom, or absence of external restrictions or hindrance; simplicity, or the directness between cause and effects; and unity, or the fact that living expression comes from one centre, and acts in all directions and harmony" (*Ibid.*). Spontaneity does not exclude the function of will or consciousness, however. On the contrary, "man is conscious of what he is doing, but the conscious volition simply directs, restrains and guides, holds each idea till it has more effectively accomplished its work upon the man's own nature, and restrains the impulse until they diffuse themselves through the whole organism" (Curry, *Province of Expression*, 192). Curry summarized the function of the will in relation to spontaneity by suggesting the simile, "Will merely acts toward the other powers of the soul as an engineer does toward his engine. He starts or stops the action, and regulates its speed and its force, but the power comes from the steam and not from the arm of the engineer" (*Ibid.*).

The entire process of the preparation and mode of delivery as it was manifested in the psyche of the actor was summed up by Curry as follows:

> The fundamental center or focus for consciousness in normal delivery must ever be upon the successive ideas, the imaginative situation must ever be in the fore-

ground; but this does not forbid in the normal action of the human mind the subordinate consciousness which recognizes the effect of emotion upon the voice and body, the whole relationship of the speaker to his audience. He abandons himself not to mere nervous impulses, but to the impulses that come from the life of the soul, *too deep for his own consciousness to fathom.* He forgets himself, only in the sense that he gives himself up to a great idea of which he is definitely and completely conscious. He leaves the great fountainhead of feeling free to pour forth its flood into his voice and body. He becomes, so to speak, two beings—becomes a great channel of thought and emotion, great impulses come to him and are given to him, the very ideas themselves that rise so vividly come out of the dim unknown, although his consciousness holds them and dominates them and lets them pass away as others rise when the voice and body, though restrained and directed in part, are kept in the background of consciousness and never displace the fundamental focus of the mind upon one great central idea or situation. It is the vividness of the central idea that stimulates the conscious actions, colors the voice, and brings that unity, freedom, variety and spontaneity which are the universal characteristics of nature. (*Ibid.*, 194. Italics mine)

It should be clear that while Curry accepted a kind of conscious control of the external aspects of delivery, he would permit no interference or control of the actor's initial creative impulses. Feeling could only be controlled in its attempt to find form. These ideas concerning the imagination and its relationship to sympathy, emotion, memory, conception and spontaneity are unique and original. Perhaps nowhere in acting theory has the imagination been more thoroughly examined, detailed and defined. Curry's ideas certainly go as far and in as much depth as those of Stanislavsky and his disciples in attempting to clarify the operation of imagination and its relationship to many complex and abstract areas. His point that the initial impetus is "identification" with the character, the thoughts, feelings and motives, constitutes a tacit acceptance of the "Magic If." But further than that, Curry considers how the "Magic If" intensifies emotion through sympathy and how the process engenders spontaneity. This is a contribution of considerable magnitude, and it was espoused as early as 1891!

The whole man as well as all the fundamental needs of expression must be considered in a satisfactory method for improving acting, asserted Curry in his first book on expression (*Ibid.*, 365). This principle remained fundamental in all his published works. Because of it, he set out to "find the psychological causes, not only of the expressive modulation of the voice, but of the conditions of mind and body required for its right training and correct use" (Curry, *Foundations of Expression*, 3–7). Furthermore, good actor training must, in his opinion, include training in three phases: vocal expression, voice, and pantomime. Such training is necessary, Curry maintained, because acting is "the expression of the human being through the human organism. It results from the right union of the modulations of the voice and actions of the body as natural signs of the . . . [actor's] experience" (*Ibid.*, 17–18).

The "ideal" actor, then, not only must have complete control of his imagination and the other faculties it influenced, he must also be a master of technique. Curry recommended three general ways of improving acting, two of which pertain to technique: stimulating the cause (psychic), opening the channels of revelation (both psychic and physical), and securing a better knowledge of the right modes of execution (physical).[12] Because Curry believed that the simplest act of expression demanded a natural unity of all the powers of the mind and the agents of the body, he believed that in good acting "the subtlest, intellectual, emotional, and physical actions and conditions must be stimulated and trained" (*Ibid.*, 5). Training, as well as stimulation is necessary, he asserted, because bad habits can interfere with immediate and natural responses of the organism. Logically, therefore, the voice and the body should be trained first. However, even though perfection of vocal and bodily techniques was of primary importance in acting, Curry maintained that both must be developed through *stimulating the cause.*

Just as the mind and the imagination were considered subject to nature's law of growth, voice, too, was conceived as being governed by the principle of "from within outward." The voice should possess the same qualities as other natural agents of expression. It must be characterized by spontaneity, freedom, simplicity, and unity.

Although Curry tried to base his theory of voice production on scientific facts and to develop his method of voice training in accordance with scientific principles, he declared that "vocal training belongs primarily to art" (*Ibid.*, 431). He meant that the voice is primarily an agent of expression. It is subjective and personal. It reveals impression; it does not represent things or facts (*Ibid.*, 445). The voice, like any artistic medium, can reveal thought, imagination and feeling, and can be used correctly only when there has been a vivid, deep impression. When the impression is adequate, the voice can be used in accordance with the laws of nature, that is, with spontaneity (*Ibid.*, 434, 435, 441).

For the actor, Curry's theory of vocal technique offered unusual freedom. He asserted, however, that in no art form is mere mechanical work so important as in vocal expression. In the development of his voice the actor must discover the connection between vocal action and the modulation of his voice and body. The actor must understand what he does voluntarily and what he does involuntarily when his thought, imagination, and emotion are brought into union. Since vocal expression is subjective and connected with the involuntary muscles and unconscious processes of the nervous system, the climax of voice perfection for the actor is reached when the voice responds perfectly to every thought and feeling (*Ibid.*, 436, 437, 438, 441).

In Curry's School of Expression, education to free the actor's body for spontaneous expression was regarded as an important part of the course of study. Indeed, to Curry, pantomimic language constituted one of the three primary

languages. Curry attempted to explain the philosophic relation of pantomime to other modes of expression. He also
endeavored to show the psychological cause and significance
of what he called "action," and to teach the principle of action
in accordance with his analysis of all expression.

Action was used by Curry as a general term covering the
visible means of thought and emotion through the body. It
and pantomimic expression were regarded as synonymous
terms indicating the most general and generic of languages.[13]
Words, Curry insisted, reveal man's opinions, tone his emotions; but action reveals the real man (Curry, *Foundation of
Expression*, 273). In fact, Curry believed that verbal language
was artificial, but that pantomimic language was a natural
language of true signs.[14] Pantomimic expression was defined
as "the display of activity which lies back of the statement, the
most natural language" (*Ibid.*, 6). Pantomimic dramatization,
therefore, was of immense importance, and its perfection was
regarded as absolutely essential to acting. From the acting
standpoint, pantomimic dramatization, like voice, was not
considered a separate discipline, but could only be considered
in relation to the total actor. On this point Curry wrote:

> We can see that all expression presupposes two things.
> First, a correct action of the faculties of the soul
> [thought, feeling, will], and secondly a normal action of
> the organic means which transmit the action of the soul
> [voice, body, speech]. (Curry, *Province of Expression*,
> 251)

The relationship of art to nature is best approached through
Curry's ideas concerning manifestation and representation.
Though Curry tends to classify representational expression as
realistic and manifestive expression as idealistic, he was quick
to point out that both modes were essential elements in all
great acting. Manifestive acting, he defined as the revelation
of subjective conditions, while representative acting was
defined as the illustration of objective things or relations.
Curry believed manifestive acting to be direct, spontaneous,

emotional, passional; whereas representative acting usually expresses pictorial or imaginative actions of the mind, and locates or describes objects or figurative conceptions.[15] While Curry admitted that both manifestation and representation were essential to acting and each fulfilled its necessary purpose, he maintained that manifestive acting was of a higher order. One important aspect of representative acting, in Curry's opinion, was that it sometimes deals with ideas as if they were things. Manifestive acting is fundamental and continuous, whereas representative acting is accidental (*Ibid.*, 278). Curry clearly favored manifestive acting and declared frequently that the American theatre was much too representative (Curry, *Province of Expression*, 440–446).

The idea of unity pervades Curry's theories of acting. The psychical man and the physical man must be merged if great acting is to take place. Throughout the writings of Curry, a fundamental concept, emphasized and reemphasized, is this: All great acting is the revelation of man's psychic nature through his physical organism. Every external manifestation is the natural outgrowth of inner activity. A clear pattern of development and approach to the role emerges from this dominant idea.

TEACHING METHODS

The philosophy of actor training at the School of Expression was proclaimed in the preface of one of Curry's early books: " 'To know a thing, we must do it,' is a fundamental principle of education" (Curry, *Imaginative and Dramatic Instinct*, 1). Curry firmly believed that the student should be set to doing. He should discover the principles for himself in his practice. Consequently, Curry supported the idea that explanation should be given only to guide the student in his work and that all instruction should be subordinate to the student's direct contact with nature (*Ibid.*).

Curry's educational theory was guided by the principle that

the teacher must arouse spontaneous impulses within the student; he rejected the idea that spontaneity was synonymous with wild impulse (Curry, *Province of Expression*, 198–200). In true education, Curry asserted, the encouragement of spontaneity meant the coordination of conscious and unconscious elements (*Ibid.*, 205–207). Curry also eschewed the idea that education of the actor embodied merely intellectual development. Intellectual development alone, Curry said, would only lead to mechanical skill. He wished to train not only the intellect, but the imagination as well.

Curry was convinced that the teacher of acting must be a thoroughly educated person: cultured, practical, artistic, and scientific. The teacher must have a knowledge of the nature of expression, its causes, methods, and modes of execution; must have a knowledge of the nature of man, his mind, voice, body, and of normal and abnormal actions of all the activities and agents of expression; must have a knowledge of the processes of nature, of how it grows and declines (*Ibid.*, 263, 418, 419). He must also know the principles of art and the most advanced methods of education (Curry, *Lessons in Vocal Expressions,* 7).

The chief duty of the teacher is to forget one's own egotistic conceptions. Curry believed that the actor was the worst trainer of other actors. The next worst, Curry said, was the stage manager or director. According to Curry's view, the actor is too egotistic, and the run-of-the-mill director is too interested in the trappings of the stage and pictorial representation to spend time on the revelation of character. Consequently, Curry believed that only a person trained exclusively in the total art of expression, with all the knowledge and dedication mentioned above, could qualify as a teacher of acting.

As a critic, the teacher was not to praise or find fault but to inspire, to encourage, and to awaken hope and enthusiasm. By all means, the teacher must not repress or inhibit the student (Curry, *Province of Expression*, 412). In this situation, the student was in many ways considered the equal of the teacher. Since Curry considered it the critic's province to compare the actual with the ideal, he stipulated that the critic should study the whole situation, including all the difficulties the actor had to encounter. According to this view, criticism was not merely external comparison; it must see the *student's* ideal intention. The teacher could then compare different actors' relative success in reaching their ideal. It was important to Curry that the student actor reach the ideal in his own way and at his own speed. Growth, to be natural growth, cannot be forced. Consequently, Curry saw improvement and development as relative. The word of the teacher, therefore, should never be the absolute standard for the work of the student. In this way, Curry attempted to protect the originality and spontaneity of the student's development (*Ibid.*, 266–267).

Some of the teacher's other functions, aside from the chief duty of helping each student achieve the greatest possible growth, were to aid in training the voice, to develop ease and grace in the body, to remove awkwardness and stiffness, and to develop the actor's power to think and feel imaginatively. Because the imagination enables the actor to penetrate to the heart of nature and the character, because it is the chief creative faculty, because it enables the actor to enter into sympathy with his character and all fellow men, because it is the foundation of all altruistic instinct, because it is the faculty upon which depends appreciation of art, because it is the faculty which enables man to realize eternity—in short, because upon its discipline depends any true education of emotions, Curry argued that the imagination must be trained. Imagination should be highly developed in both the teacher and the student (Curry, *Imagination and Dramatic Instinct,* 7–10).

The nature of the curriculum for the aspiring actor at the School of Expression was quite similar to that which was basic to the study of all forms of expression. As stated earlier in this chapter, Curry regarded fundamental training in voice, body, and imagination as essential for the actor. It was only after a thorough grounding in the fundamentals that Curry permitted specialized training in acting. Consequently, before any consideration of the specialized training in acting, it is first essential to understand the methods of the "fundamental" course work.

The basic curriculum at the School of Expression was discussed by Marianna McCann, a former student at the institution. She mentioned:

> Rigorous training in aesthetic gymnastics, movements which are modifications of the so-called Delsarte system, slow and thorough voice-building, and a general acquaintance with English, French and German dramatic and poetic literature comprise the courses of instruction exacted in this school as adjuncts to the study of characters and presentation of plays. Stage make-up, any hints as to stage dressing, and the regular stage business and 'gags,' wisely or unwisely, are quite ignored by the director [Curry, himself]. (McCann, 999)

Curry's attempts at teaching acting were not based on any particular style of acting, unless it would be manifestive. Curry contended that all acting springs from the mind; therefore, if the mind reacted well to impression and could think and feel imaginatively and if the voice and body were free, the actor would move and speak naturally and effectively regardless of whether it was a play by Shakespeare, or one by Boucicault, Herne, or Gillette.

The Curry method of teaching voice must have been unique in its time since it was designed to awaken the spontaneous action of the mind. Without spontaneity, voice development becomes training in mechanics of language, Curry charged.[16] He was convinced not only that his method was natural but that his theory and practice of voice training were different from those of most of his contemporaries as well as his predecessors. He expressed such a view when he wrote:

> It is not too much to claim that it [The School of Expression] has led an advance or reform in the training of the Spoken Word and has emphasized and placed upon a psychological basis all work for the training of

the voice and body in relation to the mind and its expressive acts.[17]

As a natural agent, the voice must be governed by nature's principle of "from within outward." It should possess the same qualities as other natural agents of expression, and must be characterized by spontaneity, freedom, simplicity, and unity. It was Curry's theory that the method of developing the voice should be psychological, not merely technical. Curry asserted that the method of voice training used in the School of Expression "consists of awakening the imagination, stimulating the feeling, and securing right actions of the mind" (*Ibid.*, 20). It was Curry's aim not to set up rules, but problems which would stimulate the "mental cause" of expression.[18] In today's terms, we would say that Curry's methods advocated a "motive" behind every utterance.

Unlike most teachers of his day, Curry eschewed mechanical training in the conventional sense. He did not appear to be interested in voice and articulation for their own sake, and asserted:

> While the training of the voice and body must be separate and must usually precede technical execution, yet we can see at once that most of the exercises to develop proper action of the mind must consist in the direct work of expression itself. (Curry, *Province of Expression*, 258)

The study of vocal technique consisted not of the study of vocal quality in isolation, but the study of voice as it manifests itself in actual interpretation of literature. As Curry emphasized: "Technique must not be practiced for its own sake, with the exception of a few elemental actions" (*Ibid.*, 259). Thus, the study of voice was actually the study of pause, inflection, change of pitch, rhythm and tone color as they are manifested in the reading of literature.

Edythe May Renshaw states that "The textbook for the first-year student in the School of Expression was *Lessons in*

Vocal Expression, though after the publication of *Foundations of Expression,* in 1907, the latter book was often used" (Renshaw, "Three Schools of Speech," 246). In addition, "For the second-year students, Curry wrote *Imagination and Dramatic Instinct* shortly after the publication of *Lessons in Vocal Expression*" (*Ibid.*, 248).

The specific purpose of the course work in voice, according to Curry, was the perfection of the vocal modulations. Briefly, he taught that pause is an indication that the mind is concentrated, while touch is used to indicate where the mind is concentrated. A change of pitch shows discrimination from one idea to another. Inflection manifests the actor's attitude and his sense of relation to ideas. Tone-color reveals feeling, while rhythm and stress change according to the actor's estimate of the value of what he says. In comparison with tone-color, texture expresses deeper and more permanent conditions and reveals the character (Curry, *Imagination and Dramatic Instinct,* 299). Curry also discussed the manner in which inflection, change of pitch, touch, and tone-color could be technically perfected through "successively focusing" on the action of the mind (Curry, *Province of Expression,* 259–60). Both *Lessons in Vocal Expression* and *Imagination and Dramatic Instinct* are full of "exercises" consisting of poems or selections designed to stimulate thought and arouse the voice to response. Each poem was considered to have in it certain characteristic thought patterns which would give special training or practice in one of the modulations. However, Curry considered *all* of the modulations to be operative in any selection of prose or poetry.

At times, Curry's "exercises" seem little more than analyses of "how to do it." All of them, however, were intended to stimulate the imagination, regardless of Curry's penchant for describing what the author intended. For instance, with reference to a passage from *Hamlet,* Curry instructed:

> Note the effect of excitement upon the abruptness of Hamlet's inflections. At first, he is indifferent, and the

inflections are slow, but in his second speech, surprise
and excitement cause them to be quick and abrupt.
(Curry, *Lessons in Expression*, 181)

Though it is not usual, there are other examples which
indicate that Curry may have contradicted his dictum: "Rarely
do two people see anything from the same point of view"
(*Ibid.*, 9).
Another device employed by Curry in the classroom served
to get control of the various vocal modulations. One exercise
which was not related to an individual selection follows:

Make one word very salient by inflection, then, after a
pause, give many words upon a lower pitch and with
shorter inflection, for the purpose of training the ear and
securing the power to subordinate the voice. (*Ibid.*, 208)

Curry's more usual procedure, however, was to stimulate the
action of the mind. He suggests the following exercise for
cultivating the imagination and dramatic instinct in vocal
expression.

Read a passage describing some real object or scene, and
also some passage involving the most ideal thought, and
note the action of the imagination in each case, and
express this as far as possible by the voice; in other
words, idealize the real, and realize the ideal. (Curry,
Imagination and Dramatic Instinct, 49)

One method of arousing dramatic instinct appears not unlike
improvisation. Curry suggested:

Another means of realizing the nature of dramatic
instinct and of developing its power is to take the most
familiar word, such as 'Yes' and 'No,' and give it with a
dozen different imaginative situations and characters.
(*Ibid.*, 237)

Though Curry frequently declared that the student should
strive for individuality and originality, some of the exercises

indicate that all imaginations will respond in the same manner. Also, one might infer that his suggestion for vocal interpretation of a selection was the correct and only one. Of one poem he asserted: "In the first six lines of the foregoing extract we find simple conceptions, given without atmosphere, or without feeling of connection with other objects" (*Ibid.*, 17). Curry goes on to say that the imagination does not come into play for the "next four lines" (*Ibid.*). While most of Curry's exercises are not tinged with his own personal responses, some contradict his concern for the student's natural growth, spontaneity and originality.

The first year work at the School of Expression was built around the different aspects of thinking or stimulating the cause, involuntary actions, abandonment and responsiveness. The second year work also studied mental causes, and their relation to imagination and dramatic instinct. In the preface to *Imagination and Dramatic Instinct,* the second year text, Curry wrote that the aim was not only to bring the student into contact with great literature or merely to analyze or study the literature from the standpoint of the voice. Rather, it was "to stimulate and awaken the faculties in the . . . actor which are awake in the writer, to study the processes of the mind in creating and assimilating ideas for the true and artistic interpretation of literature by the human voice" (*Ibid.*, 2). In order to accomplish this avowed purpose, it was Curry's custom to assign selections a week in advance for the student to work on alone. In criticizing the student's understanding, Curry urged the teacher to ask questions that test the student's conception of the deeper meanings. But Curry maintained that the student should be judged chiefly on his personal and unique rendition of the passage (*Ibid.*, 2–3). The student was also asked to train the ear to listen, but the process was always tied to the state of feeling. If the conception and feeling were right, the vocal response was bound to be correct.

The fundamental approach to training in pantomime at the School of Expression owed a great deal to Delsarte as adapted by Steele MacKaye. Curry was wary of the stigma attached to the Frenchman's concept of the trinity and the "system" to which he attributed all action,[19] but he did accept Delsarte's study "into the fundamental norm of the whole body and each agent in particular" (Curry, *Province of Expression*, 355). Curry contended that a knowledge of the "fundamental actions" of the body was essential and that an actor's "grace of movement and all the effectiveness of his expression, in pantomime especially, is dependent upon the distinctiveness of the elemental actions . . . and in this he [Delsarte] must be followed if true grace and power of expression is ever developed in the whole man" (*Ibid.*).

Although Curry firmly believed that pantomimic action stemmed from psychic action, he still insisted that a knowledge of the operation of the bodily agents was necessary. The body may have constrictions and other perversions as a result of habit which necessarily must be corrected if good expression would result (Curry, *Foundations of Expression*, 89). When the body has become constricted through neglect or abnormal use, it does not respond immediately to thought and feeling, Curry declared; therefore, training is needed to establish normal conditions of the body (*Ibid.*, 62).

The work in pantomime lasted two years at the School of Expression. The first year's work consisted of technical steps in normal adjustment and freedom as well as something called "elemental actions and cooperative steps."[20] In Curry's notes for a first-year class which he taught in "Pantomimic Expression" for the year 1897–1898, the general plan of presentation of the material included some lecture on theory, a statement of laws, and exercises. The general aim of the first-year course was "unity." It was also the goal of the exercises of the first lesson.

The exercises concerned themselves with attempting to discover the center and involved shifting the center of weight from foot to foot. The lesson also included directions for "folding and unfolding the arm," which were intended to induce relaxation. The purpose was to "establish a center," by beginning with the agents which revolved about the center (*Ibid.*, 1). The second lesson consisted of studying and practicing the walk, melodic or successive movements, harmonic or opposing movements, and elements of grace. In this lesson attention was drawn to the importance of poise and of a good walk. "A good walk is the perpetual preservation of harmonic poise" stated Curry (*Ibid.*, 3). The outline for the third class meeting indicates that Curry combined pantomimic and vocal expression. The students practiced the expression by acting in character such short phrases as 'No' and 'Yes.' This appears consistent with Curry's purpose of training the total actor. Following this practice, pantomimic problems were introduced for the eye, feet, and torso. In the next lesson, the problem was to try to act with each part of the body, to realize its function, and to become conscious that each part of the body has a language of its own. These exercises were quite similar to MacKaye's "Gamuts of Expression."

Succeeding lessons were similar, but one problem in particular has important application to acting. Curry assigned students to impersonate a noble character and illustrate all the attitudes, bearings, and gestures in a given situation and under certain circumstances. In many ways this assignment bears a marked resemblance to Sargent's improvisational techniques employed at the American Academy of Dramatic Arts. Other assignments in improvisational techniques applied to particular parts of the body: i.e., feet, arms, eyes, head, etc. Later in the year, the students practiced states of action which were considered "manifestive" or "elemental" actions of the body. These included: repulsion, appellation, protection, invitation, surprise, and many others. Actions for types of men were also practiced. Curry listed the representative actions for types such as teachers, patrons, champions, conservatives, tyrants, orators, saints and martyrs, and included brief comments about them. The last few lessons were devoted to statements of laws and principles, most of which were quite similar to MacKaye's adaptation of Delsarte and appear to have been based on "Gamuts of Expression." All expression in these exercises was examined against the fundamental universal signs and all were performed with an underlying "motive" and in imaginative circumstances.

The second year's work in pantomime is described in Curry's notes as "psychic," and was apparently the counterpart of the second year's work in vocal training. Mrs. Curry taught the course and called it "Grace and Power," or "harmonic training." The course was basically a review of the first year with "pantomimic conditions" added. According to Mrs. Curry, there were five steps in the course.[21] The first step was called "oneness" or "erectness." Of oneness, she said that the student "must lift oneness to a standard of spiritual action" (*Ibid.*, 3). No definition was given for the term in the outline. The next step was "unity" which was explained by another teacher as establishing the center about which all the parts move harmoniously. The exercises for unity were called "Normal Adjustment" and included exercises in stepping backward and forward to test poise. Mrs. Curry called these exercises "Rhythmical Balance Steps." The third step in the course, "Liberation," consisted of relaxing exercises similar to MacKaye's decomposing exercises. The purpose of the exercises was to "free the channels of expression."

> Take the weight from two feet to one foot, *energize the mind* so as to hold it [the weight] on one foot, the other leg will relax; that done, one must move in accordance with the law of gravity; as movement goes on at each point, one becomes conscious of the law of grace; becomes conscious of the sense of gravity; weight all on one foot, you become conscious of the law acting within and lifting the body; radiation from center to surface. (*Ibid.*, 3–4. Italics mine)

Mrs. Curry expected the student to supply the psychic cause for the physical exercise. In this sense, she combined the semiotic and the aesthetic in her teaching of pantomimic action.

In the fourth step, called both "elemental actions" and "elementations," there were three parts: attitudes, transitions, and modulations. Florence Lutz, who also taught the course, stated that the aim of "elementation" was to train one to know the elemental or primary action of each agent of the body.[22] The student would move successively from one attitude to another until the cycle was completed. The modulations were considered to be subtle variations of the nine basic attitudes, similar to MacKaye's "inflections." The fifth step, called "transitions," involved an overlapping with the previous step. The final section of the outline deals with theory and explanations of the elemental actions of the various agents of the body.

The final course in the actor's training at the School of Expression was rehearsal and performance. Before any consideration could be given to the aspiring actor's desire to perform in a play, Curry was convinced that the "fundamentals" had to be learned. The principle behind this position is basic to Curry's theory of training the actor.

> One who wishes to make a success in dramatic expression needs to obey the principles here unfolded, to secure control over voice and body, to develop the artistic faculties, to stimulate the imagination and the sympathies, to develop ideals of art from the depths of his own soul and from an ideal study of the best possible art of every form. Then, and not till then, should he begin to study the business of his art; otherwise he will be more conscious of the external than of the internal, he will all his life lack control of his voice and of his body, which should have been attained as the most preliminary step in his training. (Curry, *Province of Expression*, 440–41)

Because Curry believed "that histrionic art broadens and expands the human soul more directly than any art form" (*Ibid.*, 437), he was dedicated to the position that the actor should be thoroughly grounded in the fundamentals of his art. Following this point of view, then, Curry insisted on two years of work on education of the mind, imagination, feeling, voice, and body. Only then was the actor ready to act.

Curry was worried about the state of the theatre in his day. He saw only three modes of training open to the actor: imitation, or through the old stock-company training; the amateur company, which he regarded as the worst possible training ground; or elocutionary, which he regarded as artificial and mechanical (*Ibid.*, 438–440). He was convinced that his method of training in the fundamentals was best. Only after thorough preparation did he permit play rehearsal and performance.

His students met to rehearse their parts in one of the regular classrooms of the School of Expression. "These rooms contain a piano, an organ, a blackboard or two, the director's desk . . . several enormous mirrors, one hundred or more cane-bottomed chairs" (McCann, 999). The appointments of the School of Expression were a far cry from the two stages that the American Academy of Dramatic Arts possessed. Marianna McCann explained Curry's reasons for the simplicity.

> The School of Acting meets and works in these rather barren rooms, where green baize, stage properties, scenery, and all the usual paraphernalia of a mimic world are conspicuously wanting, not because the school is meanly endowed, but because Professor Curry, the director, considers the environment of stage life and all theatrical equipment harmful to the best growth of a dramatic pupil. (*Ibid.*)

Curry stated his position quite succinctly: "Students often think that dramatic action consists in scenery, stage business, and odd make-ups; but that only is dramatic which is intense and true" (Curry, *Imagination and Dramatic Instinct*, 341). The School's methods were described as "according with the instruction at the Paris Conservatoire—the absence of properties, scenery, and all the mechanical aid of stage illusion" (McCann, 999). Curry saw the situation of the theatre in

America as being merely visual and tending toward reproduction. He said:

> There is to-day very little dramatic instinct upon the stage. The methods for the development of actors, the nature of many of the plays which are produced, call for mere technical performance and not for artistic acting. ... The whole art of acting is looked at from the external aspect and not in reference to the true principles of art of the real nature of the human soul. (Curry, *Province of Expression*, 440)

At the School of Expression, therefore, "The student must imagine all; must concentrate his mind exclusively upon characterization and the dramatic situation, or spiritual *mise en scène,* if one may so express it" (McCann, 999). Curry warned that all rehearsals should proceed "without make-up or scenery. These must only be used *after* dramatic intuitions have been awakened or an amateurish trust in mere 'business' is acquired" (Curry, *Imagination and Dramatic Instinct*, 240).

Little is mentioned about the manner in which Curry actually conducted rehearsals for the plays at the School of Expression. One can imagine, however, that his methods, in theory at least, resembled those outlined in the study and approach to literature in general. The point of view that Curry's methods of directing were similar to those for studying all literature for oral expression is substantiated by Oclo M. Miller.[23] In the study of a part, said Miller, Curry urged the pupil to study lines and then to try to walk the part (Ibid., 42–43). Curry is reported to have said that if one could walk in character, he could think in character (*Ibid.*). The point appears to be consistent with Curry's view that mind affects the whole man. Moving in character implies, to Curry's way of thinking, that the organism is functioning as an organic whole and that *action may stimulate thought and emotion.* His belief was that right mental conception made it possible, in theory, for the actor to possess a completely flexible style. McCann asserted that Curry's methods were intended to produce "actors whose versatility and finish" enable them to play any role, "from that of austere classicism to that of the pretty and petty bric-a-brac farces of the hour" (McCann, 999).

The performance at the School of Expression was not considered anything more than another day of class work. This was only another phase of training, according to Curry. McCann explained the process as follows:

> On play days the pupils assemble in the stage-room, forming a semicircle about the large empty platform. No pupil is allowed to carry a play-book on to the stage. Letter perfect—or, as the veteran says, 'dead letter perfect'—is the invariable requirement, and no call [for lines] is permitted, but at the cue the pupil is expected to be in place, the right words at tongue-tip. Whole acts proceed without a single interruption, but at the end of the act the instructor in charge will descend upon the trembling pupils with a perfect cyclone of criticism. The act must be gone through again, piecemeal this time, and at each repetition of the scene or act a new cast is called. (*Ibid.*)

It is interesting to note that Curry permitted the entire play to run its course, and then had it repeated "piecemeal." This seems consistent with his theory of reserving criticism until the "total" expression of an idea is completed. The implication that the "criticism" was harsh or severe, however, seems contradictory to Curry's theory. If he followed the practice indicated in his other work, he undoubtedly asked pointed questions pertaining to conception, and then went through the play and asked the students to note their response. The emphasis on manifestive, simple, direct, and natural acting was one of the prerequisites. Since Curry admired Booth so completely, perhaps his comments on the tragedian will clarify the style of acting which Curry taught.

> Note the difference between good and bad acting. Booth, our most artistic American actor, brings out a

psychic link of unity so that one always feels that the
acting is a real manifestation. He does not assume the
character only by external tricks. He does not bring a
great labored gasp of muscles of the throat such as
elocutionists have so long taught as necessary for characters like Shylock. There is not the least hint of 'doing
things.' We see that there is an instinctive and intuitive
assimilation of a character, and no mere external,
mechanical aggregation or trickery. There is representation, but it is always transcended by manifestation.
(Curry, *Province of Expression*, 132)

This was the goal of training at the School of Expression.

The purposes and teaching methods of the School of
Expression are best summarized in a special pamphlet published by the institution in 1902. This prospectus presents a
consistent relationship between Curry's acting theory and
teaching practices and gives a clear picture of the organization
of the course work for the person interested in a career in the
professional theatre.

The courses in the School of Expression especially
arranged for those who are studying for the stage have
been gathered from the methods followed in the best
dramatic schools in the world. The President has had
thorough courses in stage business as well as many years
of training with Steele MacKaye, the pupil and successor
of Delsarte. He has had courses in Paris with Ricquier,
advice and counsel from Regnier, with the privilege of
observing the methods at the l'Ecole de Declamation in
the Conservatoire. This is as far as any American is
admitted to the Conservatoire. He has studied with over
forty of the foremost teachers in all parts of the world.

The character, thoroughness, and progressive unity of
the work in the department of dramatic action, are
difficult to explain in words. Many of the most important aims are accomplished simultaneously.

The method seeks first to awaken dramatic thinking—
to develop the imagination and dramatic instinct, and to
train the mental or artistic powers of each student, while
training the voice and body to the greatest degree of
strength, flexibility, and responsiveness to the actions of

the mind in every phase of thought and passion; it aims to develop power in Expression; first in the individual, and then to bring him in contact with other dramatic students, for a higher realization of dramatic unity.

In general the courses endeavor

1. To develop dramatic action; to prepare the body for expression by developing ease, flexibility, and responsiveness to thought and emotion.

2. To train the simple, easy, natural, and dramatic modulations of the voice; to develop its strength, and increase its resonance and responsiveness to every phase of thinking and feeling in every kind of character.

3. To study the relation of mind and voice; to develop the power to think in character; to train vocal dramatic action; to secure a vocabulary of the dramatic modulations of the voice; to develop naturalness and correctness in speech, and the power to accentuate and enlarge without departing from naturalness; to train the imaginative and artistic nature to command the rhythm and melody of speech, and the dramatic significance.

4. To master the language of each agent of the body, and to secure harmony of all actions, and to develop unity of the natural languages, tone, and pantomime, with work in dramatic expression.

5. To furnish the opportunity to secure knowledge of histrionic art in all its forms; to act and realize the true character of burlesque, comedy, farce, and tragedy; and to gain a true conception of the exalted character of the art, with thorough knowledge of stage business.

6. To afford practical training to managers, dramatic critics, and writers of plays, as well as to actors, to dramatize stories; to give examples of Burlesque, Farce, Comedy, Melodrama, and Tragedy; and to study all phases of dramatic art.

Those who are prepared are recommended for small parts in companies of the various theatres of Boston. Boston is noted as the best dramatic city in the country.

Plays at the School are produced without properties,
scenery, or make-up, according to the custom at the
foremost acting school in the world,—at the Conservatoire, Paris. This method develops the dramatic instinct
and artistic power, and trains the student to subordinate
exhibition to expression.
Dramatic applicants will receive personal examination
from the President of the School, and will be classed
carefully according to needs and purposes in study.[24]

Curry was quick to point out that many of the graduates of
the School of Expression achieved success in the profession of
acting and declared that his former students "had taken
positions in the organizations of Richard Mansfield, Quincy
Adams Sawyer, Julia Marlowe, Viola Allen, Joe Jefferson,
Leslie Carter, Mrs. Patrick Campbell, and other first-class
stock companies, and some of our graduates are prominent
stage managers" (*Annual Catalogue*: 1980, 19). Prospective
students were also advised: "President Curry has invaluable
influence with leading managers, and a student who can act,
will, with the School of Expression backing him, get a hearing
where artists are needed" (*Ibid.*). No clearer indication of the
school's willingness to compete for the privilege of training
actors can be made.

So great was the demand for additional course work in
acting at the School of Expression that in 1905, Curry hired
Herbert Q. Emery, a graduate of the school and a well known
actor and stage manager, as the director of a newly organized
"Special Summer Dramatic Term" (*Annual Catalogue*: 1905,
17). Emery remained at the school as the principal teacher of
acting and "theatre arts" until 1927. In addition to Emery,
William Seymour was a teacher of acting at the School of
Expression during the regular session from 1897 to 1912.

By 1909, the school further enlarged the scope of its
training. The *Annual Catalogue* lists courses in "1. Dramatic
Thinking. 2. Dramatic Rehearsal. 3. Stage Business. 4. Forms
of the Drama. 5. Characterization. 6. Modern Drama. 7. Old
Comedies. 8. Poetic Drama. 9. *Life Studies*. 10. Histrionic

Expression. 11. Dramatic Construction" (*Annual Catalogue:* 1909, 29. Italics mine). Makeup and Methods of Staging Plays were offered as "Adjunctive Courses" (*Ibid.*, 3). The addition of these specialized courses was probably due to the fact that Emery was appointed as teacher of acting and "theatre arts." The appearance of the courses also indicates that Curry was becoming increasingly aware of the necessity for specialized training in work he had always considered "extraneous to true dramatic expression." It should be noted, however, that these "specialized" courses were offered only when the student had successfully completed two years of work in fundamentals.

Curry's many books and articles present a formidable task for anyone interested in the essential aspects of his acting theory. Two of them, however, contain the kernel of his ideas: *Province of Expression* (1891) and *Imagination and Dramatic Instinct* (1896). In these two volumes, and the much later *Foundations of Expression* (1907), Curry set out an acting theory that is distinctly modern in thought and tone. Once the nineteenth-century volubility is grasped and absorbed, the features of Curry's acting theory provide a coherent and integrated system. Further, he attempted to make the abstract and ambiguous as concrete and demystified as possible— frequently with amazing clarity.

He was among those who advocated the process of acting as one which moved from the *inner* to *outward* expression. The process was decidedly internal, and the thrust of the theory was the stimulation of the emotions and ordering of the thought process of the character, awakening the imagination and trusting instinct. While Curry recognized the necessity for conception, he recognized also that its principal function was to stimulate imagination. He said, "conception alone, however vivid, does not result in perfect expression."

Curry called for complete identification with the character and demanded that the actor accept all the circumstances and reality of the play. This "sympathetic" act unleashed the imagination and permitted the actor to draw upon his *emotional memory* as a source for imaginative emotion: thus, real emotion fuels imaginative emotion! Further, imagination and sympathetic identification liberate the dramatic instinct which was deemed spontaneous and a reflection of the *unconscious*. This innovative conception sounds amazingly similar to many of the ideas of Stanislavsky and his American interpreter, Lee Strasberg. Yet another similarity lies in Curry's acceptance of instinct as "unconscious action [moving] toward an unconscious purpose," which may account for his encouragement of spontaneity and conviction that fine acting could be achieved not only through "think the thought" but "feel the feeling" of the character.

Another perceptive conception of Curry's was his view of *action*, which he defined as "the display of activity that lies behind statement, the most natural language." Action represents the expression of *both* conscious and unconscious motives, which are in turn the *cause* of action. Acting presupposes two things, said Curry: "First the correct action representative of thought, feeling and will, and secondly, a normal action of the organic means which transmit the action." Good *listening* also played a critical role in action; Curry believed that it is brought about through listening and the "action is the response of imagination, feeling and body to the 'ideas' uttered by the interlocutor." Curry's conception of action, therefore, also embraces "concentration of attention."

As a prescriptive acting theory, Samuel Silas Curry presents the actor with an approach that is comprehensive and one that is truly based on emotion as well as thought. It is a thorough and detailed acting theory, and it also attempts to clarify the process as well as the difficult terminology of such terms as imagination, instinct and spontaneity. What is more, Curry rejected the idea that the actor should learn either vocal or gestural "patterns" since they interfere with his view that acting is the result of imagination, instinct and spontaneity. An examination of the teaching at the School of Expression will confirm that the methods employed consistently supported his major principle: *good acting represents a psychic movement from within outward.*

Of the nearly three thousand students who graduated from the School of Expression between 1885 and 1925, fifteen to twenty per cent entered the professional theatre as actors and platform readers.[25] Of this number, Anne Deere, Domis Flugge, and Warner Olin were the most successful. Hundreds of graduates became professional teachers of expression, and still more entered the teaching profession at the high school and college level. The graduates of the School of Expression carried Curry's ideas and methods into a variety of professions.

The teaching methods husbanded the individuality of each student and each course appeared designed to assist the student to reach the potential of ability. There were no rules governing or restricting expression, but each student was urged to identify sympathetically with the character, conceptualize and identify with the thought processes, concentrate attention, listen and act, vocally and physically, in the circumstances as the character. Curry insisted that even the most mundane exercise should have a "cause" or motive behind it, whether relaxing, kneeling, practicing inflections or responding to another character. Each movement, thought, gesture or utterance must have cause or motivation. The theory was well integrated into the teaching.

Samuel Silas Curry goes much farther than most theorists in his attempts to *explicate* his theory of acting and teaching methods. He sheds a great deal of light on the depth, comprehensiveness, coherency, and more important, the unique position acting had attained in America. Curry held acting as an almost sacred trust and certainly a social and moral responsibility. His devotion to acting after his fateful meeting with Steele MacKaye subsumed his life and led to one of the most truly significant and best developed American acting theories.

LEFT: Leland Powers—founder, teacher, lecturer, and proponent of monodrama. A highly effective performer whose national reputation drew focus to his School of the Spoken Word. (Photo from *Random Recollections: A Book Commemorating the 50th Anniversary of the Leland Powers School, 1904–1954*)

RIGHT: Carol Hoyt Powers married Leland Powers and was a significant force in the governance of the school. (Photo from *Random Recollections: A Book Commemorating the 50th Anniversary of the Leland Powers School, 1904–1954*)

CHAPTER V
SCHOOL OF THE SPOKEN WORD

Leland Todd Powers was probably the staunchest advocate of the conceptual aspect of the Delsarte system. He differed from Curry and Emerson to the extent that his fundamental philosophy of expression was entirely based on the supposed correspondence between the infinite and the finite. The acceptance of this *a priori* assumption, which Powers regarded as fact, established that everything in the universe—everything he termed true or real—had a threefold nature in which the elements were coexistent, cooperative, and coessential, and, like his trinities, had no beginning or end. Powers completely accepted the correspondences of Delsarte, and upon the relationship of the Trinity to the threefold nature of man he erected his theory of expression and of acting.

Powers was a student of Lewis B. Monroe at the Boston University School of Oratory. He entered Boston University in 1878 when he was twenty-one years old and remained there after Monroe's death in 1879, graduating two years later.[1] While at Boston University he was a fellow student of Emerson and a pupil of Curry. Powers also studied with Curry's wife, Anna Baright, at her private school. He was a talented platform reader and was given a contract with the Redpath Lyceum Bureau early in his career. As a very young man, Powers had developed an individual technique of impersonating *all* the characters in a play or story. This style Powers called "monoacting," and he taught it as a speciality in both his school and for Emerson and Curry.[2] Although his teaching was acceptable to both the schools of Curry and

Emerson,[3] he had been formulating his own ideas of education, and was convinced that by using his theories all the speech arts could be taught. In 1904, Powers, along with this wife, Carol Hoyt Powers, opened the School of the Spoken Word.

When Powers and his wife first began the School of the Spoken Word, they had decided to maintain a small enrollment and to do a large part of the teaching themselves. They never permitted the enrollment to outgrow the home they bought and remodeled as a school. At first they taught six sections of fourteen students each. Later, when they had some capable graduates to employ as teachers, they added more sections, but they never permitted the enrollment to exceed two hundred. From the beginning, the students were carefully selected, and since the school's aim was to turn out professional artists, a student was not permitted to return unless he showed satisfactory talent and progress.[4] Powers was active in the school he founded until his death in 1920. Unlike Curry's School of Expression and Emerson's College of Oratory, Powers' School of the Spoken Word never attempted to evolve into a Liberal Arts institution. Its intention was always to develop professional artists in platform work and acting.[5]

Although Powers was primarily known for developing artists in the medium of "monoacting," he recognized its applicability to the art of acting as well. His theories were meant to form the basis for all expressional art employing the voice and body as a medium, and the textbooks written by Powers and his wife (an Emerson graduate) are filled with advice for actors.

Powers contended that "a man's expression is his understanding."[6] He did not believe that the actor is a creator, but a reflector of truth and beauty. He subscribed to the view that truth and beauty are, always have been, and always will be, and that the actor is a revealer of universal truth and not the originator of it. Only God can create.[7] In every work, Powers insisted, the cause is mental. The actor embodies his vision of truth, he does not create the truth. An embodiment, Powers explained, can be said to be mental when the mental concept is carried out in definite pictures of thought under guidance; when the media cease to be material and become the idea embodied.[8] All bad art has its cause in sensation and is addressed to sensation, said Powers. All good art manifestations, on the other hand, have their causation in mind and spirit. Although material symbols are used as media (body and voice) in acting, good acting is addressed to mind and spirit; it speaks in terms of mind and spirit (Powers and Powers, *Fundamentals of Expression*, 11).

The function of the actor under Powers' system is the direct reflection of Truth. More particularly, however, "It is the mission of the . . . [actor] to turn the printed page back to life;—in other words, to translate, in terms of life, form and color, the awakening which masterpieces of literature have given in his own mind and heart" (*Ibid.*, 15). Actually, Powers went further in his insistence that expression is dependent on thought. Concept and expression, he declared, are essentially the same thing, each incomplete without the other (Powers, *Talks on Expression*, 82). Therefore, "when the mental concept, becoming vital enough to demand expression, is carried out in definite thought pictures through the trained and obedient voice and body, under mental guidance, the result is *a mental concept made visible*" (Powers, *Practice Book*, 28. Italics mine).

All literature, like every other expressive manifestation, reveals thought, Powers maintained; and since thought is a trinitary reflection of the Divine Trinity's wisdom, love, and power, all works of art therefore possess the same attributes. Consequently, Powers demanded that the actor, as the interpreter of the playwright, must rethink the playwright's thought, recognizing the contribution of *each* element of the thought's trinity. By Powers' definition, expression is thought taking on embodiment, and the voice and body of the actor must be obedient to the thought as intended by the playwright.

The actor's aim is primarily to show what the playwright envisioned when he wrote the lines and, though he must be true to the author's purpose, the actor may reveal more than a person might get for himself if he read the play silently. He believed that the play stirs something in every individual so that he adds to it something from his own experiences. If the actor's sympathies and understanding of life are deeper than the playwright's, the play will be enriched by the spirit he brings to his revelations (Powers and Powers, *Fundamentals of Expression*, 42–44). As Powers phrased the idea, the truth revealed in a play may be universal, but it is presented through an individual understanding and a distinct interpretation (*Ibid.*, 19).

The actor must always strive to see the play as an entire whole so as not to destroy the continuity of the playwright's thought. He must never interfere with the onward march of the play to merely "exhibit" even a well-conceived and well-executed character. No character should stand above the play, and if the story or the atmosphere of the tonal beauty of the play is the principal thing in the playwright's mind, "the . . . [actor] must obediently subordinate his character to the author's purpose."9

Powers saw acting as an intellectual process rather than an emotional one. While he urged the actor to "understand" the emotions of the character, he never indicates that the actor "feel" the emotion of the character. On the contrary, because Powers was convinced that expression was thought or intelligence contacting intelligence, the assumption was that the actor interpreting the character should attempt to reach the mind, *not* the emotions of his audience. Any emotion that appealed to the "senses" was considered harmful and bad art (Powers, *Talks on Expression*, 91–92). The perennial question—"should the actor feel" or lose himself in his role?—was carefully discussed by Powers. His conclusion was that the actor should *never* be given over to the use of the character he is impersonating. The actor may let the character use his body and a part of his consciousness, "but the highest part of him—the judge, the life giver, the God-like part, stands and watches and guides, and sympathizes" (Powers and Powers, *Fundamentals of Expression*, 54). Emotional identification with the character was denied the actor in the Powers system.

The actor's approach to the character is always one of constantly analyzing and expressing. The play is studied until the actor's mind *understands* the thoughts and emotions the playwright intended. Constant practice and intelligent self-criticism gradually lead the actor to the right mode of expression (Powers, *Talks on Expression*, 102–103). The characterization did not come by sitting and thinking but by responding to the thought with movement of the head, the hands, or the body as a whole. By assuming some phase of the character's nature, it was believed, individual movements of the character will come to the actor. When some action results from thorough absorption in the character, that physical action should be noted and preserved. It should always be used from that point until a new and better revelation is received. When the actor is before the audience, however, Powers urged that he perform as he practiced. If an inspiration seems to come during public performance, the student should not yield to it, but should remember it and try it out later in practice (*Ibid.*, 51–52).

Powers maintained that expression has no purpose unless it makes an impression. Consequently, the relationship between the audience and the actor was given primary consideration. Powers believed that the actor should induce in his audience a certain thoughtfulness instead of physical and emotional excitement. This injunction grew out of Powers' philosophy that art should reveal man's understanding of God's infinite goodness (Powers and Powers, *Fundamentals of Expression*, 40). According to Powers, the relationship of the actor to the audience was the embodiment of the brotherhood of mankind. The actor should not affect the audience in the physical or sensory meaning of the word. Even the emotional effect of the actor's expression of character on the audience must appeal to the audience through intellectual concepts. Powers believed that subordination of the intellect to the emotions distorts the form of expression and, therefore, becomes merely physical. "Without form there will be no appeal to the intelligence of the auditor and the emotion produced in the auditor will not be legitimate but one born of sensation" (Powers, *Talks on Expression*, 88). If the expression is ideal, the actor will not appear to the audience as a "sense" impression, but as the embodiment of thought.

Since Powers saw man as an embodiment of the Holy Trinity, he believed, therefore, that man was endowed with its characteristics: divine wisdom, love, and power are reflected in man's corresponding ability to plan, feel, and express. The "ideal" actor was composed of three distinct natures which were actually one. According to Powers, it is the reflective or intellectual function which *conceives* and plans. The affective or volitional function *chooses* and decides. The effective or vital function *expresses* the decision and plan. The three general terms, by whatever synonyms they may be called, always have this general relationship of function. Furthermore, all three functions must act proportionately or thought will be unsymmetrical and imperfect. The activities of the first, or mental aspect seem to be allied to what is generally associated with reflective thinking. Under the second aspect are included not only all emotions, but ethical and volitional decisions as well. The third, or effective aspect, Powers declared, was not generally considered by others to be a part of the act of thought. In general, it was called physical. His own belief that the effective aspect is also an act of thought constituted the basis of the radical difference between his and other schools.

The place of the imagination in Powers' system and in relation to the "ideal" actor is indefinite. Nevertheless, imagination as an activity of thought was given some importance. Sometimes its meaning is clear, as when it is said that a vision is awakened in the imagination (Powers and Powers,

Fundamentals of Expression, 8). The imagination's particular operation and function appears to be to supply the vivid images which the intellect *forms,* the will *chooses,* and action *expresses (Ibid.,* 43). Since Powers believed that the will also helps to select, give purpose, and form emotion, it is clear that both mind and will also interact with the imagination. Powers insisted that expression, too, contributes to the imagination. Since the purpose of training in expression is to clear away all the obstacles that interfere with the discovery of the truth that lies latent in the mind, Powers believed that right expression reacts on one's thought, makes the thought clearer and strengthens the emotion and the form. After continued striving, the inward vision may be finally and completely realized (Powers, *Talks on Expression,* 102–103). Thus, all three aspects of the mind contribute to the formulation and perfection of the revelation of thought. It is reasonable to assume, therefore, that if the imagination has something to do with the "visionary" aspect of thought (i.e., creating pictures which are not the result of sense perception), it must, in some way, be related to and integrated with *all* the aspects of thought.

Powers' ideas concerning the nature and function of emotion in acting are somewhat paradoxical, since he had no place for physiology in his system of acting. Sensations, Powers claimed, are all destructive of expression. "Expression is not the material medium in action, it is vital thought dematerializing the intervening, interfering material" *(Ibid.,* 91–92). The five senses were called blockades between truth of art and thought. Sensation, excitement, or any consciousness of the body cause interferences. Powers concluded that intelligence, not sensation, should be the source of true emotion *(Ibid.,* 92–93).

The expression of emotion by the "ideal" actor must be under the guidance of will and intelligence. The placement of emotion in the same category with will implies that the emotions should be constantly "formed" under control. The necessity of conscious emotional control is intimately bound up with Powers' concept that uncontrolled emotions produce only physical signs which are merely a product of sensation or nerve excitement in the actor and produce the same in the audience (*Ibid.*, 14, 17, 77). Uncontrolled emotion which produces wrong expression excites the listener, inhibits his clear thought, and leaves him with a sense of fatigue (*Ibid.*, 77). Whatever spontaneously arises in practice through concentration of mind must be exposed to conscious reflection so that it may be purged of all "sensational" aspects. Thus "purified," the emotion is manifested by the voice and body as an object of spiritual or mental perception.

Because Powers judges art by ethical standards, only plays which reveal "truth" could be considered worthy of thought. It would appear, therefore, that Powers' acting theory has severe limitations. If the actor were to express envy, for instance, the manifestation could only be expressed through physical signs which would result in mere sensationalism. While Powers does not explain how the actor could use his system to portray malignant emotions, it is assumed that they, too, may be "purified" in such a way as to be perceived as an object of thought and not sensation.

What is generally considered to be intellect was regarded by Powers as the reflective aspect of thinking. He stated that "the *reflective* activity governs and is expressed in the outline of *form*" (*Ibid.*, 64). In reality, declared Powers, form is an idea in the mind; it cannot be fixed in finite outline. What seems to the senses to be shape, outline, and surface of a form is only the limit of human understanding of an intelligent plan. As understanding grows, the form seems to change. "The form present in one's consciousness is forever made up of the fading presence of the one just gone before and the dawning presence of the one just come" (*Ibid.*, 72). It should be noted that Powers conceived "form" as being the abstraction of the entire thinking process. Without the will, which supplies *purpose*; without action, which supplies *expression,* the "form" or idea cannot be manifested. All three conditions—idea, purpose, and expression—were considered necessary to complete the process of thinking.

The intellect of the "ideal" actor, therefore, was an instrument of investigation, analysis, and conception. It furnished the motivating factor of expression in acting, but it could by no means be thought of as self sufficient. Since Powers believed expression was governed by a trinitary concept, it was inconceivable to him that good acting could be an expression of the initial "form" alone. Intellect enabled the actor to understand, plan, and conceive his character and to give it initial "form." As the actor acquired more understanding through observation, study, and analysis, the "form" changed proportionately. Finally, when the "form" or idea became vivid and demanded expression, it affected the imagination. In turn, the "form" also affected the emotions and volition which reacted upon the imagination in the guided picturization of the idea. Finally, the entire process achieves fruition when it is expressed and becomes the *embodiment* of thought or "form." This explanation of the psychological processes which the "ideal" actor experiences in building a character in a play must be thought of as an organic and evolutionary phenomenon.

The use of the body and voice as expressional servants also fell under the law of the trinity and reflected mental and spiritual cause (*Ibid.,* 49–50). Powers thought that the material human body shows correspondences existing in its form (*Ibid.,* 49). In the body, the head, the torso, and the limbs are the special agents of the mental, moral, and vital factors respectively, which correspond to spiritual wisdom, love, and power of the Divine Trinity (*Ibid,* 45). The elements of voice and speech also had their own particular correspondences. Consequently, the study of the effective or expressive element was based on what Powers considered to be trinitary universal laws.

Since Powers conceived that body and voice were mind and spirit (Powers and Powers, *Fundamentals of Expression*, 10), and not merely physical aspects of man, it is difficult to discuss them in terms of technique. Powers was actually convinced that the purpose of acquiring technique was to dematerialize the body so that it may become a pure expression of thought. Thus, the objective of the actor was to be as physically unobtrusive as possible. The actor, therefore, must perfect his technique in order to "disappear" as media and appear as embodied thought.

The two chief problems in teaching acting were, from Powers' point of view, to awaken the student's vitality of thought and to help him perfect technique. He asserted that the only value of technique is that it enables the actor to be free and unconscious of physical form. But Powers pointed out that one does not begin with freedom in any art. He believed that every individual possesses at the outset in his own right all the potentialities he will ever possess, and assumed that training in technique was not a matter of learning, but of discovering the powers of expression which have been lying dormant. Technique, then, cannot be acquired, but consists in freeing the voice and body of obstructions (*Ibid.*, 28).

Technique, Powers believed, was not an end in itself (Powers, *Talks on Expression*, 33). Only technique which springs from an intelligent cause can truly express spirituality, said Powers (*Ibid.*, 89). While technique was considered absolutely essential in expression, Powers believed that it should have a subordinate function. "If the belief prevail that the embodiment in any art is anything in and of itself, if a separation be made between the concept and the expression, then the art tends toward decadence" (*Ibid.*, 33).

In order to become the "ideal" actor, it was suggested that, first, the student must learn by trial and demonstration the laws of bodily posture and gesture. Second, one must gain command of the numerous vocal qualities and connect them with their mental causation. Third, the facial muscles must be drilled into such obedience that one may present at will a contour and expression suggesting a type of character or a variation of that type. The fourth requirement, which Phidelah Rice calls the most important of all, is that one must become a student of character, learning how the human mind works. This Rice added, is a life study and will not be completed when life is done.[10]

Besides the mastery of technique the method of approaching expression was considered vitally important. In approaching the role, then, analysis is needed to discover the author's aim and, consequently, which element of the thought's trinity is dominant. The knowledge of the dominant factor is necessary to help the actor bring all activities of his mind to bear most effectively on his problem of making the author's thought clear. Such knowledge will help the actor portray the character in the light of the fundamental purpose. Through the will, the actor selects and gives purpose to the "form," and enables the body and voice to bring about "relationship of parts resulting from a subordinating of one part and the enlarging of another" (Powers, *Talks on Expression*, 41). The result of proper relationship of the parts is the creation of a character which possesses the proper form and is the ideal embodiment of thought (*Ibid.*, 40–41).

Powers' theory of acting is quite idealistic. He was not concerned with a literal transcript of life. For Powers, reality consisted of the spiritual realm; any manifestation of the physical world was utterly repugnant to him. The actor should not arouse any form of sensory reaction in the audience but should reveal only Truth. Acting, therefore, called for infinite subtlety and the complete "unity" of the expressive elements which result in the dematerialization of the physical actor. In this sense, Powers' theory of acting resembles the Platonist who accepts the only true reality as existing in the realm of the Ideal.

TEACHING METHODS

Powers claimed that every individual possesses at birth all
the knowledge he will ever possess, and maintained that the
methods and processes of education are really successful only
when they serve to clarify thought. Educational systems,
therefore, can do no more than clear away the debris of false
or hazy thinking. The function of education, according to
Powers, was to awaken the student to a realization of his
inherent birthright of intelligence (Phidelah Rice, Introduc-

**Above: The final location of The School of the Spoken Word, later
The Powers School. Powers had the building built to his specifica-
tions in 1914. (Photo from *Random Recollections: A Book
Commemorating the 50th Anniversary of the Leland Powers
School, 1904–1954*)**

tion to Powers, *Talks on Expression*, 5–6). The aims and methods of training in expression were intended to get the student to know the truth, to be willing to tell it, and to know how to tell it (Powers, *Talks on Expression*, 9). These aims correspond with Powers' belief that all expression consists of reflective, affective, and effective elements of thought.

On the basis of the validity of these three educational aims, Powers charged that the conventional educational methods and systems of his day were incomplete and unsatisfactory. He asserted that by conventional practice, thought was only two-thirds trained. The reflective, analytical process was trained in discovering truth. The ethical and volitional process, or the desire to tell the truth, also received cultivation. But, Powers maintained, too often the third function of thought, corresponding to the third aim of education, was ignored. Rarely was the student trained to bring his concepts and purposes into "working contact with the world of other men" (*Ibid.*, 10). The expressive process, the ability to speak the truth, Powers insisted, received little help from the conventional educational methods of other schools (*Ibid.*, 9–11). For Powers, then, the correct training in expression was absolutely necessary because it was regarded as a part of thought.

One of the chief functions of education, and of the teacher as an instrument of education, is to free the student of wrong habits of thought. The right thought is there waiting to be freed. This correct expression can be made habitual by getting the student to realize that the ideal is already his; it is only waiting to be embodied. Good habits can be established more rapidly if the student understands. the purpose of every exercise and if his attention is called instantly to correct behavior manifestation and if the teacher helps the student to become conscious of what took place in his thought (*Ibid.*, 41). Mental guidance is imperative, since the physical agents follow the path of least resistance if left to themselves. The relationship of the teacher to the pupil was similar to that established by Curry, Emerson, and Sargent. His function was to offer constructive criticism designed to help the student realize his *own* potential, not that of the teacher (*Ibid.*, 102–103). Patience and understanding born of love were required of the teacher who was a stimulator of thought, a guide to its formation, purpose, and expression.

Powers' system of education called for training of the body as the initial step in the development of the actor. All of the theories of body training were based on those of Delsarte, of whom Powers wrote, "Every method of teaching expressive action today unless it is so antiquated or so lacking of a scientific basis as not to be worthwhile, embodies more or less, or at least is tinged by, the discoveries and teachings of Francois Delsarte" (*Ibid.*, 7). Powers was convinced that whatever Delsarte's faults, he made a tremendous advance in the teaching of acting. "Delsarte toiled for forty years with unswerving zeal, to transform the bungling empiricism of the stage, into a perfect art growing out of a perfect science" (*Ibid*).

In the first-year course called Expressive Movement, Powers taught that the body "claims to be an animal and it insists on expressing its own life and sensation, whether or not the expression interferes with and belies the plan of purpose of the rightful master, mind" (*Ibid.*, 13). However, Powers regarded freedom of body as harmful unless it is governed by intelligent planning. Further deterrents to true expression of thought through the body were inertia and fear (*Ibid.* 16). Habit and opinion also inhibited free expression guided by intelligence. In itself, the body is nothing but an obstruction, Powers maintained. Only when it does not allow its own sensations and nerve excitements to stand in the way does the body become the embodiment of thought.

The study of the science of right expression of the body involves trinitary laws which govern the thought's vitality and the body's sensation; further, it is learning to obey the laws of thought so that the body will reflect the thought's form (*Ibid.*, 18–19, 32–33). In every idea expressed through the body the factors of the trinity of thought as embodied in the reflective, affective, and the effective processes were considered. Consequently, the bodily expression of every idea intended to present these three factors, with one dominant and the other two subordinate. This theory of expression acknowledges the complete acceptance by Powers of the Law of Trinity as formulated by François Delsarte.

Powers was confident that he had satisfactorily demonstrated the inevitability of certain physical consequences in certain given circumstances. In some persons, one of the three states of thought may become habitual to the exclusion of the other two. Such habits of thought cause men to become types since each type is dominated by the characteristic behavior. Instead of being limited to one response, a good actor should react to the whole trinity with one of the three factors dominant according to the circumstances. It is then possible for the actor merely to refer to the Law of Trinity as it applies to the body or the voice, and reveal, through conscious guidance, the proper manifestation. While Powers would deny the mechanical nature of this system, it is undeniable that the Laws of Trinity dictated the terms of characterization. Furthermore, Powers' deductions of the appropriate manifestations tended to make characterization even more rigid. While Delsarte's system had undeniable mechanical implications, in theory at least he conceived that bodily expression was natural, spontaneous, and unconsciously guided. Like so many others, Powers appears to have mistaken Delsarte's study of semiotics for his complete theory of expression.

Edythe May Renshaw, in her study of the teaching methods of the School of the Spoken Word, concluded that the theories recorded in the class notebooks of students are "in complete harmony with those of the published textbooks."[11] It was evident in the notebooks that the students studied and practiced the external manifestation of each attitude, bearing, and inflection. The method of studying and practicing in such an obviously mechanical manner was in harmony with Powers' contention that all art is conscious, not spontaneous.

Doing things the "natural" way was not reliable, contended Powers, since spontaneous movement is unguided and tends toward sensation. All unnecessary action must be pruned away, he said, reaffirming his belief that only "fundamental" actions were necessary.

The result of his attitudes toward bodily expression led Powers to adopt Delsarte's action charts. Renshaw stated that the student notebooks indicate that seventeen of the action charts were studied, each giving principles and methods of proper physical positions of the parts of the body. Each chart indicates that the Law of Trinity was the controlling factor in shaping the various positions. The teacher was the student's guide through all the training in bodily movement which was dictated by the action charts. Pantomimic dramatization classes consisted of elucidating the theory, practice, and criticism, which was followed by more practice until the student recognized the validity behind the law of movement. When the student had achieved that state, it was believed that his body, finally, was prepared to become the personification of thought.

Like the body, a good voice was considered to be latent in every individual. Consequently, the actor cannot acquire a good voice, but must discover it through the process of clearing the channels of expression and removing the bad habits and fears acquired through heredity and environment (Powers and Powers, *Fundamentals of Expression*, 28; and Powers, *Talks on Expression*, 35). Powers regarded vocal training as a great deal more elusive than training of the body. Although the laws of the Trinity also dictated the manner of voice and speech as dictated by the dominant thought, Powers recognized that the muscles controlling the vocal mechanism could not be as clearly pictured as the muscles controlling pantomimic expression. The teacher was asked to withhold explication of the principles governing the voice until the student was vitalized by thought (*Ibid.*, 46). Voice training, then, was less external and mechanical than training of the body.

The whole purpose of voice training was to induce the

conscious action necessary for voluntary action. As in body training, Powers asserted that certain muscles become inert and faultily automatic because of habit and fear, and must be brought under voluntary control. Mrs. Powers warned against the theory that "all one needs to do for general excellence, including freedom of voice, is to 'think the thought.'" Such a statement is only a half-truth. That one must think the thought goes without saying, she asserted, but one must also rid himself of habits and fears which obstruct and interfere with meaning.[12] While Powers used the same reasons as Emerson and Curry for justifying the need for voice training, it should be noted that Mr. and Mrs. Powers were strong advocates for *conscious control* of the voice mechanism at the time of delivery. Thus, while they accepted the idea of "think the thought" in part, they were diametrically opposed to the theory of Emerson and Curry concerning the role volition plays in expression.

After the initial phase of freeing the channels of expression through the kind and patient guidance of the teacher, it was assumed that the student had been made aware that a good voice was always latent and that habit and fear caused the imperfections. The process of teaching the student to become aware of this fact was quite interesting. In the beginning, the teacher should work with the student to awaken vitality of thought, and one of the first signs of the awakened vitality is a change in the timbre of the student's voice. The change may emphasize a vocal fault brought about by the student's unconscious effort to give the voice some kind of foundation. But, however wrong the change may be, comforted Powers, it will show the teacher that the student's mind has begun to arouse itself and that the body or sensation is trying to usurp the mind's function (Powers, *Practice Book*, v–vi).

The teacher must then help the student become conscious of what really took place in his thought, and Powers suggests that the student read or act the new condition of thought as teacher's guidance; this will help the student sense the difference and, sensing the difference, enable him to make the difference at will (*Ibid.*, vi). When the student has succeeded in knowing what the newly awakened mind action really is, the teacher should call attention to the signs by which the presence of vital thought are recognized. The student should be led to see which signs were right and which wrong, and the teacher should *explain* why some were right and some were wrong. Through this technique the teacher assists the student to distinguish between false vitality or sensations and real vitality or thought (*Ibid.*, vii).

The teacher must not be impatient, Powers counseled, with the student's tendency to lapse into false vitality. It will take time to establish the right habits. False vitality will always betray itself in unnecessary constriction of muscles and by misplaced emphasis or the changing of the mental form of the sentence or phrase, In helping the student recognize real vitality of thought and in training him to use the right outward signs of awakened thought, the teacher is training the student to keep his thought vital. The teacher is assisting the student in training "the thought-vitality to command the material agents" (*Ibid.*). At the same time, Powers added, the material agents are being taught to obey (*Ibid.*).

The teacher should show the student how to practice, should make clear what each exercise is for, and watch to see that it is correctly practiced. Above all, the student's thought concerning what he is trying to accomplish must be clear. He must have a pattern in his mind's ear. One hour's practice with the proper thought will accomplish more than several days spent in thoughtless repetition, said Powers (Powers, *Talks on Expression*, 41). Powers meant, of course, that the student must practice with a conscious awareness of what is occurring to the muscles and with the tonal quality.

Approximately one-fifth of Powers' only textbook in oral interpretation is given over to "exercises for elementary vocal expression" (Powers, *Practice Book*, 1). The first section contains literary selections to be used for the purpose of arousing and developing in the student's mind that particular factor of the thought's trinity which is dominant in the exercises. Following this formula, the exercises were intended to be read with particular emphasis on the reflective, affective, or effective factors of thought. The suggestions, however, apply only to the most general characteristics of each factor. For instance, when describing the vital or effective factor, Powers said that the passage should be read in a manner so that "the expression is dominated by power, largeness, freedom, animation and movement" (*Ibid.*). The thought trinity controlled whether or not the inflection should rise, fall, or be circumflex. The trinity also controlled volume and quality of the voice.

While course work in Literary Interpretation encompassed a wide range of forms of expression, Powers was primarily interested in what he called "monoacting." The principles behind monoacting were essentially those upon which all expression was based at the School of the Spoken Word. Using principles similar to the Laws of Trinity, Phidelah Rice discussed some of the things "monoacting" does and does not involve. Impersonation of this sort does not consist of making faces, taking on voice, or assuming poses or any kind of imitation, he said. Instead, it consists of thinking, feeling, and acting in accordance with the character. Half of the rule, then, is to do nothing to dispute the type being presented; the other half is to do whatever may be necessary to give emphasis to the character's fundamental characteristics. This involves careful study and careful vocal and bodily training. The impersonator must be able to do all the actor does and, in addition, must be able to make instantaneous vocal, facial, and bodily changes as he makes the transition from character to character (Phidelah Rice, "The Art of Impersonating in Play Reading," 79–83). Basically, then, the preparation of the actor and the "monoactor" was essentially the same. The difference is that the "monoactor" played several parts; the actor played one. Monoacting and acting demanded the same type of analysis, thought, characterization, and expression.

In contrasting the technique of the actor with that of the trained impersonator, Powers pointed out that the actor uses more physical signs of emotions resulting from dramatic situations. The great danger of acting is that the actor, in trying to avoid using physical signs, falls into a simple intellectual reading of the lines without sufficient emotional response. Powers also stated that the actors of his day either did too much or too little in expression. The trained actor, like the "monoactor," should know that he must use just the *essential* sign of the emotions resulting from the intelligent realization of the meaning of the situation (Powers, *Talks on Expression*, 91–92).

The practice of having the student perform before an audience in the advanced Literary Interpretation classes was considered a necessary part of the development for the would-be artist. It was Powers' belief that every person in his private practice imagines an audience before him listening and watching his finished production. When the audience is supplied, the student realizes that the performance has fallen short of expectations; not because the audience said so, but because the actor "saw" and "heard" as it saw and heard him. The class audience makes the student sense the distance between his achievement and his ideal. Being a member of the audience also enabled the student to watch others at every stage of their development, not to criticize, but to observe sympathetically the processes of growth (*Ibid.*, 97–100). Powers believed that experience before an audience of students in the classroom encouraged the actor or reader to strive for clarity and truth, to rid himself of personal mannerisms, and to clarify the vision of what was being interpreted (Powers and Powers, *Fundamentals of Expression*, 43–44).

Perhaps the most unique of Powers' contributions to the methods of teaching acting was his belief that a good voice and a free body were latent in every individual; therefore technical training was mainly a process of freeing. However, freeing the body was only one part of technique, since Powers believed that all the signs and methods of expression must be conscious and volitional. Consequently, he established Delsarte's Laws of Trinity as the controlling and definitive guide to correct vocal and bodily expression. The general purpose of all study in the Powers school was to gain technical facility and to make the body and voice obedient to vitalized thought.

The School of the Spoken Word resisted specialized training in conventional stage acting until Leland Powers' death in 1920. This fact, however, should not disguise the contribution of the school to the development of the theatre in America. As stated earlier in this chapter, Leland Powers thought monoacting superior to acting as an art form. He believed, however, that his theoretical principles and methods of teaching were equally helpful in training the actor, and recognized that many of his students desired careers in the professional theatre.[13] Haven M. Powers, Powers' son and past President of the institution, stated that the school was always interested in professional training and that over *ninety percent* of its graduates became actors or professional platform readers (*Ibid.*).

It was not until 1924 that Carol Hoyt Powers instituted a major change in the school's organization. Recognizing that the majority of the school's graduates were entering the acting profession and that there was an increasing demand for actors while the art of platform reading was dying out, Mrs. Powers changed the emphasis of instruction from the *impersonated* play to the *acted* play. By 1926, the school was almost completely devoted to acting and hired John Craig, director of the Castle Square Theatre, to head the Theatre Department.[14]

Although specialized training in acting was not a part of the curriculum until the latter part of the period under investigation, the school consistently presented at least two or three plays each year.[15] Rachel Noah France, a famous actress of the nineteenth century, came to the school in 1906 and remained for seventeen years as a member of the faculty.

> She taught the art of acting and traditional stage business of old comedies and Shakespearean dramas. (Tibbets, 42)

Throughout the history of the school, there was always an established artist from the professional theatre on the faculty.

Thus, while The School of the Spoken Word was primarily devoted to monoacting as an art form, it was also training actors for the conventional stage.

The list of well-known actors who graduated from the school is a long one. During the period between 1904 and 1925, 638 students were graduated from the School of the Spoken Word. Some of the better known graduates are Moroni Olsen, Arthur Kachel, Adelyn Bushnell, Parker Fennelly, Maude Sheerer, William Acton, Louise Lorimer, Stanley Pratt, Allan Mowbray, Carney Christie, Robert Gleckler, Lucille Adams, and Margaret Hughes. In a book celebrating the fiftieth anniversary of the school, letters written by over three hundred alumni who graduated between 1905 and 1920 attest to the influence of the teachings of Leland and Carol Hoyt Powers.[16] The school continued to graduate students for the acting profession until the mid 70's and contributed significantly to the development of the American theatre.

Certainly the views of the School of the Spoken Word represent the most idealistic of the so-called "speculative" schools of expression. The concept that the actor must express the idea in an "ideal" manner guided by the consciously controlled intellect may appear too abstract on the one hand and too mechanistic on the other. The idea of overt conscious control runs contrary to American acting tradition, which was predominantly emotionalistic in theory and practice. It should be pointed out, however, that Powers eschewed imitation of external signs of emotion and character. Instead, conscious control and the intellect were employed to communicate the purpose of art, which Powers believed was directed at understanding, not feeling. Thus, he gave a philosophical reason for the supremacy of intellect and conscious control. In merely imitating the external signs of the emotion and thought of a character, the actor represented the sensuous and not the spirit. Consequently, Powers justified the basis of his acting theory and teaching methods and aimed at a quality far removed from imitation. The actor must aspire to the Ideal.

CHAPTER VI
THE MADISON SQUARE THEATRE SCHOOL
OF INSTRUCTION

While the Madison Square Theatre School of Instruction was actively involved in training actors for only two years, it was one of the best known, best advertised, and most significant acting schools of the period. Its significance was due to the fact that one of the most highly respected men of the theatre had consented to head the operation. That man was Dion Boucicault.

Born in Dublin, Ireland in 1822, Dion Boucicault became one of the "most popular and prolific playwrights on the English-speaking stage."[1] Boucicault came to America in 1855, shortly before his engagement as actor and director at the Gaite Theatre in New Orleans. From that time until his

Dion Boucicault, well-known actor and playwright, was approached by A.M. Palmer, manager of the Madison Square Theatre, in 1888 to create and head a new Madison Square Theatre School. After two successful years, Boucicault died and the school closed its doors permanently in 1890. (Photo courtesy of New York Public Library of the Performing Arts, Lincoln Center)

death in 1890, he was recognized as an excellent director, playwright, innovator, and practitioner of the theatre. Always a keen student of the theatre, Dion Boucicault was connected with the outstanding stock companies in the nation, and was usually given the prerogative of directing his own plays. Consequently, when a man of his stature consented to become the head of an acting school, the entire movement profited from the association.

In 1882, six years before Boucicault became the director of the Madison Square Theatre School, he had concurred with Henry Irving, Joseph Jefferson, Helena Madjeska and others that "acting could only be taught on the stage."[2] In the same year, Boucicault traveled to England and delivered an address at the Lyceum Theatre at the invitation of Henry Irving.[3] The lecture represents the most complete statement of Boucicault's acting theory. While he was in London, however, a storm was raging over the advisability of establishing an Academy of Dramatic Arts.[4] The argument concerned whether or not England should have a National School of Acting similar to the Conservatoire. Boucicault could not have been unaffected by the arguments. He had certainly been cognizant of Steele MacKaye's ventures in various dramatic schools in America, since MacKaye served as his personal representative in 1877. The possibility of the dramatic school, therefore, was not a new idea to Boucicault.

Upon his return to America, Boucicault must have been aware of MacKaye's innovations at the Madison Square, where the operation was already known as the Madison Square Theatre School as early as 1882. When MacKaye broke with the Mallory brothers and opened the Lyceum Theatre, the acting school concept swept America. The success of the Lyceum project, wherein an acting school was associated with a theatre in much the same relationship as the Conservatoire to the Comédie Français, was hailed far and wide as the answer to the failure of the stock company in providing a training ground for aspiring actors. The story of MacKaye's venture at the Lyceum has already been discussed, but the developments at the Madison Square Theatre have remained somewhat of a mystery.

When MacKaye left the Madison Square Theatre, he took with him the nucleus of the entire theatre operation. First Franklin Sargent, then the Frohmans, and finally David Belasco left the Madison Square to join their former associate in his new Lyceum Theatre and School. As a result, the Mallory brothers were left with a theatre, but with little experienced personnel to run it. Not being theatre men, the Mallorys enticed A. M. Palmer, director of the Union Square Theatre, to take the directorship of the Madison Square and to run the entire operation. For Palmer's services, he was given half ownership in the Madison Square Theatre. The details of the transaction are quite vague, but it is assumed that the Mallory brothers received full value from the transaction. Recognizing the practicality of having a ready-made reservoir of talent associated with his theatre, Palmer, encouraged by the Mallorys, decided to open an acting school at the Madison Square. Undoubtedly, he was influenced by the relative success of the Lyceum project which, by 1888, was known as the New York School of Acting. Daniel Frohman ran the Lyceum Theatre and had the New York School of Acting from which to draw when he needed to fill the many positions in large casts and in road shows. Thus, Palmer saw the practicality of training new talent for his theatre and for filling his own road companies.

Boucicault frequently indicated that he had always believed that acting could be taught, but that he was convinced it could be taught only on the stage itself.[5] He had little faith in the products of the "schools of elocution," which he associated with the institutions of Curry and Emerson. He was also opposed to Sargent's methods of having "branches" of acting taught by different specialists. He believed that the best form of acting school would be one which taught acting on the stage, not in the classroom. If such a teaching method could be developed, which actually reproduced the circumstances of the rehearsal and performance of a play in such a way that the actor could be instructed as he developed the character, then, said Boucicault, "I'd offer my services" (*Ibid.*). A little later, he explained how he became director of the Madison Square Theatre School of Instruction.

> And so it came to pass that a certain manager [A. M. Palmer] in New York, having entertained similar convictions on the subject, offered the use of his theatre and all its appliances to establish a school upon this scheme. But he carried it further. He undertook to furnish all the expenses attending the enterprise so the students should obtain instructions *free*; and still further, he proposed to select 15 of the most promising and pay them a weekly salary.[6]

It should be noted that Palmer's apparent altruism was not completely unaffected by the fact that there was a serious shortage of actors at this time. The American public was clamoring for entertainment, and it was difficult to find enough actors to fill the growing number of touring companies. While there were earlier indications that the Madison Square Theatre was going to open a formal acting school, the official announcement appeared in June, 1888.

> Yesterday Mr. Palmer and Mr. Boucicault met and finally concluded the arrangement whereby the plan will be put into execution early in September next. Had not Mr. Palmer been able to secure Mr. Boucicault's co-operation the idea would have been abandoned.[7]

The Madison Square Theatre School of Instruction opened the following September. The acting theory taught at the Madison Square Theatre School was entirely that propounded by Dion Boucicault. Palmer needed the name of Boucicault to offset the growing prestige of Sargent's New York School of Acting and he gave Boucicault *carte blanche* in the operation of the school (*Ibid.*). The organization of the school was explained as follows:

> Mr. Palmer's conservatory will have no lecturers, no corps of professors to teach high-sounding 'branches.' It

will be an actual working company. In order that an absolute control shall be maintained over the members, there shall be no entrance or tuition fees demanded from them. On the contrary, the one requirement of admission will be talent, and every member will be paid a salary. This places the project immediately on the highest plane and does not tie the hands of the director. The necessity of retaining an unpromising member because he has paid a year's fee in advance cannot possibly arise.

Between now and the early Fall Mr. Palmer will receive applications from candidates for admission and Mr. Boucicault will examine into their claims and decide upon their eligibility. A sufficient number will be accepted to form a complete working company. Plays will include standard comedies . . . and new pieces whose merit warrants their production. When pieces cannot be entirely cast from the corps, professionals will be called in. A matinee performance is to be given every Wednesday afternoon at the Madison Square during the season. Mr. Boucicault will direct all the rehearsals, and every person that knows his genius for imparting instruction will readily perceive that a course under him is tantamount to a liberal stage education. . . . The members of the corps will be promoted to the regular company when they have achieved sufficient proficiency. (*Ibid.*)

Boucicault's plan for the school's operation was the direct antithesis of the "schools of expression" and of Sargent's enterprise. The epithet, "high-sounding 'branches,'" could only be directed at the multitude of course work offered at Sargent's and at other schools. Boucicault did not want his school to be identified with that he called "hearth-rug tuition."

As suggested earlier, Boucicault must have had the idea of a "practical" theatre school in the back of his mind before Palmer offered him the opportunity to direct the Madison Square Theatre School. Boucicault mentioned this fact and indicated the theory upon which the school was founded.

Mr. Palmer shares the ideas I have always had, that the theatre school is necessary, and that it should be the sort of establishment we have agreed upon. I believe hearth-

rug tuition is not of the slightest use. *Everything learned
in a room is devoid of any practical use.* I do not take pupils
nor have I ever received them in my life. I have always
refused. I have, however, taught actors and actresses,
and I mean that our young people shall begin as actors
and actresses, not as students. The process of tuition will
be actual engagement in performances from the start
and not by way of elocutionary treatment, except in
connection with the parts they will be called upon
immediately to study. (*Ibid.* Italics mine)

This, then, was the essence of Boucicault's ideas concerning
the acting school. All training of the actor was to be
"practical." That is, the training was actually the rehearsal of a
role under the trained eye of an expert. Body, voice, and
speech training were to be taught from the viewpoint of its
applicability to the character. Characterization was also to be
taught in the course of rehearsal.

Boucicault believed, oddly enough, that the function of the
actor changed with the type of play being presented. He
argued that comedy and tragedy, having two distinct and
different purposes, require different approaches to acting.
"Comedy," said Boucicault, "aspires to portray by imitation
the weaknesses to which human beings are subject; and, it
may be, to correct such frailties by their exposure to our
ridicule."[8] "Tragedy," he said, "aspires to portray the passions
to which strong natures are subject, and a resistance to their
influence" (*Ibid.*). Consequently, the distinctions which Boucicault believed existed between the function of tragedy and
comedy affected the aims of the actor. "We may surmise,
therefore, that as the object of the tragedian, the principles
and the practice of one of these branches of the same art may
not be applicable to the other" (*Ibid.*, 56).

The function of acting was always "to be the part." As
Boucicault explained:

> Acting is not mere speech! It is not taking the dialog of
> the author and giving it artistically, but sometimes not
> articulately. Acting is to perform, to be the part; be it in

your arms, your legs; to be what you are acting, to be it
all over, that is acting. (*Ibid.*, 23)

He defined character "in the dramatic sense" as "the
distinction between individuals, and it is exhibited by *the
manner* in which each bears and expresses his or her trouble,
or deals with his neighbors" (*The Art of Acting*, I, 55. Italics
mine). Boucicault asserted that comedy possessed and demanded more development of character than did tragedy.
Tragedy, he said, portrayed the passions of men of strong
natures. "But strong natures exhibit no distinctive features"
(*Ibid.*, 56). Thus, the relationship of the actor to the play
changed in terms of character according to whether he acted
comedy or tragedy, since Boucicault contended that tragedy
concerned characters of more general and broader character
traits than did comedy. Comedy demanded details and a
closer imitation of actual reality than did tragedy.
Boucicault warned the beginning actor:

> When you go upon the stage do not be full of yourself,
> but be full of your part. This is mistaking vanity for
> genius, and is the fault of many more than perhaps you are
> aware of. If actors' and actresses' minds be employed
> upon themselves, and not on the character they wish and
> aspire to perform, they never really get out of themselves.
> Many think they are studying character when they are
> only studying themselves. (*The Art of Acting*, II, 43–44)

The actor, then, should become completely absorbed in his
character. In comedy, the details of character would be
lifelike, and the actor's attitude would be objectively intellectual. In tragedy, however, the character would assume
broader proportions, but the actor was expected completely
to abandon himself to the feelings of the character.

> The dependence of the artist on mechanism, so elo-
> quently and truthfully laid down by M. Coquelin, may
> be accepted as applicable to comedy and to such parts of
> tragic plays as may contain an infusion of comedy;—
> but—with great respect to him—no further.

> The independence of the artist from mechanism, and claimed *per contra* by Mr. Irving, is admirable so far as pure tragedy is concerned, and only in scenes where much effusion is indicated by the eruptive language of the poet, which, if given with mechanical deliberation, might appear beneath the level of the volcanic passion. (*The Art of Acting*, I, 61)

Boucicault believed that all actors should approach a character "from the inside; not from the outside" (*Ibid.*, 48). He elaborated his point by referring to the methods employed by great painters.

> Great painters, I am told, used to draw a human figure in the nude form, and, when they were proposing to finish their pictures, to paint the costumes; then the costumes came right. That is exactly how an actor ought to study his art. He ought to paint his character in the nude form and put the costume on the last thing. (*Ibid.*, 48–49)

The analogy, of course, refers to the actor's gradual exploration, investigation, and growth in character. Boucicault also conceived that every character actually possessed three natures. "First there is the man by himself—as he is to himself—as he is to his God. That is one man, the inner man, as he is when he is alone; the unclothed man" (*Ibid.*, 50). The inner man, as Boucicault conceived him, was the essence of the character, the man he knew himself to be. "Then there is the native man, the domestic man, as he is to his family. Still there is a certain amount of disguise." Finally, Boucicault arrived at the third man, the man who is totally unlike his inner self. "Then there is the man as he stands before the world at large; as he is in society" (*Ibid.*). The actor who approaches a role "comic or otherwise, . . . will find that the three characters always combine in one man" (*Ibid.*, 51). Boucicault attempted to clarify his point by referring to the character of Hamlet.

> Look at Hamlet in his soliloquies, he is passionate, he is violent, he is intemperate in himself, he knows his faults and lashes his own weakness. But he has no sooner done

that when Horatio comes on the stage with a few friends. Horatio is the mild, soft, gentle companion; with his arm round his neck, Hamlet forgets the other man; he gets a little on, but he is the same man to Horatio as he is to his mother, when he gets her in the closet. But when he encounters the world at large, he is the Prince! the condescending man! (*Ibid.*)

Boucicault regarded the expression of the three characters as "one secret of the true and highest form of dramatic art, and the dramatist, if he would be true to nature and to his art, must carry them out" (*Ibid.*, 52).

The best way to approach a character, Boucicault believed, was with a sense of humility and duty. The actor must be willing to subordinate himself to the character and to his art. He must learn to adapt to the character; not adapt the character to himself. Concerning this point, Boucicault argued that most actresses and actors came to him and asked, "Have you any part that will fit me?" He believed that they should say:

Have you any part that I can fit? that I can expand myself or contract myself into; that I can put myself inside of; That I, as a Protean, can shape myself into, even alter my voice and everything that nature has given to me, and be what you have contrived? I do not want you to contrive like a tailor to fit me. (*Ibid.*, 44)

The relationship of the actor to the audience was one of Boucicault's greatest concerns. Being a practical man of the theatre, he fully recognized the fact that even though a play was a work of art, it was also meant to be presented before an audience. Most critics agree that Boucicault's plays are highly sentimental, full of high-flown language, action, pathos, and bathos. The success of his writing and directorial ability amply demonstrated that he knew what audiences wanted to see. While his acting theory was almost completely audience-centered, Boucicault abhorred "tricks and devices" which actors employed to gain applause for themselves rather than for the character. The devices of "taking leave," indicated by the actor crossing swiftly to an exit, stopping, and finishing the line at the door, was equally criticized by Boucicault (*Ibid.*, 40–41). He recognized, however, that the theatre had many conventions which the audience expected. Consequently, gestures, voice, and to some degree, character, were expected to conform with certain "conventions." Boucicault saw the relationship of the actor to the audience as similar to a person viewing a picture. The actor, as a figure in a painting should, therefore, gesture with "the arm farthest from the audience. . . . These, you will say, are slight rules; but still they will jar on the audience occasionally if they are not followed" (*Ibid.*, 34). Boucicault's concern for the audience led him to regard most gesture and movement, and to some degree, voice and speech as being dictated by convention.

Boucicault believed that it was necessary to create the illusion of an actual situation; of characters living an experience (*Ibid.*, 42–43). He was convinced that the illusion of life which the actor expressed should never be broken. Boucicault considered listening one of the most important aspects of acting since it held the attention of both the actor and the audience on the scene by the actor's focus and attentiveness to what he should hear and see on the stage. In this sense, Boucicault desired the actor to ignore the audience, as the character would ignore them in real life. He accepted, therefore, that it was the actor's duty to affect the audience indirectly through his power to involve them in a seemingly real situation.

If Boucicault ever conceived an "ideal" actor, he certainly never wrote about him. He was interested in the competent actor who knew and practiced his art according to the principles upon which it rested. The natural, untrained genius of the theatre was regarded as never having existed. Boucicault believed that "a good actor is not due to accident, that a man is not born to be an actor unless he is trained" (*Ibid.*, 22). Elaborating upon a discussion that raged in London at the time of his visit in 1882, Boucicault contended that there were no natural geniuses in the acting profession. Using the art of painting as analogous to the art of acting, he asserted: "If it be said that we cannot teach a man to be a genius, that we cannot teach him to be talented, that is a fact; but I ask you in any art what great men . . . would have existed if some kind of art had not preceded them by which they learned the art of, say mixing colors, the principles of proportion, and the principles of perspective" (*Ibid.*, 20–21). Boucicault firmly believed that the "ideal" actor must learn the principles of his art. "You must absolutely have principles in all arts. You cannot produce your own thoughts, your own feelings, unless you have principles as some guide, some ground" (*Ibid.*, 21).

Boucicault never really discussed imagination and intellect. He believed that those faculties were endowed at birth and if an actor hoped to attain success in his art, a vivid imagination and a fine intellect were absolutely essential. Unlike Curry, Emerson, and Sargent, Boucicault did not believe that training in the principles of acting included the necessity of training the imagination and the intellect. Training in the principles of acting could shape the person already endowed with a vivid imagination and a brilliant intellect into a fine actor. Training in the principles could even make the person of average endowment in imagination and intellect a competent actor, one who would fill the rank and file. Regardless of endowment, Boucicault believed that the principles of the art of acting existed for all. Imagination and intellect furnished the raw material; the principles furnished the guidance. Without principles, imagination and intellect were considered useless, and the actor erratic and ineffective (*Ibid.*, 20–21).

While imagination and intellect were accepted as essential to the "ideal" actor, the place of emotion in acting was more nebulous. Boucicault appears to have desired the best of both worlds, or he was implying "a plague on both your houses." That he believed the actor should experience the emotion in tragedy, and imitate feeling in comedy has already been established. However, the manner in which Boucicault justified his conclusion was quite interesting. A long extract from his article concerning Coquelin's and Irving's opinions on the subject may help place Boucicault's position in clearer focus. In comparing the process of playwriting to the process of acting Boucicault stated:

> May I, without intrusion, exemplify from personal experience the action of the mind under the two different affections [feeling and non-feeling] while engaged in tragic and comic composition? While writing comedy the mind of the dramatist is circumspect and calculating, careful in selection of thought, a fastidious spectator of the details of his work, thoroughly self-conscious and deliberate. Such is not the condition of his mind when writing tragic scenes, or scenes of deep pathos. The mind of the poet becomes abstract, his thoughts shape themselves into language—the passion wields the pen. The utterance is impulsive—he is an actor, not a spectator in a scene, and when he awakes from this transport of the mind he looks around to recover consciousness of where he is! Surely every author must have experienced this illusion, and under these circumstances. I have never known, in all my experience, that scenes so composed have failed, when fairly acted, to convey a like emotion to the audience.
>
> M. Coquelin says the voice of the heart is inartistic; it must be controlled and molded by the brain! Yes! in comedy—into which the emotions alluded to never enter, or, if so, in a very modified degree. I am not a tragedian; therefore can only speak with much reserve; but *if the poet, under the great impulse of tragic compo sition, can lose his perfect self-control, and in that state his thoughts shape themselves into exquisite language, if grammar and spelling become instinctive work, as the pen follows the mind without circumspection or afterthought; if this can be with a poet, may it not be likewise with the tragedian? May not the rules and principles of his art be so much a part of his nature that he can give rein to his passional spasm while retaining his seat and control of Pegasus? If he fail to do so, he becomes, I admit, ridiculous; but if he succeed, he mounts to the verge and edge of the sublime. Such a feat can only be safely attempted by the perfectly trained artist. When novices give way to their effusion they inevitably become grotesque.* (Ibid., 56–58. Italics mine)

While Boucicault's relation of the processes of the playwright to the actor may certainly be questioned, it is clear that he conceived the operation of emotion to be similar in both cases. Speaking of the difficulty of teaching acting, Boucicault once said, "I can but give you enough to make you understand what your art is, its philosophic principles" (*Ibid.*, 22). The philosophic principles of which he spoke were primarily concerned with what can be called "technique." In fact, what Boucicault considered to be the "art of acting" was, in reality, rules for gesture and voice, and some basic principles concerning characterization. His theory of acting was not based on speculative assumptions. As a playwright of note, an actor, and a director of some renown, he had met the test of audiences for over four decades. What he had to say about the body, voice, and characterization was the distillation of practical experience and observation of what he had found effective in the art of acting. Boucicault divided the art of acting into three categories.

> The subject of acting may be divided into the voice for the treatment of the production; the expression of feature or gesture. I call gesture that action of the body above the waist—the arms, the neck, the head, and the bust. The carriage is that action of the body which is below the waist.
> Then there is the study of character. Now, there is no speechifying in that. It has nothing to do with dialog, it has nothing to do with posture. It applies practically to that portion of the profession with which you have to do before you begin anything of the sort. (*Ibid.*, 23–24)

Before any consideration of voice, speech, and movement, it should be clearly understood that Boucicault believed that no actor should attempt to play a role for which he was vocally and physically unsuited. This point of view, to which Boucicault wholeheartedly subscribed, is called typecasting. Consequently, his theories of the voice, speech, gesture, and movement operate on the assumption that the actor already possessed the conventional physical and vocal attributes necessary for such a character. His theory, therefore, is composed mainly of practical suggestions and the general methods of putting the suggestions into practice.

Boucicault considered six major aspects of the actor's voice: volume, breathing, rate, quality, inflection, and articulation. Articulation, however, was frequently treated concurrently with all vocal elements, since Boucicault believed that most voice faults were primarily caused by articulatory problems. Concerning volume, Boucicault asserted that "the secret of being heard is not a loud voice" (*Ibid.*, 24). The true secret of being heard in the theatre, he contended, was speaking articulately.

> Now it is the vowel which gives support, and value, and volume to the consonants. When you want to give strong impression it is the consonant you go at, and not the vowel; but when you want to be expressive, when you want to be agreeable, you go at the vowel. (*Ibid.*)

Boucicault maintained that "Every syllable of every word is pronounced, and as far as I can every consonant and vowel is pronounced (*Ibid.*). He also claimed that articulation had a very great effect on both volume and quality.

Breathing was believed to be the major factor in phrasing, and rate the most prominent cause of poor articulation (*Ibid.*, 24–25). Good articulation required that the actor pronounce words in the best traditions of the English language, although Boucicault did not send the aspiring actor to the most current dictionary as did F. F. MacKay, who will be discussed in a later chapter. Boucicault abhorred the practice of using an artificial voice for tragedy as did actors of the past and contemporary actors in France. He insisted that the "natural" voice is best for all drama (*Ibid.*, 28–30). These general observations compose his theory of the voice. It should be remembered, however, that since he advocated type-casting for voice as well as for the physical characteristics, an elaborate body of principles was considered unnecessary.

Boucicault was much more detailed in his consideration of gesture. He asserted that there are no cardinal rules in the theatre, since great actors have frequently inverted what were considered "well-known rules" (*Ibid.*, 30). However, he maintained that certain basic principles have resisted even the attempts of genius to break them. First, all gestures should be distinct and deliberate, and if the actor should point, the action must go from the shoulder (*Ibid.*). One of the most important rules of gesture, and one that should never be broken was that "all gesture should precede slightly the words that it is to impress or to illustrate" (*Ibid.*). It was considered an exceptional circumstance to break the rule against putting the hand to the head or supplication with the palms downward. Boucicault asserted that "Common sense will tell you that many of these little matters are matters that depend upon philosophy. They are so simple, so clear, and distinct." Regardless of the obvious nature of these rules, Boucicault maintained that they were "scattered about the stage and transmitted gypsy-like, in our vagrant life from one generation to another; but . . . sometimes it takes ages before they are learned, and an actor has to go on picking up these things one by one" (*Ibid.*, 31–32).

Small gestures, called "gesticles" by Boucicault, meant nothing. Because Boucicault envisioned the stage as a picture frame, and believed that the audience was used to regarding it as such, appropriate rules were necessary in movement and gesture. He asserted that the actor always gestured with the upstage arm, knelt on the downstage knee, and never gestured across the body. Interestingly enough, he maintained that the principles of gesture in the art of acting also apply to the orator and the minister, thus, making the same claims for acting that Curry, Emerson, and Powers, made for their expressional theories (*Ibid.*, 33–35).

One of the most important forms of gesture, Boucicault called "byplay"—that is, "the gestures that are used while another person is speaking, so that the recipient, by receiving the speech from the stage, may transmit its effect to the audience." Basically, "byplay" appears to have been a gesture that is made in reaction to another person's actions or to what another person said. "Byplay," then, was thought to be the physical reaction to listening or physical impression. Its effect on the audience was considered to be immensely important to Boucicault's way of thinking, since the actor may conclude " 'if his speech has no effect on me it will not have any effect on them' " (*Ibid.*, 35).

Boucicault discussed walking at great length. The basic ideas were that the body should always be erect in walking and the legs "must be kept cleanly and clearly underneath (*Ibid.*, 38). Boucicault asserted that the Greeks and Arabs walk perfectly because they carried great weights on their heads and, as a result, had achieved perfect balance. Walking, maintained Boucicault, "is not the continuous and continual, but there is a pause in the middle" (*Ibid.*, 38–39). Referring to the picture frame, Boucicault mentioned that, in walking, the upstage leg was always "farther forward than the other." Finally, Boucicault asserted the first lesson an actor has to learn is, not to speak, it is to learn to walk on the stage, stand still, and walk off again (*Ibid.*, 42). The idea that the actor must learn to move on the stage before any other kind of instruction took place was severely criticized by many elocutionists. Boucicault maintained that learning the positions, the various conventional movements—in short, the "business" of acting—was the first, and most important lesson for an actor.

The last great lesson which the actor must learn before undertaking the study of character is to focus his attention physically and mentally. The actor should focus physically through "byplay" of gestures. Boucicault believed that listening constituted the subordination of the actor to the character and of the actor to the dominant actor in the scene. Listening, he maintained, effects the same responses in the audience. "If the man fixes his mind upon some . . . object, if the mind is over *there* not *here,* on himself, ease will naturally follow, because he is naturally there as a listener. That is the first lesson; when he has accomplished this he must come to the study of character" (*Ibid.*, 43). Finally, Boucicault cautioned:

> Whatever is done by an actor let it be done with
> circumspection, without anxiety or hurry, remembering
> that vehemence is not passion, that the public will feel
> and appreciate when the actor is not full of himself, but
> when he is full of his character, with that deliberation
> without slowness, that calmness of resolution without
> coldness, that self-possession without over-weening
> confidence, which should combine in the actor so as to
> give grace to comic and importance to tragic presence.
> The audience are [sic] impressed with the unaffected
> character of one who moves forward with a fixed
> purpose, full of momentous designs. He expresses a
> passion with which they will sympathize, and radiates a
> command which they obey. (*Ibid.*, 53)

The "ideal" actor was one capable of imitating the passions and
physical appearances of man in comedy, and of experiencing
deep emotion and reacting to it physically in tragedy. Vivid imagination, brilliant intellect, a capacity for great feeling, and a
thorough knowledge of the principles of acting were considered necessary for the "ideal" actor. However, the practical and
empirical Boucicault observed that even the greatest actors of
every period were not capable of playing all roles well. The pas-
sionate actor was considered incapable of playing the intellectual drama well, and the intellectual actor was regarded as inad-
equate for the emotional play (*Ibid.*, 49–50). In this sense, even
the best actor was believed to have limitations. Always a real-
ist, Boucicault gave the aspiring actor this final piece of advice.

> Having arrived at that conclusion as to what your line is
> going to be, always try to select those characters and the
> line that is most suited and more nearly conforms to
> your own natural gifts. Nature knows best. If you
> happen to have a short, sharp face, a hard voice, and
> angular figure, you are suited for the intellectual charac-
> ters of the drama, such as Hamlet and so forth. If you are
> a soft, passionate nature—if you have a soft voice and
> that sort of sensuous disposition which seems to lubri-
> cate your entire form, your limbs, so that your move-
> ments are gentler and softer than others, then this
> character is fitted for Romeo or Othello. (*Ibid.*, 49)

METHODS OF TEACHING

When the Madison Square Theatre School of Instruction announced that it was open in September 1888, "Upward of eleven hundred applicants pleaded for admission."[9] It was asserted that "the system employed by Mr. Boucicault is entirely new, and may be said to be the reverse of the methods in use. He considers that elocution is the last thing to be taught, but when the student has been taught to act, and the meaning of the part he plays, then he will be ready for the teacher of elocution to take him in hand" (*Ibid.*). This claim for the teaching methods of Dion Boucicault, as already indicated by his theory, represented an antagonism toward the methods of the "speculative schools" of the period. Curry, Emerson, and Sargent were included in the category of "hearth-rug tuition" which Boucicault associated with most elocutionists. "To teach the student how to 'elocute' a part before he knows how to act, is like teaching a girl how to play a tune by ear before she has learned the handling of the instrument" (*Ibid.*).

The Madison Square Theatre School of Instruction held its first auditions in the Fall of 1888. The prospective student prepared a short scene for the auditions and was admitted on the basis of its worth. Constance Morris, a onetime pupil at the school, described the tryouts for membership before Boucicault, Palmer, and Augustin Daly.[10] Only fifty-three students were chosen for the course. These, Morris reported, were divided into two groups according to ability and accomplishment as determined by the tryouts. The first group was taught by Boucicault, and the second by Theodore Corbett, who was added to the school's staff to assist Boucicault.

The course of instruction at the Madison Square Theatre School was Spartan in its simplicity. It subscribed to the practical application of Boucicault's theory of acting, which was embodied in the simple statement: In order to learn how to act, one must act. The prospectus of the school's curriculum, was as follows:

The form of instruction to be followed at Mr. Palmer's dramatic school will be new and exceedingly practical. Twelve standard comedies will be first selected, and the whole of the sixty pupils put at work studying them. In each, every male student will have to prepare himself in every male part, and every female student in every female role. Then at the assembly in the theatre Director Boucicault will each day call up to the stage at random a complete cast for the piece at hand. They will proceed with certain scenes, and their errors corrected on the moment in the presence of the observers. Every correction will be accompanied by the reason dictating it. Then the cast will be changed . . . and thus proficiency will be achieved in all roles.[11]

The relationship of teacher and pupil was obviously similar to that of the director and actor in the professional theatre, although the professional director of the period may not have been so considerate of the actor as to explain the reasons for direction. The teacher was, then, a critic who corrected and explained the reasons for error. Explanation, observation, and practice appear to have been the chief methods used in the school The object was to give the students the same experience that the professional actor received in rehearsal.

The basic teaching methods appear to have been amazingly similar to those listed in the prospectus of the school. In 1889, Boucicault explained exactly what methods he employed in teaching the aspiring actors. He explained:

When the school was formed, they were called into the auditorium of the theatre, and assembled in the orchestra seats. The following *menu* for the day had been previously issued: the Garden Scene in *Romeo and Juliet*; the fourth act of *King John*; the third act of the *School for Scandal*— each part in these scenes or acts was cast to two or three different students. *Romeo and Juliet* was called; two of the students stepped upon the stage and played the scene, while the whole school became spectators, and as the corrections were made . . . *and the faults explained*, the lesson was conveyed equally to the two performers and to the audience. In the midst of this scene, it was stopped;

one of the performers was invited to retire amongst the
spectators, and a new *Romeo* or *Juliet* was called forward to
proceed with the performance. It should be evident that
this second performer had already profited by what had
been seen, and took care to avoid similar errors. (Dion
Boucicault, "My Pupils," 435)

Constance Morris states that the students were encouraged
to offer their own interpretation of the character, blocking, and
business.[12] Following their attempts at the portrayal, Boucicault would then come up on the stage and "correct the errors."
Morris claimed that his suggestions were kindly and graciously
made (*Ibid.*). The criticism of performances covered the basic
principles discussed in the section concerning theory. Criticism, therefore, was concerned with the points mentioned
under voice and articulation; while the criticism of movement
and gesture consisted of correcting "stage business" and suggestions concerning the general and "conventional" principles of
walking and appropriate gestures. Criticism of characterization
followed comments on voice and body.

Boucicault believed that his method of teaching acting was
competitive in that it challenged the novices to attempt to
excel each other. He also saw the method as an invaluable aid
in ridding the aspiring actor of "stage fright" (Dion Boucicault, "My Pupils," 435). His idea of using a scene as a
demonstrative device for the rest of the class as well as the
performers seems prophetic of certain "laboratory" techniques of present-day actor training. The method of inter-
changing the actors in the middle of the scene appears to have
been designed to test the students' powers of observation. As
Boucicault said, "It should be evident that this second
performer had already profited by what had been seen, and
took care to avoid similar errors." It might also be added that
the method may have added a certain spontaneity and
freshness to the scene.

Frequent assignments of individual roles from plays were
made so that the student would have sufficient opportunity to
act a variety of parts. Semiannual examinations were given

before such luminaries of the theatre as John Drew, James Lewis, Ada Rehan, Helen Modjeska, Otis Skinner, Wilton Lackaye, Rose Coughlan, and Mrs. Gilbert, some of whom would act as judges. According to Constance Morris, successful students were, indeed, integrated into the Madison Square Theatre organization (Morris, 406).

The Madison Square Theatre School of Instruction was short-lived. Boucicault died in September 1890, and the school never reopened. Palmer fell victim to the Syndicate and departed from the Madison Square Theatre a few years later. In its short existence, the school demonstrated an extremely close relationship between theory and teaching methods. Boucicault claimed that there was a need for a school of acting similar in organization and method to the actual practice of the theatre. "You are aware . . . that actors and authors are in the habit on the stage of teaching the actors how the characters they have drawn should be played," said Boucicault (Dion Boucicault, *The Art of Acting*, II, 23). He mentioned that T. W. Robertson, Sardou, Alexander Dumas, Henry Irving, Mr. Wilson Barret, Mr. Bancroft, Mr. Hare, and Mr. Kendall "all teach the younger actors and actresses how to play their parts." He argued that these artists "are obliged to do so in the present condition of affairs, because there is no school in the provinces [of England] to lick the novices into shape and to teach them the ground of their art, how to walk, how to talk—that is, to teach them to act" (*Ibid.*). After explaining the nature of the principles of the art of acting, Boucicault pleaded:

> Let us give him [the aspiring actor] the sound principles of his art. Do not let us leave the managers to be obliged to take the most ignorant people, and have to do here on stage what should be done elsewhere. [It seems undeniable that Boucicault means a school such as the one he helped organize at the Madison Square.] Let them be properly and fairly prepared and brought into such a position as to be able to do some of the minor parts of the drama which they profess to follow. (*Ibid.*, 54–55)

The Madison Square Theatre School of Instruction attempted to retain the best features of the stock company tradition. The school possessed an excellent director in Boucicault, one who was vitally concerned in the training of aspiring actors and actresses. Rehearsal and performance of a variety of roles was the students' training ground, and under the guidance of Boucicault they undoubtedly benefited from the experience. Constance Morris thought the school a "wonderful opportunity for beginning actors." Daly's interest in the school seems to indicate that he thought the venture worthwhile; and the fact that many noted actors and actresses took the time to act as critic judges demonstrates their faith in the value of the institution. A surprising number of the students in Dion Boucicault's school became familiar to the theatre audiences of the time. Some of the students entered the Madison Square Theatre company, but most of the graduates found employment elsewhere. Among those who achieved success in the theatre were Maxine Elliot, Nanette Comstock, May Buckley, Roy Rockman, Nan Craddock, Dorothy Dorr, Kate Klaxton, Constance Morris, Reuben Fax, Kate Lester, Edward Belnap, Edmund Day, Kate Jordan, and Alice Sheppard (Morris, 406–407).

Like most American acting theorists, Boucicault advocated identification with the character and cautioned the young aspirant: "do not be full of yourself, but full of your part." Stanislavsky was to say something similar many years later. Boucicault also asked the actor to abandon himself completely to the character and taught that the best approach to any role was "from the inside; not from the outside." While he believed that the actor should "feel" *as* the character, he also acknowledged that a technical control monitored excessive emotionalism. Part of the technical control was achieved through the actor's undivided attention to the scene at hand. The actor was asked to listen intently and react, both physically and vocally, *as* the character in order to form a public solitude and a circle of attention, a concept Stanislavsky developed in greater detail much later. Boucicault's belief that the actor must be subordinate to the character and sacrifice ego to the requirements of the scene is also consistent with an ensemble approach to acting which, again, is reflective of the best stock company traditions.

In the final analysis, Boucicault's acting theory is representative of what most good actors of the period believed and practiced. But, recognizing that the stock company tradition of training was frequently "hit or miss," Boucicault committed himself to the newer "school" idea which advocated that acting should be based on a firm foundation of principles and that the aspiring actor should acquire technique *prior* to entering the profession. Unlike other schools, however, he believed that the best training was through rehearsal, performance and criticism: learning by doing. In this sense, The Madison Square Theatre School was more a laboratory in which students presented scenes which exposed them to many genres and styles of plays.

Although the Madison Square Theatre School of Instruction lasted only a short time, the institution did much to encourage the idea of the acting school and was influential in popularizing the "practical" approach to actor training. It also represented the first time in America that a respected "practical" man of the theatre attempted to operate an acting school.[13] Boucicault's connection with the Madison Square Theatre School of Instruction undoubtedly did much to mitigate the opposition to the idea of the acting school. He clearly understood the problems which the aspiring actor faced. Since the dissolution of the stock company, there had been no place in which to train novices. Boucicault believed that he had solved the problem in the best possible way by organizing the first "practical" school of acting—The Madison Square Theatre School of Instruction.

TOP: Adeline Stanhope, and BOTTOM: Nelson Wheatcroft. Husband and wife were co-founders and teachers at The Empire Dramatic School which was associated with the Empire Theatre from 1893–1897. After her husband's death, Adeline opened a new school at a different location in 1897. She retired in 1910. (Photo courtesy of New York Public Library of the Performing Arts, Lincoln Center)

CHAPTER VII
THE STANHOPE-WHEATCROFT SCHOOL

The Stanhope-Wheatcroft School began its first classes in October 1893, under the title of the Empire Dramatic School. It was, at first, under the management of Nelson Wheatcroft, a well-known actor of the period. Wheatcroft had "come up through the ranks" and was well respected in the community of professional actors in New York. The Empire Dramatic School was, in essence, the training ground of talent for the Empire Theatre, owned by Charles Frohman. Frohman was a man "who took inexperienced persons, groomed them and publicized them, and set them up as stars without any kind of apprenticeship."[1] But it is undeniable that Frohman was also an excellent producer who worked hard to bring new playwrights and talent before American audiences.

In 1893, Charles Frohman opened his magnificent new Empire Theatre and, it would appear, saw the advisability of having connected with it a theatre school. It should be remembered that Charles Frohman was quite familiar with the idea of the acting school, since both he and his brother, Gus Frohman, were connected with the management of the Lyceum Theatre and School at its inception in 1884. Quite probably, Charles Frohman recognized the necessity of having a constant supply of new talent to fill the stage of his new theatre. Consequently, he contacted Nelson Wheatcroft, with the result that the Empire Dramatic School was formed. The school enjoyed the association with the Empire Theatre until Wheatcroft's death in 1897, when the school merged with the American Academy of Dramatic Arts, which inherited the association with the theatre. After Wheatcroft's death, his wife, Adeline Stanhope, organized her own school which she called The Stanhope-Wheatcroft School. The school lasted until around 1910, when Mrs. Stanhope-Wheatcroft retired from public life.

The theoretical position of the Stanhope-Wheatcroft School was pragmatic, partly because of the very nature of the background of the people who ran it. Both Nelson Wheatcroft and Adeline Stanhope were highly respected. In fact, the Empire Dramatic School and later the Stanhope-Wheatcroft School were considered to be among the best acting schools in the country.[2] The methods of their teaching were most highly admired because "Practice rather than theory" was their "aim."[3] The "practical" acting school, of which the Stanhope-Wheatcroft School was the epitome, gained popularity during the end of the nineteenth century, primarily because both its purpose and methods appealed to the immediate needs of the theatre. There was growing pressure against the "speculative" school and an elevation of the "practical" school. The theatre of the time was clearly in need of young talent and did not care for them to have high-flown ideas. Even the American Academy of Dramatic Arts attempted to live down the stigma of being "speculative" by advertising in the *New York Dramatic Mirror* as "A Practical School."[4] Although the "practical" schools eschewed acting "theories," a theory emerged nonetheless. It must be inferred, however, from the methods of teaching and from practice. The Stanhope-Wheatcroft School's existence was rather short-lived, because the school depended solely on the initiative, vitality, and personal prestige of the director-manager.

Mrs. Stanhope's autobiography[5] tells the story of her training and experience. She first went on the stage at the urging of "Madame Celeste, the celebrated French actress." After that she joined a company in Brighton, England. "After my Brighton appearance I studied acting for six months with John Rider, of London, and made my London debut at the Haymarket Theatre as Juliet." Thus far, it can be seen that

Mrs. Stanhope-Wheatcroft's stage preparation was little different from that of hundreds of other actresses of her period. She enjoyed private tutoring, "debuted" in a famous role, and from that point her story takes her to stock companies in England, Scotland, South America, and finally, the United States. In America, she was James O'Neill's leading lady, and also the leading lady in Baldwin's Stock Company in San Francisco. She summarized her final years on the public stage as follows:

> I played a season under Daniel Frohman's management, two seasons with Joseph Jefferson, and was in Augustine Pitou's stock company. My last appearance as an actress was with the company of the Theatre of Arts and Letters. (*Ibid.*)

On a return engagement in London she met Mr. Wheatcroft, who became her leading man and, later, her husband.

After retiring from the stage the Wheatcrofts opened their acting school with the firm conviction that it was the only means left by which the theatre could be supplied with actors of quality. Indeed, after her own long experience in the theatre, Mrs. Wheatcroft was confident that the acting school was the *best* method for training actors. In an interview she stated:

> My present work in the school is what I'm most interested in, and I like to talk of it much better than of myself. The dramatic schools are growths of comparatively recent years, and some old actors are inclined to scoff at them, on the ground that the stage itself is the best place to learn how to act. It may have been in the old days, but the veterans should remember that these are not the old days. There are comparatively few of the stock companies now which in the past, by presenting an extensive repertoire of plays, gave the young actor or actress the training that he or she rarely gets in the company today.
> Most of the actors now on the stage never went to a dramatic school and were never members of any of the

old stock companies. They learned their business by hard knocks and experience that most of them would shrink from again facing. *I know that a year in a dramatic school will teach the young aspirant for stage honors what it took me at least ten years to learn.* The training, moreover, gives the young member of the profession confidence in himself or herself, and heaven knows that confidence and self assertion are necessary to succeed in our profession. (*Ibid.*, Italics mine)

Of course, it could have been that Mrs. Wheatcroft was extolling the virtues of the acting school because she was in the business of training aspirants "for stage honors." Yet, it appears that there is a great deal of truth in what she said. As indicated in Chapter I, the stock company picture in the nineteenth century underwent an immense change. When Mrs. Wheatcroft made her comment about acting schools there were only five resident stock companies left in the entire United States. Directors and producers like Frohman and Belasco could take unknowns and turn them into overnight successes, but the general run of actor was not as fortunate as Maude Adams or Mrs. Leslie Carter. These two actresses received a personal attention showered upon few actresses of the day. Most aspiring actors and actresses were trained on the spot for roles in road companies. They received training in only one role and might be expected to play it for a year. Then, they might be cast in another role of the same type and the experience would be repeated. Consequently, actors and actresses were not being trained in the rudiments of their craft, but only in the peculiarities of a limited number of roles. Under the existing circumstances, it is little wonder that Mrs. Wheatcroft could confidently claim the acting school as the best method of training available to the aspiring actor.

Any analysis of the methods of teaching and the theoretical position of the Stanhope-Wheatcroft School must be viewed from the standpoint of Mrs. Wheatcroft. She appears to have been the guiding beacon of the school her husband founded,

because, in 1897, only four years after the opening of the
Empire Dramatic School, a writer for the *New York Dramatic
Mirror* commented: "It is well-known that for a good while
previous to his death Mr. Wheatcroft left the conduct of the
school in Mrs. Wheatcroft's hands, giving his personal attention chiefly to its business management."[6] In a rather pointed
statement which appeared in a prospectus, Nelson
Wheatcroft stated that "energies will not be diffused by
attention to extraneous subjects, but will be devoted only to
that work which is constantly in requisition on the stage
itself."[7] What this meant is not exactly clear. It appears to be
a barbed comment intended for the ears of men like Sargent,
Curry, and the more "speculative" of the acting schools. More
than likely, however, it was a flat statement of the policy of
the school. The Stanhope-Wheatcroft School prided itself on
being "practical."

In order to reach conclusions concerning the Stanhope-
Wheatcroft School's theoretical position toward the training
of actors, some small departure in method seems appropriate.
Instead of discussing and analyzing the theory, it appears
more profitable to view the manner in which the "practical"
school was conducted. From this material some attempt to
distill the theory will be attempted.

Discussing her school in 1897, Mrs. Wheatcroft commented on the length of time that the student attended classes
at the Stanhope-Wheatcroft School.[8] "Our regular school
assembles in the Fall," she said. Then, in what appears to be
another remark intended for Sargent, Mrs. Wheatcroft
added, "It is my belief . . . that one year is ample time for this
preliminary training and instruction."[9] In another article, the
point of view that "ample preparation for the stage may be
made in a single term of six months"[10] was again expressed.
The reporter mentioned, "This proof has overcome very
nearly the ancient professional prejudice against dramatic
students." Perhaps it was true that Mrs. Wheatcroft proved
that six months was sufficient to train actors thoroughly in
their craft, but the main point appears to be that she was

emphasizing the differences between her school and Sargent's, Curry's, and other institutions that insisted that at least two years were necessary in order to train the aspiring actor.

The Stanhope-Wheatcroft school did not seem to employ the rigid entrance requirements which Sargent claimed for his American Academy of Dramatic Arts. That Sargent was as selective of students as he insisted he was is perhaps a moot point. It remains a matter of fact that the Stanhope-Wheatcroft School and its predecessor, the Empire Dramatic School, never had the personnel to run elaborate entrance tests, much less have a person whose single responsibility was the testing and interviewing of prospective students. Mrs. Wheatcroft stated simply that "We have to discriminate somewhat in admitting applicants to the school. The student must have good presence, a good voice, and a good enunciation" (*Ibid.*). The requirements out of the way, the school began its work in earnest.

In contrast to the elaborate curriculum of the American Academy of Dramatic Arts, the course work in the Stanhope-Wheatcroft School appeared Spartan in its simplicity. The school, it should be remembered, was much smaller than the Academy and could not boast the faculty necessary for an extensive curriculum. It seems questionable, however, whether Mr. and Mrs. Wheatcroft would have availed themselves of more course work had they been offered the opportunity. In any event, they employed three or four instructors to teach Modern Dramatic Art, which appears to have been very inclusive but was, in fact, the acting of recent plays. Shakespeare and the classics, Melodrama and Comedy, and Stage Makeup rounded out the curriculum. In addition, every two weeks a criticism class was held, at which time the students gave a résumé of their work before the entire school and received the criticism of faculty and students.[11]

It can be seen from the outline of the curriculum of the Stanhope-Wheatcroft School that the "practical" aspects excluded all fundamental work in voice, speech, pantomime, and theory. This school abhorred what Dion Boucicault had so fatuously called "hearth-rug tuition." Here there were no "frills" or "theory." Only the essentials of the actor, on the stage, and acting in a play, were considered. This was the predominant nature of the "practical" school.

The entire method of teaching at the Stanhope-Wheatcroft School was reminiscent of the traditions of a bygone era. Mrs. Wheatcroft apparently delighted in what teachers like Curry, Emerson, Sargent, MacKaye and Powers abhorred— imitation. Her entire system appears to have been based on the premise of the master-pupil relationship which Sargent so frequently maligned. Speaking of the initial work at her school, Mrs. Wheatcroft asserted:

> The first thing we do is to give each [student] a part to learn, and when these parts have been thoroughly memorized the students step out before the class and recite the part as they conceive it. They naturally make a good many mistakes at the start, and I correct them then. Then the student tries again, and *if he doesn't succeed in approximating the correct method after two or three trials, I do it myself to give the class a better idea as to how it should be done.* ("Adeline Stanhope-Wheatcroft," 15. Italics mine)

No clearer statement of the theoretical position could be made than was implied in Mrs. Wheatcroft's teaching method. The advocacy and practice of imitation, a time-honored tradition in the theatre, had clearly not fallen victim to the vituperation heaped upon the practice by the advocates of "the natural growth" of the student. Here, in The Stanhope-Wheatcroft School, can be seen the direct contradiction of the theory and practice of Sargent and Curry. While one may scoff at such methods as imitation, Mrs. Wheatcroft appeared to get results and retained the warm admiration of the bulk of the profession as a result. It is clear, however, that Mrs. Wheatcroft had quite definite ideas concerning the relationship of the actor to the play, character, and the audience. Her position appears to have been: "do as I do—be effective—act!"

Although Mrs. Wheatcroft was always concerned about the development of young playwrights, nothing concrete is mentioned about the relationship between the actor and the play. Nelson Wheatcroft made a regular practice of presenting students on the stage of the Empire Theatre in bills of short plays, many of which were being performed for the first time. Later, Mrs. Wheatcroft, as head of the school, gave acting instructor Rachel Crothers the opportunity not only to "jump in and act a part" but also to present her own original play.[12] One of these plays, *The Three of Us*, enjoyed its first public performance at the Stanhope-Wheatcroft School, and, from there, went on to a long run at the Madison Square Theatre (Tassin, 163). Commenting on her practice of producing original plays by young, untried playwrights, Mrs. Wheatcroft commented:

> Those [plays] we produce are mostly by young or inexperienced playwrights, you know, and they frequently require considerable revision and whipping into shape. ("Adeline Stanhope-Wheatcroft," 15)

Whether or not Mrs. Wheatcroft insisted that fidelity to the playwright's conceptions was the actor's primary consideration is questionable. She appears to have been quite emphatic about characterization as she conceived it in the play, and it is assumed that the end product of the student was the character as Adeline Wheatcroft conceived the playwright intended it. The traditions of the "practical" schools were firmly behind a faithful interpretation of what was thought to be the playwright's intention, and it seems probable that Mrs. Wheatcroft accepted this point of view.

The relationship between the actor and the character was considered after the initial experience wherein Mrs. Wheatcroft gave "the class a better idea as to how it should be done." Then, she said, "Following the mere delivery of the lines comes the conception and origination of the character" (*Ibid.*). In the section in which characterization was considered, the "criticism class" appears to have been of invaluable assistance to the student. Commenting on the class, Mrs. Wheatcroft said:

> One of the most interesting features of this part of the instruction is the criticism class, which is held twice a month. Two or three pupils act a scene and then the others criticise [*sic*] the performance. Many excellent ideas are brought out in this way, and the exercise always results in material improvement in the work of the pupil criticised [*sic*]. (*Ibid.*)

The nature of this class is unique in many ways. First, it appears to have placed the teacher and the pupil on a more equal plane—the teacher no longer being in the position of final and ultimate arbiter of taste. The class appears to have been an informal and communal moment when the entire student body and faculty could get together and exchange opinions and ideas for the mutual help of the students who were acting the scenes. This was indeed a democratic interlude in an otherwise authoritarian system. The "criticism class" served as a subsidiary class which operated in conjunction with courses in Modern Dramatic Art, Melodrama and Comedy, and Shakespeare.

The Stanhope-Wheatcroft School did believe in the "natural growth" of the student, but in different terms from Sargent, Curry, Emerson and Powers. Instead of conceiving "fundamentals" as beginning work in voice and body movement, Mrs. Wheatcroft accepted the idea of giving progressively more complex acting assignments. She kept to her basic position that a "practical" acting school gives training in "that work which is constantly in requisition on the stage itself." It was understood, therefore, that the "work" should always place the student "on the stage" and "in a scene" which was criticized.

First, as we have seen, Mrs. Wheatcroft had the student "recite" a selection. Then, gradually, the student was given a scene which was criticized by the entire group. As Mrs.

Wheatcroft explained: "When the rudiments have been surmounted we give the students scenes in standard plays, and they attempt to originate the part and create the proper atmosphere" (Ibid.). It appears that the period of greatest personal development of the student was the "acting of scenes" which were criticized by Mrs. Wheatcroft and her faculty in the course called Modern Dramatic Art. Undoubtedly, the criticism class which functioned in conjunction with the course proved invaluable to the actors, student critics, and the faculty. Here the actors had an opportunity to receive objective criticism from others besides the immediate instructor who supervised the work. In this way, the student was offered another method of learning besides the imitative.

"When a few months have been devoted to this training [work in scenes and the criticism class] we give a public appearance with the students" (Ibid.). The first matinee performance of the school usually was held in January ("The Stanhope-Wheatcroft School," 11). The second matinee performance was presented at the end of the school year, usually May. "A great deal of time and energy are expended in studying the parts and rehearsing, and the students look forward to the production with mingled feelings of anxiety and enthusiasm" ("Adeline Stanhope-Wheatcroft," 15). As might be expected, the production of the play or plays twice a year was the occasion toward which all the training had been aimed. The plays were directed by Mrs. Wheatcroft, and it can be imagined that the performance and acting turned out to be a good imitation of the way in which she would have done it had she been on the stage. The inclusion of the faculty in the plays frequently occurred, as indicated by the situation of Rachel Crothers. However, the entire production of the plays was mainly the responsibility of Mrs. Wheatcroft. The explanation of her responsibility for the production begs description, but it only serves to amplify why the production and acting were undoubtedly the product of her fertile mind and tremendous energy.

Concerning the routine of production Mrs. Wheatcroft commented:

> My own labors are not light. It is really a very difficult and anxious task to assume the responsibility and attend to all the details, great and small, of one of these public performances. It is not as if I had a company of experienced and self-confident actors and actresses to handle, or plays of certain merit. . . . I attend to the lighting and the setting of the scenes. I even ring up and ring down the curtain. (*Ibid.*)

It should be clear that the Stanhope-Wheatcroft School was different from the American Academy of Dramatic Arts in more ways than one! The curriculum, the size of the faculty, and finally, the production itself, indicate the reliance upon one woman—Mrs. Wheatcroft. Her methods, and the theory behind them, appear to have been that a good model, versed in all the intricacies of the craft, was better than all the "suggestions" in the world.

The philosophy of imitation was carried over to Stage Makeup, another course which Mrs. Wheatcroft taught. She conceived Makeup as "one more important part of the instruction," and explained her method as follows:

> I give a few preliminary hints, tell the class what to buy, and then let them learn from their own mistakes. I make up one face, with the others watching. Then they all leave the room and experiment. (*Ibid.*)

It is, perhaps, significant that trial and error was the method employed in makeup as well as in acting, with the teacher finally stepping in and demonstrating the "correct" technique. The idea of thoroughly explaining the theory behind the skill first, and then permitting the students to proceed toward some goal, seems never to have entered the mind of Mrs. Wheatcroft. This comment is not meant to be critical, but merely an observation of the old "trial and error" school of "hard knocks" and experience.

As a school of decidedly "practical" persuasion the Stanhope-Wheatcroft School maintained throughout its existence
the creed of its founder. "Mrs. Wheatcroft has carried to
perfection her late husband's idea in teaching real dramatic art
and preparing for actual stage work. *Mere theories are set aside,
and practical instruction is given by real actors, who can impart
better than others the exact knowledge that the student wants and
needs*" ("The Stanhope-Wheatcroft School," 15. Italics mine).

The Stanhope-Wheatcroft School and others like it represent just one part of the diversity of the American acting
school movement. It recognized the importance of training
prior to entering the profession, as opposed to coming "up
through the ranks." As Mrs. Wheatcroft explained, one year
of school training could make up for five years of the
traditional experience and give the student better preparation
for a career in the theatre. It should not diminish the
importance of the school that it possessed nothing more than
passionately-held ideas about acting rather than a fully articulated theory. It represented yet another successful attempt to
train actors "outside" the profession and is an example of the
experienced actor's faith in the acting school tradition.

CHAPTER VIII
THE NATIONAL DRAMATIC CONSERVATORY

The National Dramatic Conservatory was founded in New York in 1898 by F. F. Mackay, a well-known and highly respected character actor at such famous theatres as the Arch Street in Philadelphia, the Globe in Boston and the Union Square in New York City.[1] As early as 1888, Mackay expressed his faith in the idea of the acting school. The occasion was a rebuttal to Dion Boucicault which appeared in the *New York Dramatic Mirror.*[2] Boucicault had announced plans to unite with A. M. Palmer in the venture known as The Madison Square Theatre School of Instruction and attacked the position that aspiring actors were in need of training in theory, elocution, pantomime, and analysis before they un-

A distinguished and highly respected actor as well as a formidable teacher, F.F. Mackay operated his successful School, The National Dramatic Conservatory, for twenty-five years from 1898 until his death in 1923. (Photo courtesy of New York Public Library of the Performing Arts, Lincoln Center)

dertook actual stage work. His position was that the only worthwhile training for the young actor was practical work "on the stage."

Mackay attacked Boucicault immediately following the Irishman's statement of his beliefs. He defended the need for thorough training in elocution *before* the aspiring actor began his stage experience and training. Mackay summarized his position in the following manner:

> In conclusion, I would like to say that when the aspirant for dramatic honors through the art of acting has mastered his language, and through a knowledge of grammar and elocution knows how to express the emotion of a character, let him then go to the stage, for its traditions and mannerisms will not harm him, he will have learned that acting is not the art of preserving and representing stage traditions, but that the stage is merely the place for the exhibitions of his studies from nature through a dramatic author's creations.[3]

In 1888, then, Mackay had already committed himself to the idea of the acting school. Ten years later, he was to organize a school which was based on the theories he had discussed in his altercation with Boucicault. In the Fall of 1898 Mackay advertised the opening of his school in the *New York Dramatic Mirror* and commented: "The system of instruction is based on the principles taught at the Paris Conservatoire. Open all year. Class and Private Lessons."[4] Aiding Mackay in the enterprise was Eleanor Gorgen, who had taught in Sargent's school for over ten years.[5] The title of the new institution was The National Dramatic Conservatory and it endured from its beginning in 1898 until a few months before Mackay's death in 1923, at the age of ninety-one.

Any consideration of Mackay's acting theory must be predicated on an analysis of his book, *The Art of Acting*.[6] He began his approach to the theory of acting by first examining the contention that acting is an art. Mackay's definition of acting was that it is "The art of representing human emotions by a just expression of the artificial and natural language"

(*Ibid.*, 32). An elaborate and thorough definition of terms followed. First, Mackay contended, "Art is not Nature for the reason that Nature is *created* and Art is *made*," and again, "Art is not Nature for the reason that Nature *re-produces* . . . Art only *represents*" (*Ibid.*, 25–26). Seen in this light, the actor's function is "simply to re-arrange material already created. But to re-arrange—that is, to make—demands a mental and physical force, and, therefore, art is the result of the application of the impressional force to mental conceptions through muscular action" (*Ibid.*, 26). Mackay concluded: "Acting does something. It makes something. Acting makes physical pictures of mental conceptions. . . . It results from a constant application of mental force to a physical effect, in the *re-presentations* of Nature" (*Ibid.*, 32).

Pursuing his definition, Mackay considered the remaining portions, "by the just expression of artificial and natural language." By the word "just," Mackay meant "its ordinary interpretation as meaning correct, true." Expression, Mackay considered at some length.

> The word 'expression' in its original sense means 'to send out' or to 'push out.' Thus, we find that the just expression of an emotion means to enunciate, to utter the artificial language, so harmoniously blended with the natural language as to present to the mind a true physical picture of the emotion. (*Ibid.*, 83)

"Natural language," he said, "is made up of the tones of the voice with all the variations of the modes of utterance, qualities of the voice, force, stress, inflections, and time, together with the gesticulations and positions of the body" (*Ibid.*, 83–84). Mackay regarded natural language as being "the tones of the voice, the gesticulations and positions of the body . . . [which] all people of whatever nation understand, without special instruction" (*Ibid.*, 84). Artificial language was regarded by Mackay as being the system of signs and symbols that require instruction and learning. He thought of artificial language as consisting of written language "because it is

made. We must study it and agree as to what it shall mean"
(*Ibid.*).

Mackay's definition of acting and its function clearly
indicates that he was distinctly in disagreement with the
position that the actor is a "creative artist." The actor
"represents," he does not create. As such, the actor "rear-
ranges" material that has already been created in life. This
view of the actor was in direct opposition to the ideas of
Sargent, Curry, Emerson and, to a degree, Powers.

The relationship of the actor to the play, to Mackay's way of
thinking, was the first, and perhaps the most important
criterion in acting. Mackay was so insistent in his idea that the
actor must be true to the author's intentions that he relegated
the actor to a position inferior to the playwright.

> Because the artist sometimes gives scope to his imagina-
> tion and thereby seems to enhance the value of the
> author's work, some people are inclined to think that
> actors create characters; but the art of acting is not
> creative. The author arranges emotions and the actor
> illustrates them. The actor through his science studies
> the emotions that the author has described, and by his
> art he represents them. (*Ibid.*, 295–296)

Understood in this context, Mackay appears to tie the actor to
the text of the play and refuses to permit him to draw upon his
own imaginative instincts. Mackay also appears to deny
absolutely the right of the actor to draw upon his own feelings
concerning the character. This, naturally, could lead to a
number of paradoxes. Mackay flatly stated that the actor
should not present "the character as the actor thinks he
should be," but "as a positive matter of fact, deduced from the
text and situation" (*Ibid.*, 294). The basic point of Mackay's
idea concerning the relationship of the actor to the play is
clearly that "true study of dramatic character lies entirely
within the dramatic author's text" (*Ibid.*, 292). While
Mackay's concern for the truthful representation of the
author's text would be considered laudable, the limitations

which he places upon the actor appear quite restrictive. His idea that acting was basically the "imitation of facts" which the playwright has written down implies that the actor receives *all* from the playwright and draws nothing from his own experience, instincts or imagination.

Mackay warned the aspiring actor against what he considered "idealizing" a character. "This," he said, was an "imitation of facts . . . blended with *fancy*" (*Ibid.*, 294. Italics mine). He considered this approach to the character as "really nothing more than presenting the character as the actor thinks he should be instead of presenting it as a positive matter of fact, deduced from the text and situation." This restriction does, of course, seem to eliminate the human quality from the actor. How else can an actor represent a character, but as he thinks he should be? An actor has nothing else to draw upon other than his own feelings, imagination, intelligence, and experience. How can he "know" what the author intended? The actor can merely say, "This is what I *think* the playwright means." He cannot ultimately "know" in the sense that his interpretation is infallibly what the playwright intended. Mackay appears to accept the position that through analysis of character and the speeches of the character, one can reach the *absolute* truth of the playwright's conceptions, apparently without accepting the concept of the symbolic ambiguity of a text. In essence, however, Mackay is reaffirming the supreme position of the playwright in his acting theory.

In the actor's relationship to the character in the play, it is assumed by Mackay that the "artist should make himself as familiar with the natural language of all emotions of the human mind as he is with his native tongue" (*Ibid.*, 289). Thus, the actor must be physically, vocally, and mentally capable of expressing any and all emotional signs before he approaches the part. After this preparation in the fundamentals of acting the actor was warned:

> In order to apply the factors of expression correctly, it
> follows that one must be able to analyze for the true

meaning of the dramatic author's words, phrases, and sentences. Every sentence in a purely dramatic composition not only has its grammatical construction, through the study of which one arrives at the author's logical conclusions, but there must always be a recognition of the sensation underlying the very words or signs of sensation. The outcome of this sensation constitutes the emotional part, through a harmonious blending of the artificial with the natural language that the actor must strive for. (*Ibid.*, 290)

In other words, Mackay wanted the actor to strive for an intellectual understanding of the emotional aspects of the play as well as a comprehension of its "logical" elements. Mackay clarified the actor's approach to the emotional understanding of the character in the following:

How shall he obtain a knowledge of the emotional part of the dramatic character? Here begins the severe work of the artist; for the emotional nature of the dramatic character cannot be fully known until the artist has a clear conception of the psychology or mentality of the character, *which conception can only be received by the artist through logical deduction made by an analytical study of the grammatical construction of the author's sentence.* (*Ibid.*, 290–291. Italics mine)

Mackay conceived feeling to be unreliable and certainly not a faculty for making correct conclusions about the psychology of the character. He held that only the intellect could function properly, since all analysis of the character's pattern of thought and emotion could only be decided through "logical deduction" reached through a study of the script.

Mackay's position concerning the relationship of the actor to the audience must naturally spring from the material already presented. Mackay believed that the audience must be completely affected, both emotionally and intellectually, by the imitation of the author's conception of character through the actor. If the playwright did not write a realistic play, however, it is assumed that the actor must react according to the playwright's demands. Generally, Mackay accepted that while the actor must remain completely objective toward the character, he must still subjugate his identity. If he did not, the audience would be aware of this fact and the actor would be presenting himself before the audience and not the "representation" which the playwright intended. It would appear, therefore, that Mackay's concern for perfect imitation would rule out any sort of "contact" with the audience by the actor. The actor portraying character must ignore the presence of the audience in order to enhance the illusion.

Mackay's contention that the actor's function is to represent and not create has a somewhat stultifying effect on the function of the imagination in acting. "Imagination," said Mackay, "is that part of our mental action which, while it grows out of the truthful observation of realities, refuses to be limited by logical conclusions, and reaches out into infinite space for expansion" (*Ibid.*, 294). Mackay saw the imagination as functioning mainly as a faculty of comparison. Its operation was intended to supply the actor with visual comparison of reality and the product of the actor's expression. Mackay observed:

> Wonder, not always an agreeable sensation, may be the outcome of great eccentricity in this factor in mental picture making [imagination]; but true pleasure, satisfaction, repose for mentality, will result only when the works of the imagination bear so strong a resemblance to nature that the mind immediately recognizes a standard for comparison in its parts or as a whole. (*Ibid.*)

Understood in this sense, the imagination appears to be more an intellectual instrument whose basis is judgment, and is related to fanciful "picture making" that must correspond to reality as the author sees life. "The dramatic art may be idealized by this power; but the imagination of the actor must be so versatile and supple as to be always a *truthful* elaboration of the author's works in any given direction" (*Ibid.*, 295. Italics mine).

Imaginative reality in terms of the author's work was the extent to which the faculty could be applied. Mackay warned the actor:

> If versatility or suppleness of imagination be wanting, the actor will not only pervert the author, but will fall into the habit of re-presenting his own individuality, and so produce that quality in his art called 'sameness.' (*Ibid.*)

The imagination, therefore, was taken from the realm of the intuitive and instinctive and placed firmly in the realm of the practical. In acting, the imagination must always work within the framework of the play, and must be consciously under the watchful eye of judgment lest it become too fanciful and fail to compare favorably with the author's text.

Mackay had an intellectual attitude toward the function of emotion in acting. This attitude was predicated on the contention that a good or great actor does not "feel" his part, but imitates the external manifestation of feelings. In the great nineteenth-century argument between Irving and Coquelin, Mackay is emphatically on the side of the Frenchman (*Ibid.*, 25). Mackay's approach to the subject of emotion in acting was similar to Coquelin's method of approaching every aspect of acting. He described feeling as "that sense that places human nature in or out of sympathy with its surroundings whether mental or physical" (*Ibid.*, 31). Mackay stated the position that feeling is in no way related to intellect or judgment.

> Feeling is one of the senses common to animal life. It is a faculty in human nature on which no one relies— except for first impressions—when he can bring his judgement to bear, or have the advantage of deductions made by comparisons. (*Ibid.*)

Mackay believed, however, that emotion was "a faculty absolutely necessary to the art of acting." Feeling was "absolutely a motor to art; for as taste prompts to the selection, so does feeling prompt to doing. But as power without proper direction may destroy the very object for whose advancement it is raised, so feeling uncontrolled may make a lunatic instead of an artist. The modern crank [the actor who claims to "feel" his role] is a result of misdirected feeling" (*Ibid.*).

Instead of "feeling" the emotion, Mackay substituted "earnestness in doing the imitation" (*Ibid.*, 35). By this he meant that the actor must be totally aware, at all times, that he is an actor imitating the *external* signs of emotion. Mackay would ask, "Is it possible that Mme. B's [Bernhardt] Camille is only an imitation—a sham? Yes 'tis true—and no pity 'tis true—Mme. B's Camille is a sham, but the presentation is good, solid, earnest work—a severe tax on nerve and muscle for the evening" (*Ibid.*). Mackay's whole point was merely this:

> But who knows it? Not the audience; for if the audience can for a moment think that the artist is not suffering . . . then Mme. B's performance is a failure in the art of acting, which must be a perfect imitation of nature. (*Ibid.*, 36)

In general, most theorists of acting would agree with Mackay concerning the *ends* of acting. However, the great conflict arises over the *means* employed to achieve the ends. Mackay is firmly in the camp of the anti-emotionalists in acting.

"Not only does the theory of acting by feeling retard the art by obscuring from the actors the necessity of study," said Mackay, "but it must necessarily often destroy the intention of the author. . . " (*Ibid.*, 43). Mackay's point appears to be that the actor can trust his intellect more than he can depend on his feeling in matters of interpretation. He firmly believed that the actor "will find a more truthful conception of a dramatic situation or speech by seeking for it through the functions of memory and comparison than by groping for it through the operation of feeling (*Ibid.*, 46).

Unlike Sargent and Curry, Mackay found little profit in training the imagination so that it would produce "true" feeling. His reasons are quite obvious. First, Mackay did not view imagination as the "synthesizing agent" of art. Secondly, he saw no possible way for the feeling to be controlled in a spontaneous situation. He was not able, nor did he care, to consider the possibility that the imagination operated in such a way as to control the nature and expression of feeling. As a result, he believed that feeling must be controlled by "judgement and comparison" which, to Mackay, was the same as saying that feeling must "look like" but not actually "be" feeling. Mackay summed up his position in the following analogy:

> It is by the public in general contended that in order to make the auditor feel, the orator and actor must feel the sensation he is portraying. The fallacy of this argument may be illustrated thus: The farmer plants his crop of corn in the springtime. When the corn sprout rises above the ground an inch or two the crow comes from the adjacent forest and plucks it up to get the sweet swollen kernel. To frighten the crow the farmer takes a suit of old clothes, stuffs it with straw, puts a pair of boots on the legs, a hat on the top and hangs it up or stands it up in the cornfield. The crow, seeing the figure of a man, flies away. May we not fairly assume that the crow flies away because it feels fear? What does the figure of the man feel that produced the fear in the crow? Nothing. The more perfect the sign, the stronger will be the responsive sensation. Now add to the actor the love of approbation as a driving force and the tone, pose and gesture are the signs of the author's mental intention. (*Ibid.*, 42–43)

The operation of the emotions were considered thus:

> Every circumstance—every environment—that affects self-love, either by elating or by depressing the mind, must produce its effect through the force of impression, begetting a sensation in the nerve system, presents exterior signs which we call emotion. It will thus be seen that an emotion is made up of three parts, impression, sensation, and exterior action—expression. (*Ibid.*, 70–71)

The actor was asked to study emotion, not from the standpoint of familiarity which the actor might have with "feeling" the emotion, but the effects which his exterior expression has on the audience. Mackay's system was based on a speculative, pseudo-scientific view of emotion and its operation.

> Emotions are either elating, and therefore tensive in their muscular action, or they are depressing and consequently relaxing to the muscular system. Again, each emotion is a sign of good or evil intention; therefore emotions are either benevolent or they are malevolent. (*Ibid.*, 71)

If one were prepared to accept these statements as fact, Mackay proceeded with the following example.

> For example: Joy is a benevolent emotion, tensive in its action—a bold, abrupt, strong outburst of self-love, proclaiming its gratification and satisfaction with exterior circumstances—past or present environments. (*Ibid.*)

Such generalizations of the expressional and impressional aspects of emotions were applied by Mackay to all forms of feeling. In turn, Mackay observed the mode of expression and the effects it has on the receiver, beginning with "Benevolent Emotions, Malevolent Emotions, Tensive and Elating Emotions, Relaxing and Depressing Emotions, and Restive Emotions" (*Ibid.*, 71–75). The entire basis for the study of emotion was to familiarize the actor with the effect his expression had upon the audience and the effect on the character he might portray.

> Study of the action of an impression is an absolute necessity if the artist would know how to imitate the effect through the dramatic author's medium, his words and sentences. (*Ibid.*, 75)

Mackay was confident that under the control of the mind, the external signs of emotion could be imitated to perfection.

> We know that acting is doing something; and we know
> that doing is the result of muscular force under mental
> control; and we know that under mental control muscle
> can be trained to do anything. (*Ibid.*, 55–56)

The function of the intellect was far-reaching in the acting
theory of F. F. Mackay. It was all-pervasive, indeed was the
cohesive force in the study of acting and the faculty most
responsible for the selection of the appropriate emotional
sign to be expressed to the audience. Thus, intellect functioned as a faculty of taste for the selection of proper feeling
for expression.

> Although the function of taste in acting is as genuine as
> it would necessarily be in the selection of this or that
> kind of discourse for a serious or joyous occasion . . . yet
> the feeling that appears, or seems to be, in acting, is not
> necessarily the genuine sensation of the emotion of the
> dramatic character represented, but a likeness of the
> emotion in accordance with the actor's conception of his
> author's presentation. (*Ibid.*, 32–33)

The consciousness of the act of judgment is forcefully shown
in the following statement:

> In the art of acting, sensation may be absent but
> judgement resulting from observation and comparison
> must, through the faculty of memory, and the mimetic
> force, direct the physical action so as to produce a
> likeness of emotion. (*Ibid.*, 33)

Taste functions in the following manner:

> Taste is the result of mental action. It may be inherent
> and it may be cultivated and its function is to accept or
> reject, to approve or disapprove of a thing already made.
> Taste never makes anything—it never does anything
> except to select or to reject, for its own gratification.
> Taste is a mental quality and not a factor in physical
> force. Taste is a kind of censor that sits in judgement on
> all exterior circumstances of life; and its services are just

> as necessary to the acknowledged arts or Poetry, Music
> and Painting as to the disputed art of Acting. (*Ibid.*,
> 30–31)

Taste, then, is in no way related to the intuitive. It is the mind's ability to make comparisons and choices of external emotional signs in acting which can be cultivated, or learned, through applied observation and study. It is completely intellectual and absolutely necessary to good acting.

The intellect also functioned in the realm of analysis of both the script and the character. In the traditions of the elocutionary movement, Mackay was greatly interested in "correct" analysis of the playwright's ideas. First, "The actor must comprehend the logic of the author's sentences" (*Ibid.*, 291). Secondly, "He must know the mentality of the character; for if he does not know the mentality of the character, he cannot know what emotions are to be portrayed." Thirdly, the actor must be a scholar, especially adept at grammar and analysis of mental states through the artificial language of the playwright. "Other things being equal, the better scholar will always be the better artist." The actor's intellect enables him to understand, through an analytical process, the artificial language of the playwright and to better employ the artificial language and blend it with the natural language of emotional expression.

> It is the presentation of this emotional part, through a
> harmonious blending of the artificial with the natural
> language that the actor must strive for. (*Ibid.*, 290)

Analysis, then, furnishes the actor with the logical evidence to support his conclusions, the "correct" mental states and the specific techniques of emotional expression.

Mackay's attitude toward technique embodied two areas: the learning of the fundamentals and the actual application. In defense of his attitude regarding the emphasis of technique in acting, Mackay commented:

In nearly all discussions on technique, there has been expressed the fear that technique, if pursued with special care, might destroy or cover up the true meaning of the phrase or sentence to which it is applied. This fear is fancy to be discarded; for technique is nothing more than the premeditated use of the forms of the voice, pose and gesture, through which sensation presents itself in nature. (*Ibid.*, 56–57)

Mackay was quite emphatic in his distrust of the methods which he understood to be impulsive.

It is not improbable to thinking people that some teachers of elocution object to technique because they rather choose to rely on the impulse of the moment, than do the mental and physical drudgery of training themselves in this kind of work. But 'nothing can come of nothing,' and even genius cannot impart its specialty except by a deliberately systematized mental action expressed in physical illustration. (*Ibid.*, 60–61)

Mackay did not pursue his ideas concerning genius, but the implication appears to be that genius abhorred the intuitive and impulsive and preferred premeditated, systematized planning of the imitation of external signs of emotion.

There is a science underlying all truthful acting; and, therefore, acting is both a science and an art. As a science it recognizes emotion, dissects it, arranges it, and presents for study the factors that produce it. As an art it puts into practice the appropriate natural and artificial means by which an emotion can be expressed. (*Ibid.*, 61)

Voice, speech, and movement were studied from the basic premise that the signs of emotion could be classified, systematized and studied objectively. Because the emotions and their external signs were conceived to be the "natural" language of mankind, they were universally "true" under any and all circumstances. The actor's purpose was to acquire sufficient ability to recall and imitate as many as possible. Then, when the actor was confronted with a script, he would be able to bring to bear mimetic skills, both vocal and pantomimic, and through a careful analysis, determine the most appropriate signs for the occasion as dictated by the playwright's script.

As an example of the fundamental training in technique, Mackay listed the emotions of joy, grief, anger, etc., and then described what occurred as a result of impression. He employed voice, speech, and movement as the stimuli for his analysis. For instance, concerning the effect of the voice on the audience's emotions Mackay had this to say:

> We hear this effect of the voice in all themes of tenderness—sentiments of love and friendship. With light force it prevails in the language of melancholy, and awakens sympathy in the tones of regret. And even when force or loudness of voice is applied to the words, this form of stress has the power to prevent the mind of the auditor from dwelling on the facts in a statement by impressing the hearer with a conception of intense feeling on the part of the speaker, which conception begets feeling in the listener, sometimes overwhelming the judgement. The mind loses its power of comparison and the auditor often responds in an uncontrolled outburst of feeling in harmony with the speaker. (*Ibid.*, 80)

"This effect of the voice" of which Mackay spoke was "an effect in speaking, produced by the application of force to the middle of the sound—a kind of crescendo and diminuendo movement of the voice, which being musical in its nature has a soothing, quieting influence on the auditor" (*Ibid.*, 78–80). Mackay proceeded to list a series of techniques of voice which were designed to arouse a specific effect that held true for all audiences. Voice, or the sound of the utterance, was considered by Mackay to be a part of natural language because it impressed the auditor and caused a sensation which he called emotion.

Speech, both articulation and pronunciation, was vastly important because it carried the "logical message" of the playwright. It was conceived by Mackay as being the artificial language of man, a system of signs upon which men agreed for the purpose of better understanding.

> To neglect articulation and pronunciation is to throw away two powerful assistants to the dramatic art; for, with perfection in articulation, the sounds, by the muscular action of the lips and tongue, are compacted and driven through the auditorium of a theatre to strike the auricular nerve of the auditor with a proper effect, like a bullet sent to the bulls-eye of a target. (*Ibid.*, 91–92)

Speech, then, was considered to be the necessary conveyance for logical thought, and its lack of effectiveness considerably hampered the clarity of the playwright's intentions. The body constituted the other form of natural language.

> Gesticulation and position include all the actions and all the postures of the entire human body. Whatever may be the exterior prompting to action or repose; and they are therefore a part of expression. Because these factors of expression may be truthfully suggestive even while the vernacular of the speaker is not understood, they constitute a part of natural language. Just as one may recognize distress in the vocality or gladness in laughter, so may one recognize mental intents and physical sensations in the gestures and poses of the body. (*Ibid.*, 190–191)

Mackay recognized the necessity of gesture and pose in acting, but his general attitude appears to be that the voice is the most important conveyance of emotion. The operation of gesture and pose is similar to that outlined for the voice.

> All human action must be the outcome of mental impressions and physical sensations; and as the impression is always an effect of some exterior circumstance, past or present, it will be readily seen that gesture, like any other part of expression, should not be without cause. There can be no motive without force. In gesture

the force results from impression, and action is the
result of force in motion. . . . There is a time and a place
for everything. That time and place in gesture and
position may be summed up in the word 'fitness.' (*Ibid.*,
191)

Mackay did not develop his idea of "fitness," although his
general attitude regarding natural language of pantomime
would appear to be similar to his position regarding the voice.
That is, just as there are certain sounds which will have
predicted results, "There are some positions and gestures that
are so common that all people readily understand their
meaning" (*Ibid.*, 193).

While Mackay does not say that it is possible to "classify
and systematize" the outward signs of bodily expression, the
implications are undeniably present. Mackay gave a multitude
of examples of gesture and pose which are common to all
people. He prescribed positions which he believed were the
best outward sign of the state. For "repose" he listed the
following positions:

Repose of body is expressed by simply throwing the
weight of the body on one leg, the feet remaining in the
same position while the knee of the opposite leg is
relaxed or bent a little. Moving the released foot
forward will express aggressiveness, while a step to the
rear must mean retreat. Each foot according to the
governing circumstance. The extension of any of these
positions will depend upon the force of the emotional
sensation of which the action is the outcome. (*Ibid.*,
194–195)

From the many examples which Mackay employed to
illustrate his point of view toward technique, it is amply clear
that his theory of acting verged on the mechanical. Certainly,
Mackay would have been the first to deny that it was
mechanical, but from his manner of analysis of the characters
in the script and the description of the external signs of
emotion in both movement and voice, there is always the

implication that *his* analysis is the most acceptable and the external signs which *he* suggested were the most appropriate. Mackay would not stand for imitation of another actor, however, and when it came to the representation of a character on the stage, he would say, "go to nature" ("F.F. Mackay," *N.Y. Dramatic Mirror*, August 7, 1897, 2). Mackay's suspicion of "idealizing" and his emphasis on observation and accuracy of detail lead one to conclude that he considered acting to be the closest possible imitation of actual reality. While he did insist on loyalty to the playwright's intention, there is a strong tendency to treat even Shakespeare quite realistically. For Mackay there was one yardstick of good acting: Was it "a true, visible, auricular picture of the author's conceptions?" (Mackay, *The Art of Acting*, 94). Mackay leaned toward a realistic portrayal of actuality, but since he believed that the playwright dictated the form, one must conclude that he was eclectic in his ideas concerning the relationship of art to nature.

TEACHING METHODS

The course work at Mackay's National Dramatic Conservatory in 1900 included Vocal Gymnastics, Techniques of Speech, Dancing, Fencing, Swedish Gymnastics, Analysis of Emotions, Reading and Rehearsing Plays, and General and Dramatic Literature. This basic curriculum remained unchanged throughout the duration of the school. The nature of the course work and the titles indicate a very intimate relationship between Mackay's textbook, *The Art of Acting*, and the methods of teaching at the National Dramatic Conservatory.

Mackay's book, like the course work, began with the fundamentals of dramatic art. In the one-year course (like Mrs. Wheatcroft, Mackay believed that the aspiring actor could be trained in a year's time), Mackay first taught Vocal and Swedish Gymnastics. These two courses were designed to "free the channels" of expression. The manner in which the courses were taught, however, differed greatly from the methods employed by Sargent, Curry, and Emerson. While no course description of Swedish Gymnastics exists, it is known that these exercises were designed more for physical culture than for acting. Exercises were taught to accomplish the limbering of the muscles, teach proper posture and bearing, and rectify awkwardness by developing grace. There is no indication that they resembled Sargent's, Curry's or Emerson's method of movement motivated by "thought." These exercises were purely technical and designed to instill physical freedom, continuity, and confidence in movement.

Vocal Gymnastics was a phrase borrowed from the Murdoch-Rush system of vocal expression. In many ways, Mackay's ideas concerning voice are quite similar to those taught by Murdoch as amplified in his book, *Analytic Elocution*.[7] This book carefully analyzed, in what was called "a scientific" manner, the vocal and speech sounds of the English language. Murdoch was extremely interested in categorizing sound and its effect on the audience. Such sounds as *orotund, stentorian, pectoral* and *guttural* were thought to have predictable and definite effects upon an audience, and the study of the voice was the study of imitating these sounds in the appropriate situations for the desired effect. Mackay's book is filled with examples of speeches which he conceived as demanding a specific sound of voice to achieve the maximum effect upon the audience. Students studied, analyzed and practiced the speeches employing the various sounds in the appropriate selections. This method, it was assumed, would give the aspiring actor vocal flexibility, an analytical formula and a technique of expression.

Techniques of Speech was primarily devoted to articulation, although Mackay was also interested in pronunciation. He frequently mentioned that correct pronunciation was expected of the actor and that the latest dictionary was the ultimate source for correct pronunciation. Mackay had conceived his own system of vowel and consonant division. His interest in the relationship of correct articulation of sounds and a free and flexible voice was similar to that of other elocutionists of the period. It is assumed that Techniques of Speech was taught in a somewhat imitative manner, since it depended upon training the ear of the actor so that he might retain the *correct* enunciation of the sound and the ability of the teacher to criticize the accuracy of the produced sound.

Analysis of Emotions appears to have been quite intimately related to his text, *The Art of Acting*. The material which was presented in Mackay's theories of emotion appears quite representative of the course content. The students were first lectured on the subject of emotion in general, with careful definitions. Then, Mackay introduced them to the "tensive" and "relaxive" emotions, which he listed and categorized in a quite definite manner. It was assumed by Mackay that no involvement of feeling should be experienced by the student. Consequently, the course work in Analysis of Emotions was probably confined to the listing of the various emotions and systematizing them into categories such as "Benevolent Emotions," "Malevolent Emotions," "Relaxing and Depressing Emotions," "Tensive and Elating Emotions," *etc.*

This part of the student's training was designed to employ the "fundamental" work of the courses in Vocal Gymnastics, Swedish Gymnastics, Techniques of Speech, Dancing, and Fencing. These "fundamental" courses had, theoretically, laid the groundwork by freeing the vocal and physical mechanism so that it was completely pliable. The course work in Analysis of Emotions tested the student's ability to imitate the external signs of emotion through voice and movement. The study of "tones" of the voice was, at this time, applied to a specific emotional expression. It was assumed that the student was sufficiently conversant with the "tones" of the voice so as to be able to apply appropriate expression of emotion.

Mackay had the system of acting organized into what he called a "science." Operating on the premise that certain sounds and movements were understood by all people regardless of environment or nationality, Mackay conceived that it was quite possible to be infallible with regard to expression of emotion. He was not, however, ignorant of the fact that there are certain subtleties of expression and combinations of expression that would defy systematizing. He would then send the student to observe similar phenomena and to learn to reproduce the expression. Mackay also believed that his "system" could be utilized for the more subtle expressions by employing combinations of the more general categories.

General and Dramatic Literature was basically a course in analysis. Again, his book is invaluable since it gives vivid clues to Mackay's methods. He believed that the actor *must* subjugate his ideas to the playwright's conceptions. Consequently, any course which proposed to teach basic techniques in analysis must have been considered of great importance. If Mackay's book can serve as a guide to his methods, it must be said that while Mackay showed deep insight into character, he appears to suggest that *his* interpretation is the correct one. His book is filled with specific suggestions to the aspiring actor concerning how best to interpret a role. In this sense, Mackay appears to cling to the traditional way of training actors. While he does not particularly refer to the manner of portrayal by a specific actor, he implied that there was one correct interpretation—his. Mackay believed that imitation of other actors was absolutely wrong, but it appears that he found it satisfactory for the student to accept his interpretation of a character. It is unfortunate that Mackay's methods cannot be recreated, since speculation will never replace facts. Perhaps Mackay was not so insistent about his own interpretations and analyses. However, the evidence of his well-considered opinion in the text, *The Art of Acting,* indicates the opposite conclusion.

Reading and Rehearsal of Plays was the final course offering of the National Dramatic Conservatory. Mackay's ideas concerning the value of training in the acting school situation appear to have been similar to those of most elocutionists of the period. He was definitely opposed to performances *during* the period of training. Algernon Tassin quoted Mackay as having said "the first round of applause kills the student for classroom work."[8] Consequently, Mackay permitted public performances by his students only at the conclusion of their training. Unlike Sargent, Mackay believed that once the student "felt" the presence of an audience, he was prepared to abandon his training. It was only when the student had fulfilled his period of "training" and learned the basic fundamentals that Mackay would permit a performance.

The teaching methods of the National Dramatic Conservatory did not completely adopt the idea of a graded curriculum with each course taught by a specialist in the field, although Mackay shared teaching responsibilities with Eleanor Gorgen, who taught the movement course. In basic idea, Mackay elevated the teacher as a kind of master who was the final arbiter of the manner and modes of interpretation and delivery. While there was an intimate master-pupil relationship, the teacher does not appear so much as guide who made suggestions and provoked thought, as he does honored critic whose opinions were valued because of experience.

The value of Mackay's experience was obviously appreciated, since his school managed to stay in existence for over twenty-five years, and then closed only because of his death. The classes at the National Dramatic Conservatory were always small, and the total number of students in any given year never exceeded thirty.[9] Mackay believed that he had found the best means of training actors for the stage and frequently asserted that the methods exposited in his book, *The Art of Acting,* were the most effective in developing a true dramatic artist.[10]

He trained such recognized stars of the period as Kathryn Kidder and Harriet Ford, but it should not be overlooked that Mackay, like so many directors of other acting schools, was primarily interested in preparing the rank and file of the acting profession. Because of the thoroughness of its training methods and the quality of the graduates, Mackay's National Dramatic Conservatory was acknowledged as one of the three "leading dramatic schools" in America.[11]

Mackay appears to have added little to the development of teaching methods of acting and his approach resembles that of the elocutionists of the period. Mackay believed that acting could be reduced to an exact science and the principles of that science could be applied to delivery. His ideas concerning the relationship of his theories to practice appear to have been consistent, with intellect and analysis, control of emotion, and faithfulness to the playwright's conceptions as the basis of his theory and methods of teaching. His faith in what he considered to be the "scientific" validity of his theories tended to make his teaching methods "mechanical." For Mackay, the art of acting was reducible to a clear-cut system, and once the actor succeeded in imitating the external signs of the system, he was considered competent to enter the ranks of the professional actor.

Mackay's contributions to acting theory rest on the fact that he was one of America's foremost proponents of the intellectual or "anti-feeling" method of acting, and firmly stated that Coquelin was correct in his position concerning acting. Mackay was an intellectual in a country of emotionalists. His textbook is one of the few, besides Powers', in the entire period that maintained that intellect, not feeling, was the key to acting.

In many ways, Mackay represented the passing of an old and honored tradition in acting, insisting that "impulsive" theorists were wrong. He was a teacher in the tradition of Murdoch and Vandenhoff and one of the last in a long line of distinguished actors, trained by elocutionary methods, who successfully competed with the modern trends of the "impulsive" school. At the same time, his school's theoretical position was considerably more developed than that of any "practical" school of the period and possessed a much more comprehensive theory and method than any "mechanical" or elocutionary system which preceded it. The National Dramatic Conservatory was highly successful in its attempts to train the aspiring actor, and its place in the professional acting school movement adds emphasis to the diversity of the phenomenon.

CONCLUSION

Motivated by a deep desire to raise the standards of acting and believing that the theatre had a significant social and aesthetic purpose, the American professional acting schools held that acting was an art and that it possessed principles that could be taught. Generally, the schools founded on the "speculative" ideas of the Delsarte system subscribed to a varied curriculum taught by experts in their field, a revolutionary and distinctly original American conception for acting training. The more "practical" schools advocated either an adaptation of the stock company tradition or elocutionary methods. All the schools believed that a theory of acting was an essential foundation whether or not such principles embraced a philosophical or a pragmatic view of acting. Further, all were convinced that certain principles form the basis of acting and should be mastered *prior* to entering the profession. The schools were convinced that if actors received thorough grounding and training in their craft, the theatre would be better served and the profession of acting would be respected in common with other established professions.

These views, then, formed the basis for the emergence of "a new school of dramatic art" in America in the last quarter of the nineteenth century. The period between 1875 and 1925 saw a revolution in actor training that was unprecedented in the history of the American theatre. The schools recognized that the time-honored tradition of "learning on the job" was no longer viable, since the resident stock company was in decline and the long run had supplanted the repertory system. While there were still a few resident companies during this period, the American theatre faced a unique situation: the public's burgeoning demand for theatre required more competent actors than were available in the theatrical centers of the nation. The consequence of this dilemma literally required the emergence of the acting school.

Initially, there was a great deal of resistance to the concept of training actors in a setting apart from the stage, much less training actors prior to entering the profession. But since the tradition of apprenticing to a stock company was nearly impossible, the profession grudgingly accepted the upstart schools, especially when reliable professionals were also offering such instruction. Also, when graduates of the schools proved capable of assuming positions in professional companies and plays, the prejudice against such training dwindled. As the century closed, the schools were a significant source of new talent for the theatre and their contributions slowly won qualified acceptance. "The new school of dramatic art" had secured a place in the American theatre. But perhaps the most remarkable aspect of the schools which emerged and flourished during the period under investigation, especially those with a more theoretical bent, is that they were teaching, writing about, and exploring many areas so often reserved as the domain of Stanislavsky.

Although the "practical" schools stated that "one year" was sufficient to grasp the principles of acting, the "speculative" schools believed that it took much longer. It goes without saying that the schools never encouraged students to believe they were accomplished actors after the completion of training; they recognized that acting requires a lifetime of learning. The "speculative" schools ranged widely in their views concerning actor training. The American Academy of Dramatic Arts and The School of the Spoken Word had two-year programs; Curry required two years of expressional work and at least a year of specialized training in acting, while Emerson's School of Oratory required four years including the study of acting. Steele MacKaye wrote in several places that to learn the fundamentals of acting, a student could not complete the task in under four years.

All the schools subscribed to the tenet that the play was supreme in its integrity. Consequently, they eschewed exhibitionism and acting that selfishly diminished the play's central position in the theatre. All the actor's energies were devoted to interpreting the character and serving the idea of the play. "Love the art in yourself, not yourself in the art," said Stanislavsky, and all the schools subscribed to that dictum.

They preceded Stanislavsky's belief that relaxation was essential not only in initial training but in the performance itself. All the "speculative" and one of the "practical" schools possessed some system within their training methods to assist relaxation, a principle considered absolutely critical for the freedom necessary for spontaneous acting. The schools also subscribed to the principle that before one can learn, one must unlearn bad habits. Consequently, all the "speculative" schools had elaborate exercises for (1) uncovering bad habits, and (2) replacing them with habits that were constructively designed to "open the channels of expression." MacKaye, Sargent, Curry and Emerson demanded that each exercise must be validated through a motive and a defined objective behind each physical act.

All of the schools taught that the actor must accept the imaginative reality of the play wholeheartedly, recalling Stanislavsky's "Magic If." All but two of the schools subscribed to the position that the actor should experience the emotions of the character. They also believed that the actor must "yield" or surrender completely to the character as well as to the imaginative reality of the play. All but two of the schools believed that the actor must identify with the character, think and feel *as* the character and totally take on the physical and psychic processes of the role. This theoretical position accomplished two quite important functions: first, it provided the actor with the focal point of concentration; and second, it enabled the actor to maintain a form of "public solitude" as a result of concentration on an objective. As well, concentration liberated both body and mind from tension during performance. Several of the "speculative" schools possessed the best developed and clearest discussion of the process which Stanislavsky later developed in even greater detail.

Several schools, notably Sargent's American Academy of Dramatic Art, Curry's School of Expression and Emerson's School of Oratory, anticipated "emotional" or "affective memory" by several decades. To my knowledge no credit is given to a specific psychologist (except William James), although all mentioned that they were strongly influenced by the "latest" theories. These three schools trained actors to return to their real-life experience as a source for the imaginative emotive life of the character. Returning to emotional experience was thought to vivify and stimulate the imagination as well as verify the "truth" of the "felt" emotion through aroused sympathetic identification. Consequently, the actor's feeling was thought imaginatively "real," but real nonetheless, as it was transformed from actual experience. While Stanislavsky's mature position diminished "affective memory" and elevated "physical actions" to a place of primacy in his system, it was the former that particularly appealed to his principal interpreters in America.

Instinct and spontaneity were important ingredients in the acting theories of MacKaye, Sargent, Curry and Emerson. Curry best summarizes the position by stating that there "is always an unconscious element in all true acting,"[1] and he concluded that mental action can be represented by both the conscious and unconscious. MacKaye, Curry, Sargent and Emerson also held the position that all physical action must be spontaneous and instinctive at the moment of expression, and that the imagination and memory played a vital role in the process.[2] The essential view is similar to the principle that Stanislavsky developed: there exists a bond between the inner psychic activity and the outward physical expression.

The culmination of such views led to yet another unique

contribution to American acting theory, one that achieved great popularity during the years prior to Stanislavsky's first interest in codifying a system. It became known as the "think the thought" process of acting, which was first clearly articulated by Samuel Silas Curry. The theory was essentially accepted by all the "speculative" schools (except Powers') as the final achievement of the actor's preparation and the capstone of their theory. Essentially, it held that if the motive and objective were totally embraced by the actor as imaginatively real and kept vitally alive, the passionately held psychic purpose would find right and truthful expression without inhibition or conscious awareness. If trained well in all that precedes the right psychic activity (careful and thorough analysis and conception, the "Magic If," emotional memory and its interaction with the imagination, concentration, *etc.*), the result will be right physical expression that is instinctual, spontaneous, appropriate and truthful. For many, this was the essence and appeal of the early Stanislavsky "system" for America and as it appeared to be interpreted by Strasberg.

Imagination, "emotional memory" and feeling, instinct, spontaneity and sympathetic identification were significant aspects of the training programs at four of the "speculative" schools and accepted as "a matter of course" in several of the "practical" institutions. That these schools worked to develop the actor's "inner technique" is truly significant, and an almost universally unrecognized aspect of what they stood for. Since their establishment, the schools of MacKaye, Curry, Emerson, Sargent and, to a degree, Powers recognized these elements of the mind as the "inner" nature of the actor and the springboard to all fine acting. They discuss at great length the nature, function and the operation of the "inner technique," and not only on a theoretical basis; they saw to it that the student integrated the internal with any expressional work on the body, voice and speech. Contrary to popular opinion, the schools went to great length to disentangle their reputation from those who corrupted both their system and Delsarte's. But it was to little avail and the public and the profession continued to associate their work with that of charlatans. That these schools were so long-lived is testimony to the effectiveness of the theories and the teaching.

The concept of natural growth permeates the teaching philosophy of the schools. Criticism was almost universally constructive and there was great emphasis placed upon the value of leading the students to make their own discovery. Indeed "self discovery" was a critical factor in at least one of the "practical" schools, the Madison Square Theatre School under Boucicault. Perhaps the Stanhope-Wheatcroft School was the most imitative. But the overall tendency of the schools was to guide, encourage and nurture the natural growth of the student and not to proceed to the next aspect of training until the foundation had been firmly laid for the previous one.

In order to cultivate the imagination and the development of instinct and spontaneity, many of the schools encouraged exploration "without text and without *guidance*." This teaching technique developed into what we regard today as improvisation and it was employed extensively at the American Academy of Dramatic Arts and at Curry's School of Expression prior to the twentieth century. The origins appear in some of the techniques developed by MacKaye in his attempts to create fictitious scenes as students moved from smaller to ever larger units of action and to test how well they had integrated the principles and practice of their craft. In such a manner, Franklin Sargent and, later, Curry developed improvisational exercises. Training the actor to observe life carefully was central to Sargent's "Life Study" class at the Academy, a part of a unit called Action. Many of the exercises remind one of those in *An Actor Prepares* as students are asked to go out to study real life and return and present *improvised* scenes based on their observations, or when they are confronted with a pile of various clothes and asked to create a living character based on what they selected. This course in "Life Studies" has been described by at least two outside observers who report objectively the improvised nature of the exercises. It is important to note that this was well before Stanislavsky developed the technique in any of his Studios, and long before it became central in teaching acting.

Several other schools, including Sargent's, employed improvisation as a means of developing the imagination, trusting instinct and cultivating spontaneity, all of which, they were convinced, could be enriched through training. Indeed, at least three of the schools believed that it was essential to their theory of acting, and integrated imaginative exercises into *every* aspect of training. Using principles and techniques apparently borrowed from MacKaye, the more "speculative" schools believed that *every exercise, regardless of how mechanical it may appear in description,* should be performed with attention to "thought" and feeling. Further, the students were encouraged to perform the exercise as their own personal instincts demanded. Thus, every gesture made in the much criticized "Harmonic Gymnastics" or "Gamuts of Expression" would have behind it an imaginative circumstance and a clear purpose as students were asked to "verify" for themselves, trusting to their own instincts. It was believed that without the imaginative framework, the exercises would become a sterile drill. It may be true that the student "practiced" exercises in a more mechanical manner *initially* in order to make discoveries about flexibility, centering, etc., but once that was accomplished, the feeling, thought, imagination and instinct came into play. This was not conceived merely to placate critics or avoid the stigma of being mechanical or formularistic; it was a natural outgrowth of acting theory and educational philosophy.

All the schools (except F. F. Mackay's) accepted that actor training was a matter of organic and natural growth from "within-outward." The "pragmatic" schools, strangely enough, subscribed to this idea even though they had no developed method to insure it through philosophical or educational bases. At times, imitation was practiced in the "practical" schools but explanation followed by further experimentation was more commonly the custom. The "speculative" schools, however, cultivated an "inner" technique that provided the actor with a method of tapping the "unconscious" as well as a means for responding to the conscious. Their method was decidedly one that gave the actor a system of expressing the inner feeling and thought of the character and a "system," at least in its broad outlines, as well cultivated and developed as Stanislavsky's.

The matter of the degree of "control" an actor should exert over expression deeply concerned the American professional acting schools of the period between 1875 and 1925. Indeed, the problem has been a major concern of acting theorists since Thespis initially stepped out of the chorus as the first protagonist. Only two schools subscribed to a "cool" approach to acting: Powers' and F. F. Mackay's. Mackay subscribed to the view that the actor should imitate the external signs of emotion to perfection; that he should study emotion and its expression in great detail; but should *not* give over to emotional involvement during performance. Powers, too, was opposed to emotional involvement *except* in the preparation for a role, when the actor was permitted to exercise "sympathetic identification." After becoming more familiar with the "truth" of the response and the effects it had on the body and voice, the actor was expected to "study" his response and become consciously aware of the external signs in order that they could be produced and imitated, but not felt. Dion Boucicault wanted the best of both worlds and claimed that comedy demanded objectivity while tragedy required the actor to feel the emotions.

Of the remaining schools, *all* believed that the actor should "feel" emotion during every aspect of preparation and performance. They recognized that there is "a part" of the actor that monitors the expression of emotion and believed it necessary. Their position was similar to that described by Joseph Roach in his penetrating analysis of Stanislavsky's position:

The advantage to the actor of such physical automism is that it liberates his critical faculties to observe, and correct his performance in accordance with the established score. Stanislavsky's wide-eyed Kostya marveled at the power and control that his dual consciousness gave to his acting: 'I have divided myself, as it were, into two personalities. One continued as an actor, the other was an observer. Strangely enough this duality not only did not impede, it actually promoted my creative work. It encouraged and lent impetus to it.' (*Building a Character,* 19.)[3]

It should be clear that just as Stanislavsky would have the actor "score his role," so did the "speculative" schools encourage the actor to "think the thought" of the character. The "speculative" schools expected the actor to "think the thought" *as* the character at each and every moment. It is in the practice of the method during the conception, preparation, rehearsal and performance of a play that the actor engenders the *habit* of sequence and action that liberates and permits true spontaneity. "This is the second nature, looking for all the world like the first"(*Ibid.*). Seen in this light, which is not at all stretching the point, the "speculative" schools of the American professional acting school movement again mirror one of Stanislavsky's views.

It is surprising that scholars have not perceived the nexus of the "think the thought" school of acting and the early Stanislavsky "system." Certainly, a detailed study of the matter should be undertaken in order to compensate, in some small way, for the years of neglect and denigration the schools and their ideas have experienced. So much has been written about the legacy of Stanislavsky that one would easily suppose that nothing of significance in American acting theory occurred prior to January 1923, the date of his arrival with the Moscow Art Theatre in New York City. The "speculative" schools, those of MacKaye, Sargent, Curry, Emerson and Powers, have been shrugged off as "merely" Delsartian, and consequently regarded as inconsequential by most scholars and critics. At best, they are considered as formularistic. The

kindest comment reserved for the "pragmatic" schools has
been that they perpetuated either the elocutionary or "imitative" methods of training.

There remains a distinctly negative conception of the
significance of the American professional acting schools that
existed between 1875 and 1925, and an almost universal lack
of appreciation of their contributions. While a few people are
aware that many of today's professional acting schools and
virtually *all* of the "professionalized" university acting programs are modeled on a curricular structure first suggested by
Steele MacKaye and/or Franklin Sargent, there is much less
awareness of the schools' significance and contribution to the
area of acting theory and teaching. And, sad to say, it is little
appreciated that the motivations and convictions concerning
theatre's place in society that so stirred Stanislavsky were the
very ones that aroused Steele MacKaye and his associates in
the 1870s and 1880s in America.

Why, then, has this movement to establish "a new school of
dramatic art" gone so unrecognized? There can be little doubt
that America's professional acting school movement lost
momentum at the end of the period under investigation. The
attitudes and forces at work were considerable and they
resulted in the decline and eventual eclipse of the schools.
Above all, the founders of the schools had died by 1925 and,
while two schools still exist, the rest either closed permanently or evolved into academically recognized institutions,
responding to one of the major forces that exerted so much
pressure after 1925. It was no small matter that the college
and university theatre movement began to compete with the
schools for the right to train actors, nor is it a coincidence that
many of the professional acting schools' graduates played
significant roles in the formation of departments of theatre
within academic environments.[4] Today colleges and universities represent one of the principal sources of acting talent for
the American theatre.

The unfortunate association of the schools with commercial
theatre also took its toll. As Garff Bell Wilson analyzed the

problem, both Broadway and the "road" were dominated by a theatrical system that offered the worst sort of plays "to appeal to the largest number of customers . . . which critics deplored."[5] This situation, claimed Wilson, created a condition that appeared to lower the standards of acting generally, and "it was inevitable that much of the acting would be routine and stereotyped"(*Ibid.,* 189). As they were the principal source of trained acting talent for a discredited system, the schools were dogged with "guilt by association."

Near the end of the period, many critics and magazines celebrated European models and movements as the panacea for addressing the "ills" of the commercial theatre system, and the solutions did not include the professional acting schools. Instead, major changes were advocated to train actors. Writing in *Theatre Arts Magazine,* Kenneth MacGowan echoed a popular critical sentiment that America had some "unusually good actors. . . . But without permanent companies and repertory theatres in which . . . three types of talent [designers, directors and actors] can come to know one another and achieve fusion, the difficulties that stand in our way of reaching the fullest and finest art of the theatre are gigantic."[6]

As early as October 1920, *Theatre Arts* devoted an entire issue to the "world's first theatre," the Moscow Art Theatre under Stanislavsky's direction; and when it arrived in New York in January of 1923 there was an eruption of lavish (and deserved) praise in all the print media of the time. Accompanying the praise was the clarion call for training actors in the spirit of the Stanislavsky "system," in association with and as part of an ensemble repertory company such as the Moscow Art Theatre. It was clear that the American professional acting school and its identification with the commercial theatre of the day would have no role in such an enterprise. It is ironic that many of the schools had formed actor training associations with theatres during the period—but with commercial theatres.

The tremendous publicity campaign surrounding the

Moscow Art Theatre and Stanislavsky is well documented and the money spent on press agentry was considerable.[7] Stanislavsky was hard pressed to maintain his sanity attempting to keep up with scheduled interviews and appearances and with writing *My Life in Art,* which "unquestionably originated as an adjunct to the publicity campaign waged by Morris Gest . . . in the tradition of his father-in-law David Belasco [who] created an aura of aesthetic sanctity around the players even as he noisily promoted them"(*Ibid.,* 201). Clearly, America was well-primed to listen to Stanislavsky's ideas. The history of what followed the appearances of the Moscow Art Theatre in 1923 and again in 1924 is too well documented to bear repeating. The undeniable superiority of the company was self-evident and the impact of the Stanislavsky "system" drove all theories before it as Russian emigrés established "laboratory" theatres and "studios" to teach what many American actors clamored to learn about. The theories advocated by the American professional acting schools were ignored, forgotten and buried beneath an avalanche of favorable opinion toward the new "system" and the resultant articles and books which detailed it. They never fully recovered as new and different institutions favoring the Stanislavsky "system" emerged to displace both the schools and their theories. The spirit of Stanislavsky was in the air.

Throughout the period, neither MacKaye nor the "speculative" schools completely shed accusations made against them by members of the profession and some critics. Though they disavowed the mechanical posing, fixed gesture patterns, formularistic "signs" that guaranteed effects on audiences, and claims that anyone could be taught to act, they were frequently identified with practices that debased the art of acting, and had no defense against the corruptors of both Delsarte and their own systems. As Garff Bell Wilson so aptly put it:

> The Delsarte principles [as taught by the schools] benefited many performers, but these principles were

> easily distorted and misapplied. Unhappily there was as
> much misapplication as there was sound teaching, so
> that the principles are remembered for the grotesquer-
> ies they spawned rather than the good they did.(Wilson,
> 102)

One could say that the principles of Stanislavsky, Brecht and
Grotowski have, many times, met with a similar fate.

The schools included in this study, limited only to the best
known, graduated nearly ten thousand students and, of these,
approximately five thousand entered the acting profession!
Since a school's viability rested to a large extent on the
achievements of its graduates as an indication of the quality of
training, few resisted the opportunity to capitalize on the
fame of former students. While the schools principally
trained the "rank and file" actor, a significant number of
graduates became respected luminaries.[8] Even a cursory
examination of the names of notable graduates included at the
end of each chapter should persuade one that the schools
offered an effective training ground for actors. But fame is
fleeting and many actors trained by the American professional acting schools have faded from our view, their names
and reputations no longer recognized or familiar. They were
not as fortunate as actors of the following generations who
achieved far wider fame more through film and television
than through the theatre.

Still, one of the most compelling arguments for the
effectiveness of the professional acting schools of the period
lies in their longevity. Two schools (The American Academy
of Dramatic Arts and Emerson) continue to train actors to this
day. The remainder, except for one, were vigorous for
decades, only closing their doors or changing focus following
the death or retirement of their founders. The brief, two-year
existence of the Madison Square Theatre School was strongly
supported by the professional community and the quality of
its known graduates is ample evidence of the efficacy of the
program. The fact that the theatre of the time has been

stigmatized as "commercial" should in no way diminish the quality of the actor or the acting. Without the schools, the American theatre of the period could not have expanded as it did nor could it have whetted America's appetite for theatre as never before. It is more a testimonial to the actors than the quality of the plays that the American theatre flourished during the period.

There can be little doubt that the American professional acting school movement revolutionized the manner in which acting was taught and their contributions to acting theory are much more significant than previously thought. Within the movement there was a wide diversity of approaches to the practice of acting that contradicts the almost universally held view that America possessed no worthwhile prescriptive acting theory until it received one from Stanislavsky. To the contrary, America was deeply concerned with the fundamental place of theatre in society and the fundamental principles that underlie acting. There developed not one, but several, effective methods of acting that proved worthy and viable. What is more, acting theory espoused by three of the schools was amazingly ahead of the times and, to a significant degree, prophetic of what eventually overshadowed and displaced them: the Stanislavsky "system." And just as significant, the theories and practices of these schools resonate positions which, even today, constitute a canon of acceptable ideas and practices concerning acting. Responding to the needs of a theatre in crisis, the American professional acting schools gave to acting what it so desperately required: a foundation of principles and the means of achieving them. The acting theories, methods and curricular organization of the schools were central to the American theatre and we are inheritors of what they pioneered.

NOTES

Introduction

[1]Francis Hodge, "The Private Theatre Schools in the Late Nineteenth Century," in *A History of Speech Education in America,* ed. Karl R. Wallace (New York: Appleton-Century-Crofts, 1954), 552. Also see Fred C. Blanchard, "Professional Theatre Schools in the Early Twentieth Century," 617–640, which appears in the same book as Hodge's article. While useful, both are historical overviews and contribute little in the way of acting theory.

[2]See Edwin Duerr, *The Length and Depth of Acting* (New York: Holt, Rinehart and Winston, 1962), 325–327. Duerr casts a jaundiced eye toward the schools influenced by Delsarte without *any* attempt to analyze their theories or methods. It is doubtful that he read the works, views, theory or teaching methods of the schools but, nevertheless, he dismisses them completely: "In an esoteric mood they grasped at externals." He credits Delsarte with "an attempt to explore the actor's 'interior memory—that storehouse where inherited tendencies, traits and aptitudes are found,'" but concludes that it is a "weird attempt." Duerr includes a brief, but mocking citation concerning Steele MacKaye, choosing not to deal with available material critical to an understanding of Delsarte's theory of acting. But this cavalier attitude only reflects views held by many people in the post-Stanislavsky era which were formed, in part, by the uninformed opinion of contemporary critics and the acknowledged corruption of the MacKaye-Delsarte "system" as evidenced by the many simplistic books published during the period by teachers who misapplied and distorted the essential nature of the acting theory. With this in mind, it is understandable why Delsarte, MacKaye and the schools influenced by them have been dispatched to the dustbin of theatrical history. Indeed, the professional acting schools influenced by MacKaye-Delsarte are simply dismissed as too "speculative," while those of a more "practical" bent are regarded as too elocutionary, imitative or mechanical.

[3]Some twenty-five years later, Michael Brian Friedman's unpublished dissertation, "Advice to Players: Acting Theory in America, 1923 to 1973," Indiana University, 1987 (see 5), perpetuates Duerr's sentiments which are misleading and, as the reader will see, unwarranted.

[4]Friedman, 18–19.

[5]A "prescriptive" acting theory makes assumptions about the nature of acting and the actor, at the same time establishing a method or system for carrying them out. As such, it is deductive: theory is followed by specific practice and moves from general principles to particular cases.

[9]For an excellent study of the American stock company, see Edward W. Mammen, *The Old Stock Company of Acting* (Boston: Published by the Trustees of the Public Library, 1945).

[7]In 1844, *The Drunkard* played 100 performances at the Boston Museum; *Uncle Tom's Cabin,* produced at the National Theatre in New York, achieved a run of over 200 consecutive performances in 1853.

[8]Alfred L. Bernheim, *Business of the Theatre* (New York: Actors' Equity Association, 1932), 30–31.

[9]Magnus, "The Condition of the Stage," *North American Review,* CXXXXIV (January, 1887), 169.

[10]This brief pamphlet is available in the New York Public Library and portions of it appear in Percy MacKaye, *Epoch: The Life of Steele MacKaye,* Vol. I (New York: Boni and Liveright, 1927), 166.

[11]Edythe May Renshaw, "Three Schools of Speech: The Emerson College of Oratory; The School of Expression; and the Leland Powers School of the Spoken Word," unpublished Ph.D. dissertation, Cornell University, 1940.

[12]Edwin Duerr, *The Length and Depth of Acting* (New York: Holt, Rinehart and Winston, 1962); Garff Bell Wilson, *History of American Acting* (Bloomington: Indiana University Press, 1966); and Marvin Carlson, *Theories of the Theatre* (Ithaca: Cornell University Press, 1984).

[13]The Lyceum Theatre School will also be examined in conjunction with The American Academy of Dramatic Arts. While Steele MacKaye undoubtedly founded and headed the Lyceum Theatre School project, Franklin H. Sargent administered the operation. Since both MacKaye and Sargent claimed to have originated the idea for the school and both appear to have incontrovertible proof for their assertions, it seems equally appropriate to discuss the Lyceum Theatre School's evolution into the American Academy of Dramatic Arts.

Chapter 1

[1]See Percy MacKaye, *Epoch: The Life of Steele MacKaye,* 2 vols. (New York: Boni and Liveright, Co., 1927). While many sources acknowledge MacKaye's contribution to acting theory, and the establishment of the first acting school in America, the references are slight and lack sufficient detail to properly evaluate his significance. As previously noted, Garff Bell Wilson's *History of American Acting* discusses MacKaye and Delsarte from an historical viewpoint; and Edwin Duerr's *The Length and Depth of Acting* makes note of MacKaye and the Delsarte movement. All other references tend to make only the most general statements concerning MacKaye's vital role. Only his son, Percy MacKaye, presents a detailed, though biased, analysis of his place in the acting school movement, but he makes little attempt to treat his father's theory of acting in an organized manner.

[2]*Ibid.,* pp. 91–92. Italics Percy MacKaye's. The argument about MacKaye's "dramatic exercises" is long and extended and will be considered in a later place. Let it suffice that MacKaye asserted that he had invented the "aesthetic gymnastics" and had added them to the Delsarte system. His son would have us believe that the 1861 record of his father's "exercises" gives ample indication that the "gymnastics" were, indeed, the invention of Steele MacKaye.

[3]Francois Joseph Regnier, actor, director and head of the Conservatoire and director of the Théâtre Français.

[4]The many letters which appear in *Epoch* from Alger and Monroe to Steele MacKaye only serve to amplify and justify the comment that they regarded MacKaye as the final authority on the Delsarte system.

[5]Samuel Silas Curry, *Province of Expression* (Boston: School of Expression, 1891), 336.

[6]See Virginia Morris, "The Influence of Delsarte in America as Revealed Through the Lectures of Steele MacKaye," unpublished M.A. thesis, Louisiana State, 1941. Miss Morris discusses twenty-three lectures which MacKaye delivered for the studio of Mrs. Hall. The lectures bear such titles as: "Philosophy—Aim of Artist, Nature of Perception," etc.; "The Trinities—Love, Wisdom and Power"; "Feet—Primary Expressions and Attitudes," etc. These manuscripts give a reasonably clear picture of MacKaye's interpretation of the Delsarte system and of his teaching of it.

[7]Claude L. Shaver, "The Delsarte System of Expression as Seen

Through the Notes of Steele MacKaye," unpublished Ph.D. dissertation, University of Wisconsin, 1937.

[8]*Werner's Voice Magazine,* XIV (March, 1892), 59.

[9]Novalyne Price, "The Delsarte Philosophy of Expression as Revealed Through the Lectures of Rev. William R. Alger," unpublished Master's thesis, Louisiana State, 1941.

[10]Claude L. Shaver, "Steele MacKaye and the Delsartian Tradition," *A History of Speech Education in America,* ed. Karl R. Wallace (New York: Appleton-Century-Crofts, Inc., 1954), 211.

[11]Preface to MacKaye's bulletin, "School of Expression," published in New York, 1877.

[12]Shaver, "The Delsarte System of Expression as Seen Through the Notes of Steele MacKaye," 40.

[13]E. T. Kirby, "The Delsarte Method: 3 Frontiers of Actor Training," *Drama Review,* March, 1972. Kirby argues persuasively that Delsarte's methods are as valid today as they were when MacKaye first advocated them.

[14]See, for example, an excerpt from an article by S. S. Curry written for *The Voice,* March, 1885. In the article, Curry urges that something should be done to stop the debasement of Delsarte by unqualified "teachers." His fears were well-founded since the abuses led to the discredit of the system and those associated with it. To this day the damage has not been repaired by historians of theatre who still regard the Delsarte tradition as "peculiar," "mechanical," and "imitative." The excerpt appears in Percy MacKaye, *Epoch,* II, Appendix lii.

[15]Claude Shaver, "The Delsarte System of Expression as Seen Through the Notes of Steele MacKaye," 42.

[16]François Delsarte, *My Revelatory Episodes,* as reprinted in John W. Zorn, *The Essential Delsarte* (Metuchen, N.J.: The Scarecrow Press, Inc., 1968), 39. The five chapters, undoubtedly incomplete, are all that remain of the more than forty years of Delsarte's work. There were attempts to recover what was considered a room full of notes, but the Franco-Prussian War intervened. Afterward, everything disappeared and has never been recovered.

[17]*Ibid.,* 29. Italics mine. "Reason" is a term employed that, today, we would call the "conscious," and "instinct" the "unconscious."

[18]M. L'Abbé Delaumosne in *The Essential Delsarte,* 165.

[19]Delsarte, 26–27.

[20]M. L'Abbé Delaumosne, 108.

[21]Shaver, "The Delsarte System of Expression as Seen Through the Notes of Steele MacKaye," 47.

[22]See Arthur Hobson Quinn, *A History of the American Drama*

from the Civil War to the Present Day, I, (New York: Crofts, 1936), 126.

[23]Sonia Moore makes the same claims for the Stanislavsky System in *The Stanislavsky System* (New York: Viking, 1974), 10–11. Moore claims, "Stanislavsky's teachings are not the result of guesswork: they form a science based on human functioning according to the laws of nature. . . . Through the system actors learn nature's laws and how to use them consciously in re-creating human behavior on stage."

[24]Angelique Arnaud, *Delsarte System of Oratory*, 3rd ed., trans. Abby L. Alger (New York: Edgar S. Werner, 1887), 375.

[25]Shaver, "The Delsarte System of Expression as Seen Through the Notes of Steele MacKaye," 103.

[26]This brief pamphlet bears the title *A Plea for a Free School of Dramatic Art* and is available in the New York Public Library. See George Odell, *Annals of the New York Stage*, IX (New York: Columbia University Press, 1927–1949), 194.

[27]Quoted from a letter of Sargent's. Reprinted in Percy MacKaye, *Epoch*, I, 456.

[28]Under Regnier's direction, MacKaye was the first non-Frenchman to act in France at the Conservatoire where he performed the role of *Hamlet*. While in London in 1873, he performed Wilkie Collins' *Hamlet* to great acclaim as well as appearing at the Olympic Theatre as a member of the company. During the remainder of his stay abroad, MacKaye toured a Tom Taylor play, *Arkwright's Wife*, as well as Collins' *Hamlet* throughout England and in Dublin, Ireland. The reviews of his acting extolled the relaxed naturalism of his performances. It should be added that his acting represented his sole form of financial support.

[29]*Ibid.*, 268. It is interesting to see MacKaye identified with the "visual realism" by Michael Friedman when his whole approach to acting was diametrically opposed to it. See Friedman, 12.

[30]*Ibid.*, 289. It was during this period of the activity that Steele MacKaye first came into contact with two of his most famous pupils in the art of expression: Franklin H. Sargent and Samuel Silas Curry.

[31]See "Franklin H. Sargent," *New York Dramatic Mirror*, March 21, 1896, 23. In this article Sargent discussed his function at the Madison Square Theatre.

[32]Philip G. Hubert, Jr., "New York's Lyceum School for Actors," *Lippincott's Magazine*, XXXV (May, 1885), 485.

[33]*Werner's Directory of Elocutionists, Readers and Lecturers*, ed. Elsie M. Wilbor (New York, 1887), 259.

[34]George Blumenthal, *My Sixty Years in Show Business 1874–1934* (New York: F. C. Osberg, 1936), 11.

[35]Arthur Edwin Krows, "Condensed Experience for Actors," *New York Dramatic Mirror,* March 25, 1914, 3.

[36]Franklin H. Sargent, "Conservatoire, Shall We Have One?" *Century Magazine,* VI (July, 1884), 75.

[37]*New York Dramatic Mirror,* April 4, 1885, 7.

[38]Mrs. Steele MacKaye, "Steele MacKaye and François Delsarte," *Werner's Voice Magazine,* XIV (July, 1892), 187.

[39]E. Miriam Coyriere, "Mme. Geraldy's Visit to America," *Werner's Voice Magazine,* XIV (April, 1892), 103.

[40]Genevieve Stebbins, *The Delsarte System of Expression* (New York: Edgar S. Werner, 1885). Genevieve used the stage name, Agnes Loring.

[41]See particularly Lee Strasberg, "Working with Live Material," *Drama Review* (Fall, 1964), 121; and Lee Strasberg, "Acting and the Training of an Actor," in *Producing the Play,* ed. John Gassner (New York: Dryden, 1941), 141.

[42]Shaver, "The Delasarte System of Expression as Seen Through the Notes of Steele MacKaye." 69. This chart represents Shaver's codification of MacKaye's notes concerning the "Attitudes of the Feet." Stebbins' book has a similar chart.

[43]The term "Gamut of Expression" was employed by MacKaye as early as 1874. See Percy MacKaye, *Epoch,* I, 231. Here, Percy MacKaye reprints a Redpath circular indicating the contents of one of Steele MacKaye's lectures. In it, MacKaye was to lecture on "I. The relation of Emotion to Motion and Form. . . . II. Aesthetic Gymnastics. . . . VI. Gamuts of Expression in the Face."

[44]Shaver, "The Delsarte System of Expression as Seen Through the Notes of Steele MacKaye," 63. MacKaye's notes have only inflections for the head.

[45]E. T. Kirby, *The Drama Review,* Vol. 16 (March, 1972), 56.

[46]*New York Dramatic Mirror,* August 9, 1884, 3.

[47]Speech to the Lyceum Theatre School. Reprinted in Percy MacKaye, *Epoch,* I. 476.

Chapter 2

[1]Quoted from a letter written by Sargent in 1923. Reprinted in Percy MacKaye, *Epoch,* I, 457.

[2]Franklin H. Sargent, "Conservatoire, Shall We Have One?" *Century* VI (July, 1884), 75. Italics mine.

[3]*New York Dramatic Mirror,* February 28, 1885, 7.

[4]*New York Dramatic Mirror,* January 4, 1885, 10.

[5]*New York Dramatic Mirror,* January 31, 1885, 7.

[6]*New York Dramatic Mirror,* January 4, 1885, 3.

[7]*New York Dramatic Mirror,* June 6, 1885, 7.

[8]*New York Dramatic Mirror,* December 5, 1885, 12.

[9]Philip G. Hubert, "New York's Lyceum School for Actors," *Lippincott's Magazine* XXXV (May, 1885), 487–488. Italics mine.

[10]Franklin H. Sargent, "The Preparation of a Stage Neophyte," *New York Dramatic Mirror,* July 19, 1911, 5.

[11]"Franklin H. Sargent," *New York Dramatic Mirror,* March 21, 1896, 23.

[12]Arthur Edwin Krows, "Condensed Experience for Actors," *New York Dramatic Mirror,* March 25, 1914, 3.

[13]Aristide D'Angelo, *The Actor Creates* (New York: Samuel French, 1939), 5. The book by D'Angelo, a former student and instructor at the Academy, presents a consistent picture of the Sargent theories.

[14]Eleanor Cody Gould, *Charles Jehlinger in Rehearsal,* Academy of Dramatic Arts Pamphlet, 1958, 11. These words, said Eleanor Cody Gould, may have been those of Sargent, himself. She asserted that frequently it was impossible to separate the ideas of Jehlinger from Sargent's. Hereafter cited as *Jehlinger in Rehearsal.* The material covers the years 1917–18.

[15]"Franklin H. Sargent," *New York Dramatic Mirror,* March 21, 1896, 23.

[16]D'Angelo, 23. D'Angelo italicized *"during."* The other italics are mine.

[17]*Jehlinger in Rehearsal,* 1; D'Angelo, 23; Sargent, in *Jehlinger in Rehearsal,* 13.

[18]Jehlinger or Sargent, in *Jehlinger in Rehearsal,* 16.

[19]*Jehlinger in Rehearsal,* 6. See Lee Strasberg, "Working With Live Material," *Drama Review,* Fall 1964, 121. And "Acting and the Training of the Actor, in *Producing the Play,* ed. John Gassner (New York: Dryden, 1941), 141.

[20]D'Angelo, 40–41. It should also be noted that early in the career of the American Academy of Dramatic Arts, the students violently objected to Sargent's emphasis on pantomimic training to the detriment of vocal training. See the *New York Dramatic Mirror,* May 27, 1887, 3. Indeed, Sargent's outline of curriculum for the school and the number of hours of training for 1887 indicated that four times as much time was spent on pantomime as work on voice and speech. See the *New York Dramatic Mirror,* June 4, 1887, 10.

[21]Hubert, 488. Hubert is here quoting Sargent concerning his position on Delsartian exercises and philosophy of expression.

[22]Bronson Howard, "Our Schools for the Stage," *Century Magazine,* LXI (November, 1900), 28.

[23]"Franklin H. Sargent," *New York Dramatic Mirror,* March 21, 1896, 23.

[24]Franklin H. Sargent, "Preparation of a Stage Neophyte," *New York Dramatic Mirror,* July 19, 1911, 5.

[25]"Franklin H. Sargent," *New York Dramatic Mirror,* March 21, 1896, 23.

[26]"A School for Actors," *The Nation,* XXXIX (September 4, 1884), 195.

[27]See footnotes 3 and 8 this chapter for comparison.

[28]Letter in *New York Dramatic Mirror,* May 27, 1887, 3.

[29]*New York Dramatic Mirror,* June 4, 1887, 10.

[30]*Ibid.* The apparent discrepancy in the teacher and pupil hours in voice is accounted for by the fact that the class "averaged six members each." The small size of the class meant more teacher hours and less pupil hours. The student supposedly benefited by the personal attention of the small class.

[31]This material has been drawn from the *Catalogue of the American Academy of Dramatic Arts* for 1899 which outlines the work in detail.

[32]Algernon Tassin, "American Dramatic School," *Bookman,* XXV (April, 1907), 158–161.

[33]Mariana McCann, "Two Schools of Acting," *Harper's Weekly,* XXXV (December 12, 1891), 999.

[34]See *Dramatic Studies,* I (November, 1893), a publication of the Academy which first appeared in 1893.

[35]Alfred Ayres, "A Student's Matinee," reprinted from his collection of articles and essays titled *Acting and Actors* (New York: D. Appleton and Co., 1899), 172–73.

[36]For criticism of Academy productions see Norman Hapgood, *The Stage in America, 1897–1900* (New York: 1901), 373, 386, 391 and 393. This little book has eight different reviews of plays presented by the Academy. The plays were *Tartuffe, Pierre Patelin, A Failure* by Bjornson, *Un Caprice* by Marivaux, Congreve's *Love for Love,* Beaumont and Fletcher's *The Coxcomb,* and Tolstoi's *Power of Darkness.* Also, see Hubert, 484; McCann, 999; Tassin, 162.

[37]"Franklin H. Sargent," *New York Dramatic Mirror,* March 21, 1896, 23.

[38]*Annual Catalogue of the American Academy of Dramatic Arts, 1901–1902,* 78–80. This is the last year that the catalogue listed all

the graduates from the year 1886. After 1902, only the graduates of a current year appear in the catalogues.

[39]Interview with Bryn Morgan, Director of Admission, American Academy of Dramatic Arts, December 20, 1962. The number of graduates is also verified by the lists which appear in the catalogues from 1886–1925.

[40]While neither Delsarte nor MacKaye utilize the term, followers such as the American Academy of Dramatic Arts, Samuel Silas Curry and Charles Wesley Emerson totally embraced the idea. Essentially, it presumes that if one concentrates totally on the passionately held thought of a character that right external expression will naturally follow.

Chapter 3

[1]See Clifford Eugene Hamar, "College and University Theatre Instruction in the Early Twentieth Century," *A History of Speech in Education in America,* ed. Karl R. Wallace (New York: Appleton-Century-Crofts, Inc., 1954), 580, 583, 586, 589.

[2]Edyth May Renshaw, "Five Private Schools of Speech," *A History of Speech Education in America,* ed. Karl R. Wallace (New York: Appleton-Century-Crofts, Inc., 1954), 304, 305, 307.

[3]Edythe May Renshaw, "Three Schools of Speech: The Emerson College of Oratory; The School of Expression; The Leland Powers School of the Spoken Word," unpublished Ph.D. dissertation, Columbia University, 1950, 36.

[4]Hereafter, the word "actor" will be substituted for the word "orator" in order not to confuse the reader.

[5]Charles Wesley Emerson, *Evolution of Expression,* I (29th ed.; Boston: Emerson College of Oratory, 1913), 15.

[6]Julia King Parsons, in "Alumni Meeting," *Emerson College Magazine,* X (January, 1902), 4.

[7]*Emerson College Magazine,* XX (May, 1912), 348, unsigned article quoting Jessie E. Southwick's *Principles of Oratory, An Outline of Emerson College Methods* (Boston: The Everet Press, 1912).

[8]Cecil Harper, "The Emerson College of Oratory—Its History, Methods of Teaching and Courses of Instruction," *Emerson College Magazine,* I (May, 1893), 108–113.

[9]Charles W. Emerson, "Relation of Physical Culture to Character," *Emerson College Magazine,* V (March, 1897), 127–128. Emerson used the terms "soul" and "mind" synonymously.

[10]Mary Margaret Robb, *Oral Interpretation of Literature in American Colleges and Universities* (New York: H. W. Wilson Company, 1941), 133–137.

[11]Charles W. Emerson, "Wholeness," *Emerson College Magazine,* VI (November, 1897), 3.

[12]Charles W. Emerson, "The Voice in Relation to Intellect," *Emerson College Magazine,* II (January, 1894), 45–46.

[13]May Greenwood, "The Relation of Mind to Voice," *Emerson College Magazine,* V (February, 1897), 119–120.

[14]Charles W. Emerson, "Our College Work," *Emerson College Magazine,* V (November, 1896), 23.

[15]Henry L. Southwick, "Opening Day Address," *Emerson College Magazine,* XV (November, 1909), 2–9; and "Welcome," *Emerson College Magazine,* I (December, 1892), 7.

[16]Charles W. Emerson, *Expressive Physical Culture* (Boston: Emerson College of Oratory, 1900), 27.

[17]Grace B. Loverin, "Quotations from a Student's Notebook," *Emerson College Magazine,* XXI (March, 1913), 153–155.

[18]Charles W. Emerson, "Power and Perfection in the Use of the Voice," *Emerson College Magazine,* XI (April, 1903), 167.

[19]Charles W. Emerson, "Vocal Techniques," *Emerson College Magazine,* III (February, 1895), 72.

[20]*Emerson College Magazine,* VI (April, 1898), 152.

[21]Henry L. Southwick, "Opening Address," *Emerson College Magazine,* X (November, 1901), 19–20.

[22]Charles W. Emerson, "The Orator as a Power," *Emerson College Magazine,* V (December, 1896), 40.

[23]It seems reasonable to assume that this is a reflection of the influence of Williams James's psychology.

[24]Charles W. Emerson, "The Voice in Relation to the Intellect," 43.

[25]Jessie Eldridge Southwick, *Expressive Voice Culture* (Boston: Emerson College of Oratory, 1908), 26–28.

[26]Charles W. Emerson, *Lecture XIII* (December, 1894), 109.

[27]Emerson, *Psycho Vox* (Boston: Emerson College of Oratory, 1897), 101.

[28]Charles W. Emerson, "The Emerson Philosophy of Gesture," *Emerson College Magazine,* II (April, 1894), 92.

[29]*Ibid.,* 97. Emerson pointed out that this was a distinctive aspect of his method and distanced himself from schools which employed charts. But as we have seen, neither MacKaye nor Sargent used them as indicators of the emotional states, but as methods of establishing control and confidence in order to achieve relaxation.

[30]Emerson, *Evolution of Expression,* I, 13.

[31]Charles W. Emerson, "The Teacher," *Emerson College Magazine,* II, (May, 1894), 143–149.

[32]Joseph S. Gaylord, "Emerson System of Physical Culture," *Emerson College Magazine,* IV (April, 1896), 145.

[33]Charles W. Emerson, "The Demosthenes Departure," *Emerson College Magazine,* II (February, 1894), 75.

[34]Mary Ann Greely, "Gleanings from Dr. Emerson," *Emerson College Magazine,* XX (April, 1912), 329.

[35]Henry L. Southwick, "Opening Address," *Emerson College Magazine,* XIII November, 1904), 12.

[36]Charles W. Emerson, *Lecture IX,* January 12, 1895, 126.

[37]Henry L. Southwick, "The Scholastic Year of 1903–1904," *Emerson College Magazine,* XII (May, 1904), 202.

[38]Jessie E. Southwick, "The Principles of Gesture," *Emerson College Magazine,* XIII (May, 1905), 209–209.

[39]The writer is indebted to Edythe May Renshaw's dissertation "Three Schools of Speech" for much of the following material. Her study of the teaching methods of Emerson School of Oratory presents a clear and concise picture by comparing and contrasting various student notebooks and lecture notes.

[40]Jessie E. Southwick, "The Principles of Response in Voice and Gesture," *Emerson College Magazine,* XVIII (March, 1909), 243. The idea that a "motive" should be behind all Delsarte gestural patterns was first expressed by Steele MacKaye as we have seen and was not new or original. It is interesting that the reason for the motive sprang from a desire to avoid mechanical reproduction.

[41]*Annual Catalogue of the Emerson College of Oratory, 1886–1892.* It should be noted that the school's *Annual Catalogue* from 1886 to 1891 was the *Annual Catalogue of the Monroe College of Oratory.* Emerson named the school after his former teacher, and give it his name in 1891.

[42]Interview with John R. Chase, Director of Alumni Relations, December 18, 1962.

[43]These facts come from material tabulated in the Alumni Office of Emerson College and have been verified by examination of *Emerson College Magazine,* 1893–1925, and *The Alumni News,* 1900–1925.

Chapter 4

[1]*New York Dramatic Mirror,* October 31, 1885, 10.
[2]*New York Dramatic Mirror,* October 15, 1892.

[3] School of Expression, *Fourth Annual Catalogue,* 1888, as quoted in Mary Margaret Robb, *Oral Interpretation of Literature in American Colleges and Universities* (New York: H. W. Wilson Company, 1941), 131.

[4] Marianna McCann, "Two Schools of Acting," *Harper's Weekly,* XXV (December 10, 1891), 999.

[5] Samuel Silas Curry, *Province of Expression* (Boston: School of Expression, 1891), 110.

[6] Samuel Silas Curry, *Imagination and Dramatic Instinct* (Boston: The Expression Company, 1896), 225.

[7] *Ibid.,* 120–122. It should be noted, however, that Curry did not conceive "histrionic art" to be manifested only in acting. He believed that platform reading and recitation could also use the playwright's product.

[8] Curry, *Foundations of Expression* (Boston: The Expression Company, 1920), 143–145.

[9] Samuel Silas Curry, "Glimpses of Art and Character," *Expression,* I (March, 1894), 144.

[10] Samuel Silas Curry, *Spoken English* (Boston: Expression Company, 1913), 178.

[11] Samuel Silas Curry, *Mind and Voice* (Boston: Expression Company, 1910), 435.

[12] Curry, *Lessons in Vocal Expression* (Boston: Expression Company, 1891), 1; *Province of Expression,* 169, 259–260.

[13] Samuel Silas Curry, "Pantomimic Expression," notes for a course taught in 1897–1898, 6. As quoted in Edythe May Renshaw, "Three Schools of Speech: The Emerson College of Oratory; The School of Expression; and the Leland Powers School of the Spoken Word," unpublished Ph.D. dissertation, Columbia University, 1950, 326.

[14] Curry, "Pantomimic Expression," notes for 1897–1898, 7.

[15] Curry, *Foundations of Expression,* 227; and "Pantomimic Expression," notes for 1897–1898, 1.

[16] Samuel Silas Curry, "Report on Founder's Day Celebration," *Expression,* XVIII (December, 1911), 9.

[17] Samuel Silas Curry, "Foundation and Aim," *Expression,* XIV (September, 1907), 11.

[18] Samuel Silas Curry, "A Message from the Alumni," *Expression,* XVI December, 1909), 4.

[19] Percy MacKaye, *Epoch,* II, 51–52 in Appendix. Curry's letter to *Voice,* edited by Edgar S. Werner, March, 1885 expresses his deep concern at the corruption of Delsarte by "former pupils of MacKaye's pupils." Curry states that MacKaye was a genius and his

finest teacher, but the system has been warped and twisted by those with incomplete knowledge.

[20]Curry, "Pantomimic Expression," notes for class in 1897–1898. The bulk of the material presented in the analysis of the class work in pantomime is derived from Edythe May Renshaw, "Three Schools of Speech," 337–352. Miss Renshaw makes available material from the lectures of S. S. Curry, Mrs. Anna Baright Curry, and Florence Lutz for the period spanning the study.

[21]Anna Baright Curry, "Grace and Power," an outline for a course in Action, 1.

[22]Florence Lutz, graduate of the School of Expression, 1907; instructor in the School of Expression, 1907–1914; assistant professor, University of California, 1917–1922; dean of the School of Expression, 1923–1924. Lutz's definition comes from her notes for a course similar to Mrs. Curry's which was taught at least by 1923 and probably before. The title for the course was "Harmonic Training Program."

[23]Oclo M. Miller, "The Psychology of Dr. S. S. Curry as Revealed by His Attitude Toward the Mind-Body Problem," unpublished Master's thesis, State University of Iowa, 1929.

[24]*School of Expression,* a pamphlet announcing Courses in Dramatic Art, October 10, 1902.

[25]Interview with Dr. Donald Miller, December 17, 1962. Dr. Miller was the President of Curry College and an expert in the area of Curry's theories and teaching methods. Dr. Miller's estimate is verified by the alumni reports that appear in *Expression,* 1895–1917. The exact number of graduates from the founding of the school to 1925 is 2,268. The lists of alumni which appear in *Expression* include date of graduation, address, and present occupation.

Chapter 5

[1]*Who's Who in America,* Vol. XI, ed. Albert Nelson Marquis (Chicago: A. H. Nelson and Co., 1920–21), 2292.

[2]Samuel Silas Curry, "The Monologue as a Dramatic Form," *Expression,* II (September, 1896), 209–210.

[3]Unsigned announcement, "The Graduate Course in Platform Art," *Emerson College Magazine,* X (May, 1902), n.p.; unsigned announcement, "Leland T. Powers," *Expression,* VII (Spring, 1899), n.p.

[4]Edythe May Renshaw, "Five Private Schools of Speech," *History of Speech Education in America,* ed. Karl R. Wallace (New York: Appleton-Century-Crofts, 1954), 307. Renshaw reports conclusions from interviews with Hortense Creedle Railsback in 1944, with Adele Hoose Lee in 1945, and with Elizabeth Pooler Rice in 1945.

[5]Fred C. Blanchard, "Professional Theatre Schools," *History of Speech Education in America,* ed. Karl R. Wallace (New York: Appleton-Century-Crofts, 1954), 626–627. Blanchard quotes a letter received from Powers' son, Haven M. Powers, dated March 2, 1953.

[6]Leland T. Powers and Carol Hoyt Powers, *Fundamentals of Expression* (Boston: Groom and Co., 1916), 57.

[7]Leland T. Powers, *Practice Book* (Boston: Thomas Groom and Company, 1916), 5–6.

[8]Leland T. Powers, *Talks on Expression* (Boston: Thomas Groom and Company, Inc., 1917), 76–77.

[9]Phidelah Rice, "The Art of Impersonating in Play Reading," *Studies in the Art of Interpretation,* ed. Gertrude E. Johnson (New York: D. Appleton-Century Company, 1940), 84. Rice was one of Powers' pupils who won fame as a platform reader. He also taught at the School of the Spoken Word.

[10]Phidelah Rice, 83–84. This is a summary of Phidelah Rice's list of requirements necessary for attaining perfection in monoacting. Mr. Rice taught for years at the School of the Spoken Word and wrote the introduction for Mr. Powers' book, *Talks on Expression.* In this article, he states the basic beliefs of Powers in clear, concise terms.

[11]Edythe May Renshaw, "Three Schools of Speech: The Emerson College of Oratory; The School of Expression; and the Leland Powers School of the Spoken Word," unpublished Ph.D. dissertation, Columbia University, 1950, 437.

[12]Carol Hoyt Powers, *The Speaking Voice,* pamphlet consisting of three articles copyrighted by *The Christian Science Monitor,* November 9, 16, 23, 1938, 12–14.

[13]Interview with Haven M. and Lilian R. Powers, December 19, 1962.

[14]Maude McGarry Tibbets, "Traditional High Lights," *Random Recollections* (Boston: The Leland Powers School, 1954), 49–50. This enlightening book was published on the fiftieth anniversary of the school. It contains the reminiscences of the alumni and other invaluable material concerning the development of the School of the Spoken Word.

[15]Interview with Haven M. Powers, December 18, 1962.
[16]"Alumni Memories," *Random Recollections*, 85–155.

Chapter 6

[1]Dion Boucicault, *The Art of Acting*, Publications of the Dramatic Museum of Columbia University, I (New York: Columbia University Press, 1926), 57. This quotation is taken from editorial notes which were written by Brander Matthews.

[2]Joseph Jefferson and others, "Success on the Stage," *North American Review*, CXXXV (December, 1882), 58lff.

[3]The lecture was reproduced from the stenographic report printed in *Era* of July 29, 1882 for the Dramatic Museum of Columbia University. See footnote 1.

[4]See Hamilton Aide, "A Dramatic School," *The Theatre*, V (March, 1882), 73–76.

[5]Dion Boucicault, "My Pupils," *North American Review*, CXXXXVII (August, 1889), 435ff.

[6]*Ibid.* It should be noted that Steele MacKaye called for the free training of promising dramatic students as early as 1871.

[7]Announcement of the formation of the Palmer-Boucicault school, *New York Dramatic Mirror*, June 16, 1888, 6.

[8]Constant Coquelin, Henry Irving and Dion Boucicault, *The Art of Acting*, Publications of the Dramatic Museum of Columbia University, II (New York: Columbia University, 1926), 55.

[9]*New York Dramatic Mirror*, July 28, 1888, 2.

[10]Constance Morris, "Dion Boucicault's School of Acting," *Green Book Album*, VI (August, 1911), 401–407.

[11]*New York Dramatic Mirror*, July 28, 1888, 8. It should be noted that this prospectus is dated two months previous to the opening of the school. Morris clearly indicates that the "sixty" pupils turned out to be "fifty-three" after the tryouts.

[12]Morris, 405. Most likely, however, they followed standard blocking and business when preparing the scenes.

[13]It will be remembered that Steele MacKaye's St. James (1871) and Union Square (1877) schools undertook training actors in a situation quite similar to Palmer and Boucicault, but MacKaye was neither as established nor as well-known at the time. As well, MacKaye taught a "system" much more developed and "speculative" and was not at all in sympathy with Boucicault's fundamental view of training since, to him, the Irishman was merely perpetuating the old, stock company tradition.

Chapter 7

[1]Barnard Hewitt, *Theatre U.S.A.: 1668 to 1957* (New York: McGraw-Hill Book Company, Inc., 1959), 278.

[2]Algernon Tassin, "American Dramatic Schools," *Bookman*, XXV (April, 1907), 152. Also see Bronson Howard, "Our Schools for the Stage," *Century Magazine*, LXI (November, 1900), 29.

[3]*New York Dramatic Mirror*, June 19, 1897, 13.

[4]*New York Dramatic Mirror*, October 1, 1898, 27.

[5]"Adeline Stanhope-Wheatcroft," *New York Dramatic Mirror*, June 19, 1897, 15.

[6]*New York Dramatic Mirror*, June 19, 1897, 13.

[7]Undated article titled "Nelson Wheatcroft," from the *New York Dramatic Mirror, Clipping File*, New York Public Library Theatre Collection.

[8]Mr. Wheatcroft died in June, 1897. During the summer the Empire Dramatic School, which was in the Empire Theatre, merged with the American Academy of Dramatic Arts. It appears that Mrs. Wheatcroft preferred to maintain her autonomy rather than join the Sargent organization. Consequently, beginning in October, 1897, she opened her own school in the Holland Building, at Broadway and Fortieth Street under the name The Stanhope-Wheatcroft School. It seems inconceivable that she and Sargent could have been compatible when one understands their separate theories and teaching methods.

[9]"Adeline Stanhope-Wheatcroft," *New York Dramatic Mirror*, June 19, 1897, 15.

[10]"The Stanhope-Wheatcroft School," *New York Dramatic Mirror*, October 1, 1898, 11.

[11]Undated article titled "Nelson Wheatcroft," *New York Dramatic Mirror, Clipping File*, New York Public Library Theatre Collection. This material is verified in another article titled "Adeline Stanhope-Wheatcroft," *New York Dramatic Mirror*, June 19, 1897, 15.

[12]Henry James Forman, "The Story of Rachel Crothers," *Pictorial Review*, XXXII (1931), 56.

Chapter 8

[1]"F. F. Mackay," *New York Dramatic Mirror*, August 7, 1897, 2.

[2]"The Art of Acting," *New York Dramatic Mirror*, September 22, 1888, 2.

[3]"F. F. Mackay," *New York Dramatic Mirror*, September 22, 1888, 2.

[4]*New York Dramatic Mirror*, October 1, 898, 23.

[5]See *New York Dramatic Mirror,* June 4, 1887, 10 and "Franklin H. Sargent," *New York Dramatic Mirror,* March 21, 1896, 23. Mrs. Gorgen taught pantomime and elocution for Sargent, and the length of her association with the American Academy of Dramatic Arts leads one to assume that Sargent had been well pleased with her methods of teaching.

[6]F. F. Mackay, *The Art of Acting* (New York: Published by the author, 1913).

[7]James E. Murdoch, *Analytic Elocution* (New York: American Book Company, 1884).

[8]Algernon Tassin, "American Dramatic Schools," *Bookman,* XXV (April, 1907), 162.

[9]*New York Dramatic Mirror,* July 27, 1907. *Clipping File,* New York Public Library Theatre Collection.

[10]"Developing a True Dramatic Artist: Interview with F. F. Mackay," *New York Dramatic Mirror,* August 21, 1912, 5; "A Talk with F. F. Mackay," *New York Dramatic Mirror,* December 23, 1899. *Clipping File,* New York Public Library Theatre Collection.

[11]Tassin, 152. Also see Bronson Howard, "Our Schools for the Stage," *Century Magazine,* LXI (November, 1900), 29.

Conclusion

[1]Curry, *The Province of Expression,* 226.

[2]Curry, *Imagination and Dramatic Instinct,* 137–138.

[3]Joseph R. Roach, *The Player's Passion* (Newark: University of Delaware Press, 1985), 214.

[4]See Clifford Eugene Hamar, "College and University Theatre Instruction in the Early Twentieth Century," *A History of Speech Education in America,* ed. Karl R. Wallace (New York: Appleton-Century-Crofts, Inc., 1954), 580, 583, 586, 589.

[5]Garff Bell Wilson, *A History of American Acting* (Bloomington and London: University of Indiana Press, 1966), 187–188.

[6]Kenneth MacGowan, "The Centre of the Stage," *Theatre Arts Magazine,* V (April, 1921), 91–92.

[7]See Laurence Senelick, "Stanislavsky's Double *My Life in Art,*" *Theatre Survey,* XXII (November, 1981), 201–203.

[8]See the index of Daniel Blum, *A Pictorial History of the American Theatre* (Crown Publishers Inc.: New York, 1969) 402–416. The names of forty-seven notable actors of the schools appear in the index, many of them with numerous citations for appearing in the outstanding plays of the various seasons during the period.

BIBLIOGRAPHY

Aide, Hamilton. "A Dramatic School." *The Theatre,* V (March, 1882), 73–76.

Arnaud, Angelique. *Delsarte System of Oratory,* 3rd ed. Trans. Abby L. Alger. New York: Edgar S. Werner, 1887.

Ayres, Alfred. "A Student's Matinee." Reprinted from Ayres, Alfred. *Acting and Actors.* New York: D. Appleton and Co., 1899, 172–73.

Bernheim, Alfred L. *Business of the Theatre.* New York: Actors' Equity Association, 1932.

Blanchard, Fred C. "Professional Theatre Schools in the Early Twentieth Century." In *A History of Speech Education in America.* Ed. Karl R. Wallace. New York: Appleton-Century-Crofts, 1954.

Blumenthal, George. *My Sixty Years in Show Business 1874–1934.* New York: F. C. Osberg, 1936.

Boucicault, Dion. "My Pupils." *North American Review,* CXXXXVII (August, 1889), 435ff.

————. *The Art of Acting.* Publications of the Dramatic Museum of Columbia University. Vol. I. New York: Columbia University Press, 1926.

Carlson, Marvin. *Theories of the Theatre.* Ithaca: Cornell University Press, 1984.

Coyriere, E. Miriam "Mme. Geraldy's Visit to America." *Werner's Voice Magazine,* XIV (April, 1892), 103.

Curry, Anna Baright. "Grace and Power." An outline for a course in action, unpublished, n.d.

Curry, Samuel Silas. *Province of Expression.* Boston: School of Expression, 1891.

―――. *Imagination and Dramatic Instinct.* Boston: The Expression Company, 1896.

―――. *Foundations of Expression.* Boston: The Expression Company, 1920.

―――. *Spoken English.* Boston: Expression Company, 1913.

―――. *Mind and Voice.* Boston: Expression Company, 1910.

―――. *Lessons in Vocal Expression.* Boston: Expression Company, 1891.

―――. "Glimpses of Art and Character." *Expression,* I (March, 1894), 144.

―――. Written for *The Voice,* n.p., March, 1885.

―――. "Report on Founder's Day Celebration." *Expression,* XVIII (December, 1911), 9.

―――. "Foundation and Aim." *Expression,* XIV (September, 1907), 11.

―――. "A Message from the Alumni." *Expression,* XVI (December, 1909), 4.

―――. "The Monologue as a Dramatic Form." *Expression,* II (September, 1896), 209–210.

D'Angelo, Aristide. *The Actor Creates.* New York: Samuel French, 1939.

Duerr, Edwin. *The Length and Depth of Acting.* New York: Holt, Rinehart and Winston, 1962.

Emerson, Charles Wesley. *Evolution of Expression,* I, 29th ed. Boston: Emerson College of Oratory, 1913.

―――. *Psycho Vox.* Boston: Emerson College of Oratory, 1897.

―――. *Expressive Physical Culture.* Boston: Emerson College of Oratory, 1900.

————. "Relation of Physical Culture to Character." *Emerson College Magazine,* V (March, 1897), 127–128.

————. "Wholeness." *Emerson College Magazine,* VI (November, 1897), 3.

————. "The Voice in Relation to Intellect." *Emerson College Magazine,* II (January, 1894), 43–46.

————. "Our College Work." *Emerson College Magazine,* V (November, 1896), 23.

————. "Power and Perfection in the Use of the Voice." *Emerson College Magazine,* XI (April, 1903), 167.

————. "Vocal Techniques." *Emerson College Magazine,* III (February, 1895), 72.

————. "The Orator as a Power." *Emerson College Magazine,* V (December, 1896), 40.

————. "The Emerson Philosophy of Gesture." *Emerson College Magazine,* II (April, 1894), 92.

————. "The Teacher." *Emerson College Magazine,* II (May, 1894), 143–149.

————. "The Demosthenes Departure." *Emerson College Magazine,* II (February, 1894), 75.

————. *Lecture XIII.* n.p., December 1894.

————. *Lecture IX,* n.p., January 12, 1895.

Forman, Henry James. "The Story of Rachel Crothers." *Pictorial Review,* XXXII (1931), 56.

Friedman, Michael Brian. "Advice to the Players: Acting Theory in America, 1923 to 1973," unpublished Ph.D. dissertation, Indiana University, 1987.

Gaylord, Joseph S. "Emerson System of Physical Culture." *Emerson College Magazine,* IV (April, 1896), 145.

Gould, Eleanor Cody. *Charles Jehlinger in Rehearsal* (pamphlet). New York: American Academy of Dramatic Arts, 1958.

Greely, Mary Ann. "Gleanings from Dr. Emerson." *Emerson College Magazine,* XX (April, 1912), 329.

Greenwood, May. "The Relation of Mind to Voice." *Emerson College Magazine,* V (February, 1897), 119–120.

Hamar, Clifford Eugene. "College and University Theatre Instruction in the Early Twentieth Century." In *A History of Speech in Education in America.* Ed. Karl R. Wallace. New York: Appleton-Century-Crofts, Inc., 1954; 580–589.

Hapgood, Norman. *The Stage in America, 1897–1900.* New York: n.p., 1901.

Harper, Cecil. "The Emerson College of Oratory—Its History, Methods of Teaching and Courses of Instruction." *Emerson College Magazine,* I (May, 1893), 108–113.

Hewitt, Barnard. *Theatre U.S.A.: 1668 to 1957.* New York: McGraw-Hill Book Company, Inc., 1959.

Hodge, Francis. "The Private Theatre Schools in the Late Nineteenth Century." In *A History of Speech Education in America.* Ed. Karl R. Wallace. New York: Appleton-Century-Crofts, 1954.

Howard, Bronson. "Our Schools for the Stage." *Century Magazine,* LXI (November, 1900), 28–29.

Hubert, Philip G., Jr. "New York's Lyceum School for Actors." *Lippincott's Magazine,* XXXV (May, 1885), 485–488.

Jefferson, Joseph *et al.* "Success on the Stage." *North American Review,* CXXXV (December, 1882), 58lff.

Kirby, E. T. "The Delsarte Method: 3 Frontiers of Actor Training." *Drama Review* (March, 1972), 56.

Krows, Arthur Edwin. "Condensed Experience for Actors." *New York Dramatic Mirror* (March 25, 1914), 3.

Loverin, Grace B. "Quotations from a Student's Notebook." *Emerson College Magazine,* XXI (March, 1913), 153–155.

McCann, Marianna. "Two Schools of Acting." *Harper's Weekly,* XXV (December 10, 1891), 999.

MacGowan, Kenneth. "The Centre of the Stage." *Theatre Arts Magazine,* V (April, 1921), 91–92.

Mackay, F. F. *The Art of Acting.* New York: Published by the author, 1913.

MacKaye, Mrs. Steele. "Steele MacKaye and Francois Delsarte." *Werner's Voice Magazine,* XIV (July, 1892), 187.

MacKaye, Percy. *Epoch: The Life of Steele MacKaye.* 2 Vols. New York: Boni and Liveright, 1927.

MacKaye, Steele. *A Bulletin of The School of Expression.* New York: School of Expression, 1877.

Magnus, "The Condition of the Stage." *North American Review,* CXXXXIV (January, 1887), 169.

Mammen, Edward W. *The Old Stock Company of Acting.* Boston: The Trustees of the Public Library, 1945.

Marquis, Albert Nelson, ed. *Who's Who in America,* Vol. XI. Chicago: A. H. Nelson and Co., 1920–21.

Miller, Oclo M. "The Psychology of Dr. S. S. Curry as Revealed by His Attitude Toward the Mind-Body Problem," unpublished Master's thesis, State University of Iowa, 1929.

Moore, Sonia. *The Stanislavsky System.* New York: Viking, 1974.

Morris, Constance. "Dion Boucicault's School of Acting." *Green Book Album,* VI (August, 1911), 401–407.

Morris, Virginia. "The Influence of Delsarte in America as Revealed Through the Lectures of Steele MacKaye," unpublished M.A. thesis, Louisiana State, 1941.

Murdoch, James E. *Analytic Elocution.* New York: American Book Company, 1884.

Odell, George. *Annals of the New York Stage,* IX. New York: Columbia University Press, 1927–1949.

Parsons, Julia King. "Alumni Meeting." *Emerson College Magazine,* X (January, 1902), 4.

Powers, Carol Hoyt. "The Speaking Voice." *The Christian Science Monitor,* November 9, 16, 23, 1938.

———, and Leland T. Powers. *Fundamentals of Expression.* Boston: Thomas Groom and Co., 1916.

Powers, Leland T. *Practice Book.* Boston: Thomas Groom and Company, 1916.

———. *Talks on Expression.* Boston: Thomas Groom and Company, Inc., 1917.

Price, Novalyne. "The Delsarte Philosophy of Expression as Revealed Through the Lectures of Rev. William R. Alger," unpublished Master's thesis, Louisiana State, 1941.

Quinn, Arthur Hobson. *A History of the American Drama From the Civil War to the Present Day,* I. New York: Crofts, 1936.

Renshaw, Edythe May. "Five Private Schools of Speech." In *A History of Speech Education in America.* Ed. Karl R. Wallace. New York: Appleton-Century-Crofts, Inc., 1954; 304–307.

———. "Three Schools of Speech: The Emerson College of Oratory; The School of Expression; and the Leland Powers School of the Spoken Word," unpublished Ph.D. dissertation, Columbia University, 1950.

Rice, Phidelah. "The Art of Impersonating in Play Reading." In *Studies in the Art of Interpretation.* Ed. Gertrude E. Johnson. New York: D. Appleton-Century Company, 1940.

Roach, Joseph R. *The Player's Passion.* Newark: University of Delaware Press, 1985.

Robb, Mary Margaret. *Oral Interpretation of Literature in American Colleges and Universities.* New York: H. W. Wilson Company, 1941.

Sargent, Franklin H. "Conservatoire, Shall We Have One?" *Century Magazine,* VI (July, 1884), 475.

———. "The Preparation of a Stage Neophyte." *New York Dramatic Mirror* (July 19, 1911), 5.

Senelick, Laurence. "Stanislavsky's Double *My Life in Art.*" *Theatre Survey,* XXII (November, 1981), 201–203.

Shaver, Claude L. "Steele MacKaye and the Delsartian Tradition." In *A History of Speech Education in America.* Ed. Karl R. Wallace. New York: Appleton-Century-Crofts, Inc., 1954.

———. "The Delsarte System of Expression As Seen Through the Notes of Steele MacKaye," unpublished Ph.D. dissertation, University of Wisconsin, 1937.

Southwick, Henry L. "Welcome." *Emerson College Magazine,* I (December, 1892), 7.

———. "Opening Address." *Emerson College Magazine,* X (November, 1901), 19–20.

———. "The Scholastic Year of 1903–1904." *Emerson College Magazine,* XII (May, 1904), 202.

———. "Opening Address." *Emerson College Magazine,* XIII (November, 1904), 12.

———. "Opening Day Address." *Emerson College Magazine,* XV (November, 1909), 2–9.

Southwick, Jessie Eldridge. *Expressive Voice Culture.* Boston: Emerson College of Oratory, 1908.

———. "The Principles of Gesture." *Emerson College Magazine,* XIII (May, 1905). 209–209.

———. "The Principles of Response in Voice and Gesture." *Emerson College Magazine,* XVIII (March, 1909), 243.

Stebbins, Genevieve. *The Delsarte System of Expression.* New York: Edgar S. Werner, 1885.

Strasberg, Lee. "Working With Live Material." *Drama Review,* Fall (1964), 121.

————. "Acting and the Training of an Actor." In *Producing the Play.* Ed. John Gassner. New York: Dryden, 1941.

Tassin, Algernon. "American Dramatic School." *Bookman,* XXV (April, 1907), 152–162.

Tibbets, Maude McGarry, ed. *Random Recollections.* Boston: The Leland Powers School, 1954.

Wilbor, Elsie M., ed. *Werner's Directory of Elocutionists, Readers and Lecturers.* New York: 1887.

Wilson, Garff Bell. *A History of American Acting.* Bloomington: Indiana University Press, 1966.

Woodard, Debra J. "Steele MacKaye's *Marriage*: The Beginning of a Movement Toward American Realism." *Theatre Survey,* XXIII, Number 2, (November, 1982), 191–8.

Zorn, John W., ed. *The Essential Delsarte.* Metuchen, N.J.: The Scarecrow Press, Inc., 1968.

Interviews

Chase, John R. Director of Alumni Relations, December 18, 1962.

Miller, Dr. Donald, (then) President of Curry College, December 17, 1962.

Morgan, Bryn, Director of Admission, American Academy of Dramatic Arts, December 20, 1962.

Powers, Haven M., December 18, 1962.

———and Lilian R. Powers, December 19, 1962.

Other Publications

The Alumni News, Emerson College, 1900–1925.

Annual Catalogue of the American Academy of Dramatic Arts, 1899, 1901–1902, 1939–1940.

Annual Catalogue of the Emerson College of Oratory, 1886–1892, 1893, 1894, 1898–99, 1903, 1905, 1907, 1909, 1914, 1917, 1921.

Annual Catalogue of the School of Expression, 1905, 1908, 1909.

Dramatic Studies, I. November, 1893; a publication of the American Academy of Dramatic Arts.

Emerson College Magazine, 1893–1925.

Emerson College Magazine, VI, (April, 1898), 152.

Emerson College Magazine, X (May, 1902), n.p.; unsigned announcement, "The Graduate Course in Platform Art."

Emerson College Magazine, XX (May, 1912), 348; unsigned article quoting Jessie E. Southwick's *Principles of Oratory, An Outline of Emerson College Methods.* Boston: The Everet Press, 1912.

Expression, VII (Spring, 1899), n.p.; unsigned announcement, "Leland T. Powers."

The Nation, XXXIX (September 4, 1884), 195; "A School for Actors."

New York Dramatic Mirror, August 9, 1884, 3.

New York Dramatic Mirror. January 4, 1885, 3 and 10.

New York Dramatic Mirror. January 31, 1885, 7.

New York Dramatic Mirror. February 28, 1885, 7.

New York Dramatic Mirror, April 4, 1885, 7.

New York Dramatic Mirror. June 6, 1885, 7.

New York Dramatic Mirror, October 31, 1885, 10.

New York Dramatic Mirror. December 5, 1885, 12.

New York Dramatic Mirror. May 27, 1887, 3.

New York Dramatic Mirror. June 4, 1887, 10.

New York Dramatic Mirror, June 16, 1888, 6; announcement of the formation of the Palmer-Boucicault school.

New York Dramatic Mirror, July 28, 1888, 2 and 8.

New York Dramatic Mirror, September 22, 1888, 2; "The Art of Acting," and "F. F. MacKay."

New York Dramatic Mirror, October 15, 1892.

New York Dramatic Mirror, March 21, 1896, 23; "Franklin H. Sargent."

New York Dramatic Mirror, June 19, 1897, 13.

New York Dramatic Mirror, June 19, 1897, 15; "Adeline Stanhope-Wheatcroft."

New York Dramatic Mirror, August 7, 1897, 2; "F. F. MacKay."

New York Dramatic Mirror, October 1, 1898, 11; "The Stanhope-Wheatcroft School."

New York Dramatic Mirror, October 1, 1898, 23 and 27.

New York Dramatic Mirror, December 23, 1899; *Clipping File,* New York Public Library Theatre Collection; "A Talk with F. F. Mackay"

New York Dramatic Mirror, July 27, 1907. *Clipping File,* New York Public Library Theatre Collection.

New York Dramatic Mirror, August 21, 1912, 5; *Clipping File,* New York Public Library Theatre Collection; "Developing a True Dramatic Artist: Interview with F. F. Mackay"

New York Dramatic Mirror, Clipping File, New York Public Library Theatre Collection, undated; "Nelson Wheatcroft."

School of Expression, a pamphlet announcing Courses in Dramatic Art, October 10, 1902.

Werner's Voice Magazine, XIV (March, 1892), 59.

INDEX

Aesthetics, 8, 9, 10, 14, 173, 178

Alger, Rev. William R., 3, 5, 20

American Academy of Dramatic Arts: xvi, 45, 51, 52, 54, 55, 56, 57, 58, 59, 60, 61, 62, 63, 64, 65, 66, 67, 68, 69, 70, 72, 73, 74, 77, 78, 79, 80, 81, 82, 83, 84, 85, 89, 90, 91, 92, 93, 140, 149, 171, 244; acting as a two-fold process, 57, 58; bad habits, 66; and certain changes to MacKaye-Delsarte theories, 45, 46; concentration 55, 59, 63, 64, 81, 87, 92, 93, 243; conception, analysis, expression, 86–87; corrective and formative, 81, 83, 84, 85; courses during middle years, 80–81; dwindling faculty, 47; early acting theory, 49–50; early curriculum, 74–80; early emphasis on pantomime, 78–80; emotion, 55, 57, 59–62, 65, 83, 243, 245, 248, 249; emotional memory 57; evolving methods of teaching, 51; faculty of New York School of Acting, 48–49; freeing body and voice, 65, 67; function of the actor, 49–51; function of the school, 50–51; function of teacher in stage rehearsal, 87–89; gamuts of expression, 75; graduates, 91; harmonic gymnastics, 81; ideal or total actor, 51, 57, 65, 67, 74, 92; ideas similar to Stanislavsky, 54, 55, 58, 59, 64, 89, 92, 93; ideas similar to Strasberg, 65, 93; identification with character, 59; imagination, 52, 57, 58, 243, 244, 245, and imaginative feeling, 59–64, 65, 243, 245; and memory, 57, 60, 61; imaginative truth and "magic if," 52, 53, 54; an improvement over stock company method, 50; improvisation, 67, 81, 83, 84, 85, 246, 247; influences of MacKaye, 56, 65, 76, 81, 86, 92; influences of MacKaye-Delsarte "system," 48, 58, 59, 67, 68, 69, 74, 78, 79, 83, 84, 93; inner technique, 57, 93, 245; instinct (impulse), 57, 61–62, 244, 245; intellect, 57–58, 64,, 86–87; internal to external, 81, 85, 86, 90, 91, 92, 247, 248; large number of faculty at opening of Lyceum School of Acting, 47; length of program, 80; Lyceum School of Acting changes to New York School of Acting, 48; MacKaye departure, 48; motive and objective, 67, 81, 92; natural growth, 81, 84, 85, 86, 90, 91; opposed to empirical and imitative methods, 46, 47; opposed to imitation, 45, 48, 50, 69, 72, 89, 91; overcoming criticism, 91; philosophy of American Academy of Dramatic Arts, 57; philosophy of Lyceum School of Acting (1885), 47; philosophy of physical training, 65; physical and vocal training, 65–67; practical courses, 87; relationship of actor to audience, 56–57; relationship of actor to character, 52–55, 59, 63, 64, 92; relationship of actor to the play, 52, 243; relationship of art to nature, 56, 67–69; relaxation, 65, 66, 81, 83, 93, 243; Sargent, Franklin H. acknowledges MacKaye his principal master, 45, clearly head of school, 48, head of school after MacKaye's departure, 45,

ABOUT THE AUTHOR

JAMES H. MCTEAGUE graduated from Carnegie-Mellon University with a BFA and MFA in Directing and completed the Ph.D. in Dramatic Art at the University of Iowa. Trained as a director, Dr. McTeague has worked in both the professional and university theatre. He is currently at the University of Alberta where he teaches in the professional training programs of Directing(MFA) and Acting(BFA). In addition, he also teaches Acting Theory and Aesthetics in graduate seminars for the academic area. Dr. McTeague served as Chairman of the Department of Drama as well as Head of Drama at the prestigious Banff School of Fine Arts where he was instrumental in the development of its Professional Master Class in Acting. Dr. McTeague's background and experience in both the creative and scholarly aspects of theatre are a rare combination and the more than 120 productions he has directed contributed significantly to his insight into acting theory and aesthetics.